Consumer behavior
selected readings

Consumer behavior
selected readings

edited for the

American Marketing Association

by JAMES F. ENGEL

Professor of Business Organization
College of Administrative Science
The Ohio State University

AMA Reprint Series

1968

RICHARD D. IRWIN, INC., Homewood, Illinois
IRWIN-DORSEY LIMITED, Nobleton, Ontario

Library of Congress Catalog Card No. 68-30850

Printed in the United States of America

Preface

Hopefully this is not just another book of readings. If so, one might legitimately question its addition to the already long list of such efforts. Indeed, little is required to "clip" articles and assemble them between two covers.

Upon receiving this assignment from the American Marketing Association, the writer made an early decision that it was necessary to establish a rationale for the assembly of this volume which would serve both to aid in selecting the readings and to facilitate the organization of its contents. Therefore, the first section consists of a model of buyer behavior which provides an overview of the complex process underlying what the consumer does. Articles then were selected which illuminated key elements of this process or otherwise contributed to an understanding of consumer motivation and behavior. Certainly some articles of merit had to be omitted because of space limitations.

One of the difficulties faced is that the literature published by the American Marketing Association covers only a relatively limited segment of the total set of relevant interdisciplinary contributions. Some topics could, as a result, be covered rather thoroughly, whereas others have received little or no mention. This, however, was unavoidable.

One of the prime objectives of the book is to enable the reader to gain some understanding of the areas where knowledge is most scanty and research most greatly needed. A concerted research tradition in consumer behavior unfortunately has been sadly lacking in the field of marketing, and it is hoped that this volume can contribute in some small way to stimulating and focusing the needed inquiries.

July, 1968   JAMES F. ENGEL

Table of contents

Introduction

This short book is one of a new series being published by the American Marketing Association. It is designed to make available in a convenient form the latest scholarly research and writing on a series of topics which are of continuing interest to practitioners, students, and teachers in the field of marketing. It is our hope that this format will be successful in bringing such material to the attention of persons who are not members of the Association as well as of those who are members of the AMA but who have not had the opportunity to read, in their original sources, the articles that have been included in this volume. Many of the publications that have been drawn upon in connection with this endeavor have had a relatively limited circulation in spite of the fact that they contain a substantial number of significant contributions to the literature dealing with various aspects of Consumer Behavior.

JOHN J. WHEATLEY
General Editor

Part I

FUNDAMENTAL CONCEPTS AND PSYCHOLOGICAL PROCESSES

The reading in Part I, by James F. Engel, presents a model of buyer behavior. Its purpose is to offer a perspective that, hopefully, clarifies much of the complexity of buyer behavior, and indicates significant variables and relationships. In turn, it serves as the outline for the remaining readings, each of which is concerned with a specific area of the model.

It is necessary from the beginning to make a sort of road map that permits the serious student to make sense out of the available literature, which, quite frankly, has never been related in any kind of meaningful fashion. This is the role of the *conceptual model*—a formal structure that specifies and clarifies the nature of relationships between those factors that influence and shape consumer behavior.

A model of buyer motivation and behavior, presented in this section, explicitly assumes that buyer behavior is a process with a clearly defined beginning, significant intervening steps, and an ending that consists of a purchase as well as the consequences that result from this action. As such, the model is a simplified representation of the phenomena studied, and it thereby provides a tentative explanation of the system or process.

"The Study of Human Behavior" begins with a review of the traditional way of analyzing human behavior. Using this background the model is presented, and several examples illustrate its application and use. Each of the readings presented in later sections is then used to explain *aspects of the total process*. It is hoped that the reader will thereby gain insights that otherwise would be difficult to attain.

1. THE STUDY OF HUMAN BEHAVIOR*

James F. Engel

The study of human beings presents real methodological difficulties, which in turn have led to the variety of conceptual and empirical approaches that confront the student. The major types of psychological influences and their interaction are discussed first, followed by a review of empirical problems.

THE PSYCHOLOGICAL FIELD

Man is influenced by many forces, the sum total of which is designated, in Figure 1, the *psychological field*. As the diagram indicates, each person is motivated by basic needs or drives activated in the present time, without particular influence from the past or anticipated future. In this sense, man does not differ greatly from other animals. The human being, however, is not time bound in that he is fully capable of recalling and being influenced by the past as well as anticipating the future consequences of what he does. The past functions, in part, through learned patterns of behavior and ways of thinking. In addition, man is more profoundly influenced than other animals by the environment in which he lives, and he is especially affected by the social role of others. All these factors are significant, and any realistic theory of consumer action must comprehend each major element in a consistent manner.

FIGURE 1

THE PSYCHOLOGICAL FIELD

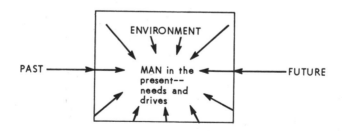

By taking the perspective that man is subject to compound and, at times, conflicting motivational determinants, it is possible to understand the overwhelming complexity of the forces underlying behavior. Each

---

*From parts of several chapters in James F. Engel, Roger D. Blackwell, and David T. Kollat, *Consumer Behavior* (New York: Holt, Rinehart & Winston, Inc., 1968).

person must adapt to his unique psychological field, and to him this field is reality. He will establish patterns of behavior which permit a workable and meaningful pattern of adaptation.

EXPLAINING HUMAN BEHAVIOR

The complexity of the psychological field is not the only difficulty faced by the analyst of human beings, because mental processes cannot be observed directly. The result is that explanations of what takes place can only be inferences about what must have happened to cause the individual to act as he did. A diagram (Figure 2) will clarify the nature of this dilemma.

FIGURE 2
THE BASIC MODEL FOR STUDY OF HUMAN BEHAVIOR

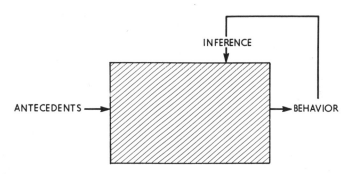

Antecedents are the inputs or stimuli that trigger action, and behavior is the output or result. The individual's mental processes stand between inputs and outputs, and are forever hidden from view. For that reason, they are sometimes referred to as being located within an impenetrable *black box*. Any explanation of what took place within the black box, therefore, can only be an inference made by the analyst.

As an example, assume that a person reacts negatively and perhaps violently when he picks up his telephone and discovers a voice that says: "Good evening; we are pleased to tell you that you are one of the very few in this city who will be permitted to purchase *Blab* magazine at half price." He may slam the receiver in the salesman's ear. A relationship is thereby established between the antecedent (the call) and the behavior (slamming the receiver). This relationship is affected by something within the black box, but this something, whatever it might be, cannot be observed directly from this sequence.

Perhaps the analyst will conclude that the person has a strong attitude against telephone solicitation. Yet, what is an attitude? It is only an inference made concerning some variable that intervened between the stimulus and response. More is said about attitudes later.

THE INFERENCE PROBLEM

It should be apparent from this brief discussion that many of the terms in common use to explain human behavior (need and attitude are examples) are nothing more than inferred intervening variables. For this reason, many schools of thought have arisen, *each viewing the same phenomenon and postulating different intervening variables.*

In part, these differences arise because analysts have different purposes and, hence, focus on different variables or concepts. The result, of course, is that there can be real disagreement on the meaning of such terms as need, motive, and attitude, and nobody is clearly right or wrong! This suggests, among other things, that great caution be exercised in borrowing concepts from the behavioral sciences without a clear understanding of definitions, meanings, and uses to which the concept is put. In marketing, this seemingly commensense warning too often is violated with unfortunate results.

A MODEL OF CONSUMER MOTIVATION AND BEHAVIOR[1]

The essence of the black box model is a good starting point, for it conceives of the human being as a *system* with outputs (behavior) in response to inputs. It is necessary, however, to expand the black box to specify the nature of the significant intervening variables. Then it is possible to discuss what happens when inputs are received (the *comparison process*) and what type of output results (the *decision process*). From here on, the black box is referred to as the *central control unit*.

THE INDIVIDUAL'S PSYCHOLOGICAL MAKEUP

The basic components of an individual's psychological makeup are represented in Figure 3.

The central control unit may be called the psychological command center, for it includes both memory and the basic facilities for thinking and analysis. Stored in memory are the various personality characteristics or predispositions, past information and experience, and values and attitudes. These components are illustrated in Figure 3 separately so that their relationships to each other can be made clearer; this does not mean, however, that they stand *outside* the control unit. Each is an integral component with its own unique function, as will become more apparent shortly.

Personality characteristics. Each person has certain ways of behaving

[1]This section first appeared in simplified form in James F. Engel and M. Lawrence Light, "The Role of Psychological Commitment in Consumer Behavior: An Evaluation of the Theory of Cognitive Dissonance," Frank M. Bass, Charles W. King and Edgar A. Pessemier (eds.), *Applications of the Sciences in Marketing Management* (New York: John Wiley & Sons, Inc., 1968), pp. 39–68.

and responding, which characterize him in a unique way. First, certain patterns of behavior that are seen as successful in satisfying needs become learned and stored in memory. These are designated in Figure 3 as *motives*. One individual, for example, may have a strong achievement motive, and will orient much of his behavior to this end, whereas another may show quite different activities because of a strong affiliation motive. Everyone has a complex organization of motives ranging from physical (hunger, etc.) to such psychological predispositions as those mentioned above, and they can singly or in combination exert a powerful influence on thinking and behavior.

FIGURE 3
THE CENTRAL CONTROL UNIT

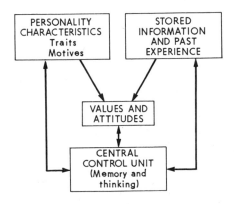

In the process of behaving, it is common also to develop ways of thinking and reacting, called *response traits*. One person may be quite persistent in all that he does; another may have a tendency or trait to give up more easily. These traits are quite individualistic, and they can pervade a variety of related actions.

Clearly, motives and traits as defined here are similar both in nature and in function. As such, they are pervasive predispositions which resist change from outside influences.

Past information and experience. Nearly all that we do is somehow retained in the central control unit as either conscious or unconscious memory. As a result, we learn to respond to situations and stimuli of all types in consistent and predictable ways. If this were not possible, one's world would be nothing more than blooming confusion. Other information is retained in less organized fashion, but, as is pointed out shortly, it is of importance in what the individual thinks and does.

Values and attitudes. Each of the personality characteristics discussed thus far is stored in memory and affects behavior in its own right. Each also interacts with stored past experience and information to form values and attitudes— ". . . an organization of concepts, beliefs, habits and motives associated with a particular object."[2] This interaction is depicted in Figure 3.

The consumer, for example, develops characteristic ways of evaluating various brands, which usually are referred to as brand images or attitudes. One brand may be highly preferred, whereas others are regarded as unacceptable. Truly, this set of orientations toward objects and persons represents an individual's map of his world. As such, values and attitudes are a prime target for persuasive advertising because of the assumption that behavior will change once an attitude is modified or redirected. The importance of this concept in understanding consumer motivation and behavior can scarcely be overemphasized.

Values differ from attitudes only in the sense that they are generally considered to be somewhat more basic. A person may have a value favoring free enterprise, for instance, and may therefore hold a negative attitude toward socialized medicine.

Inputs to the system

Everyone is continually bombarded with stimuli of all types from environment. These are represented in Figure 4 as being of two basic types—(1) physical and (2) social. They are received by the five senses (sensory receptors) in the form of a physical sensation, such as the firing of a retinal cone or some other physiological reaction.

FIGURE 4
Inputs to the System

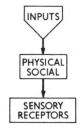

One important stimulus input, of course, is the array of available alternative products and services. Another is the demands of family members, expected patterns of behavior in social settings (norms), and the behavior of friends. Still others are such physical stimuli as weather, the volume of traffic on a given road, or the size of nail necessary to attach plywood paneling to a wall. Many others could be mentioned, but the actual form (physical or social) is of little importance. The key question focuses on what an individual does to make sense out of them.

[2] Wilbert J. McKeachie and Charlotte L. Doyle, *Psychology* (Reading, Mass.: Addison-Wesley Publishing Co., Inc., 1966), p. 560.

AROUSAL

The system must be turned on before behavior can occur; this is the function of arousal. This can occur internally through *need activation,* in which case the individual becomes alert, responsive, and vigilant because of a feeling of discomfort triggered by his sensory receptors.[3] Similarly, arousal can be achieved through an outside stimulus of some sort. Both of these types are shown in Figure 5.

FIGURE 5
AROUSAL

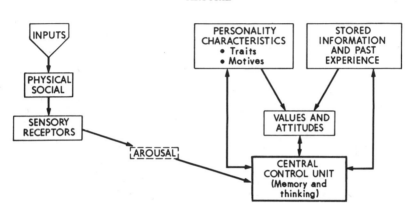

It is generally assumed that a need must be activated or aroused before behavior can occur. This is not necessarily true, but there is no question that physical and psychological needs perform this function. The result is arousal of a state of *drive,* which, in turn, provides for an energizing of need-satisfying action. The consumer, for example, becomes hungry; his system now is activated because of this state of felt discomfort.

Arousal also can occur through awareness of an external stimulus. Assume that a consumer is thumbing through a magazine and sees an advertisement for a German Chocolate Cake mix. The picture of the cake, in itself, can make him feel hungry and thereby initiate behavior. Such an outcome, however, should not be predicted in all situations, because the incoming stimulus also could conflict with his preferences and lead him to distort or ignore what he sees or hears. Nevertheless, incoming stimuli can trigger arousal, a point sometimes overlooked by students of motivation.[4]

---

[3] D. O. Hebb, *The Organization of Behavior* (New York: John Wiley & Sons, Inc., 1949).

[4] See J. McV. Hunt, "Motivation Inherent in Information Processing and Action," in O. J. Harvey (ed.), *Motivation and Social Interaction* (New York: The Ronald Press Co., 1963), pp. 35–95.

PERCEPTION

Let it now be assumed that the system is active and vigilant (that is, attentive to relevant incoming stimuli), for that is the normal state of affairs. How does a person make sense out of what he sees, hears, or senses in other ways? Clearly, he cannot consciously attend to all stimuli that reach him, for they easily number into the millions during the course of a day. This implies that the individual perceives, or sizes up, inputs selectively through a process of *comparison* whereby inputs are compared with all that is stored in memory. He thus will be highly selective and will not attend to irrelevant stimuli in most circumstances. The comparison process is illustrated in Figure 6.

FIGURE 6
THE COMPARISON PROCESS

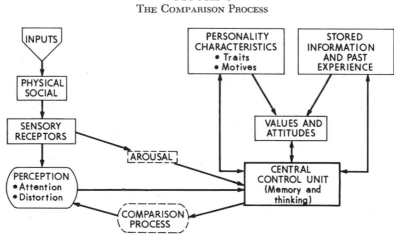

If the individual is aroused by a state of need, it is logical to expect that he will be highly selective in what he sees, hears, touches, feels, and smells. He is now especially alert to those inputs that are relevant in satisfying the aroused drive. To continue with the previous example, those stimuli known from past experience to be relevant to hunger satisfaction are likely to be attended to. For instance, a picture of a juicy steak on the outside of a restaurant or a huge piece of chocolate cake in an advertisement are now likely to be noticed, whereas previously they were largely ignored.

Meaning is attributed to incoming inputs through a decision process in which the individual evaluates input cues and selects the most appropriate category of meaning. All the components of the central control unit become relevant by serving as categories in their own right or by enhancing the probability that a given category will be chosen. The state of hunger referred to earlier, for example, raises the probability that hunger-relevant categories will be chosen.

Perception is selective, however, even in the absence of aroused drive. Human beings seem to resist a challenge to their values and attitudes. When one occurs, perhaps through an advertisement challenging their brand preference, it is natural to avoid a state of *dissonance or imbalance,* which would probably result if the message were consciously weighed and evaluated.[5]

Perception is selective in two ways—(1) *attention* and (2) *distortion.* Selective attention has already been described. It refers to the fact that the system usually attends to those stimuli that are seen to be relevant. Furthermore, the components of memory can function to screen out or distort inconsistent stimuli, while at the same time enhancing the probability of action on those that are relevant. For instance, Ohio-grown tomato juice may be preferred as an appetizer when several other alternatives would do, simply because of an attitude that favors consumption of Ohio products. An equally acceptable product from another area, on the other hand, may be evaluated negatively and thereby become distorted in the comparison process.

The outcome. The outcome from the comparison process is illustrated in Figure 7. Action results if it is perceived that some change is necessary to improve the present state of the system and to restore the balance disturbed by arousal. Nothing will be done, of course, unless it is possible for the individual to act (he has the financial means, etc.). If he can

FIGURE 7
OUTCOMES OF THE COMPARISON PROCESS

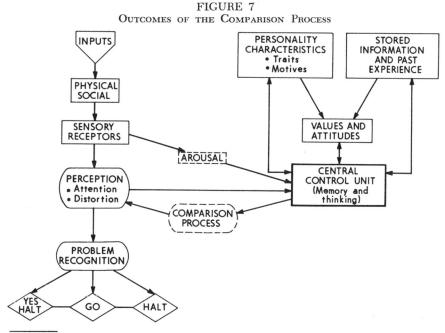

_____
[5]See Leon Festinger, *A Theory of Cognitive Dissonance* (Evanston: Row, Peterson & Co., 1957).

act, it is said that the person *recognizes a problem* and does something about it (designated "go"). Otherwise, the process halts at this point.

Notice that a problem can be recognized and not acted on, even though such action is feasible (shown as "yes, halt"). No doubt there is some minimum level of perceived difference between the results of action and inaction which must be surpassed before the flow proceeds. It should be noted that this level, or threshold, probably is learned and will vary with circumstances. In some instances, it is quite reasonable that one can achieve greater total satisfaction by no action at all.

THE DECISION-MAKING PROCESS

Problem recognition often is only the beginning step in a somewhat complex process of decision making, which also can include the following stages represented in Figure 8: (1) search for alternatives, (2) evaluation of alternatives, and (3) purchase. Each is discussed later.

Notice that a decision to search for external information on alternatives is shown by an arrow that designates new inputs to the system. This means that the information acquired is subject once again to selective perception, as discussed earlier. The purchaser of a color television set may, for example, screen out perfectly acceptable brands because they conflict with his values and attitudes. Therefore, there is no certainty that the information gathered during search will survive perceptual screening in undistorted fashion. The same can be said, of course, about information acquired when search is undertaken to evaluate alternatives.

An arrow also is shown extending downward from the control unit labeled as *response sets*. Those predispositions that affected perception can function to shape the action followed by the individual. For example, a consumer may have a response trait that leads him to perceive considerable risk and doubt in many buying situations. Thus, he most likely will be predisposed to search for information to justify his actions. This is only one example of how one's psychological makeup can function in the decision-making process; many others are given in the readings in this book.

Whatever the consumer does as he proceeds toward a decision, each action is stored in memory. Storage, in turn, is shown by a return loop extending directly into memory. Whether the outcome at the problem recognition stage is, for example, "yes, halt," "go," or "halt," the outcome is retained in memory. It might be argued that this arrow should extend upward and enter as an external stimulus subject to the comparison process, but it is shown as it is in Figure 8 to avoid undue complexity. The primary point, of course, is that the person learns from what he does, and the results of past experiences are retained for future use.

Finally, it should be pointed out that decision making ranges from true or extended problem-solving to virtually routine decisions. On the one hand, much will be done in the way of search and evaluation, whereas an action based on habit usually will bypass alternative search and evaluation altogether. The model easily accommodates these varying situations, as is explained later.

FIGURE 8
THE DECISION-MAKING PROCESS

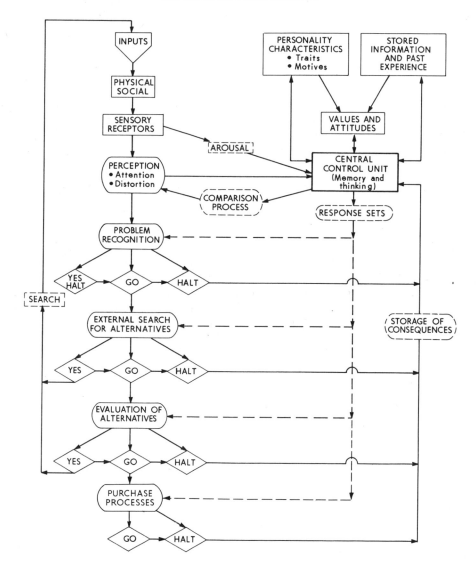

Search for alternatives. In some instances, a problem is perceived, and the individual has little knowledge of the alternatives for action. A husband and wife, for example, may make a decision to consider the purchase of a color television set and have little or no awareness of available brands. Therefore, they probably will begin to ask friends and relatives, look for advertisements, consult product-rating agencies, or turn to other external information sources. This probably represents an illustration of true problem-solving where a conscious attempt is made to discover many feasible alternatives and to weigh their advantages and disadvantages. Search will continue until apparently enough is known to proceed—shown in Figure 8 as a "go" decision.

In other situations, however, the alternatives will be known, and a decision to "go" is made *without search* for alternatives. Where the purchase is based on habit, this step will be completely bypassed without thought or consideration (i.e., a "go" decision is made almost automatically).

Evaluation of alternatives. Some persons are known to be cautious and unwilling to act without augmenting the information stored in memory; they are, therefore, "set" to seek information. In other instances, one alternative may be seen as satisfactory, but the perceived risk of a wrong decision is too great to warrant action without justification. In any event, action is not taken on the existing information base, and the system triggers the search process. When adequate information is procured or the costs of additional search are seen to outweigh the gains, a decision to "go" is made.

Search for information is most likely to occur in nonroutine decisions or true problem-solving. Even though search may have been bypassed at the earlier stage (i.e., the domain of alternatives is known), it still may be necessary to find out more about each. Even in these circumstances, however, evaluation may be bypassed because of an awareness that the time and energy required for search outweigh any expected gains.

One outcome of search may be to terminate action at this point because no alternative is seen as "good enough" (shown as "halt"). Moreover, this stage also may be bypassed in routine buying decisions in that strong preference for one alternative over all others leads to an automatic "go" decision.

Purchase processes. Finally, the preceding steps can lead to a decision to buy. Also, action can be terminated at this stage. Circumstances may change or other variables not apparent earlier may become introduced.

Outcomes of the purchase. Matters do not cease once a decision is made to purchase or not to purchase, because, as is shown in Figure 9, two additional things can happen: (1) perceived doubt about the wisdom of the action can trigger a search for information to justify the decision; (2) the outcomes may change circumstances enough to serve as a stimulus for further behavior. Postdecision evaluation is represented by an extension of the "search loop" mentioned earlier, and the triggering of further behavior is shown as a new input.

Once the family has purchased the television, for instance, they may

FIGURE 9
A Complete Model Showing Outcomes of the Purchasing
Decision

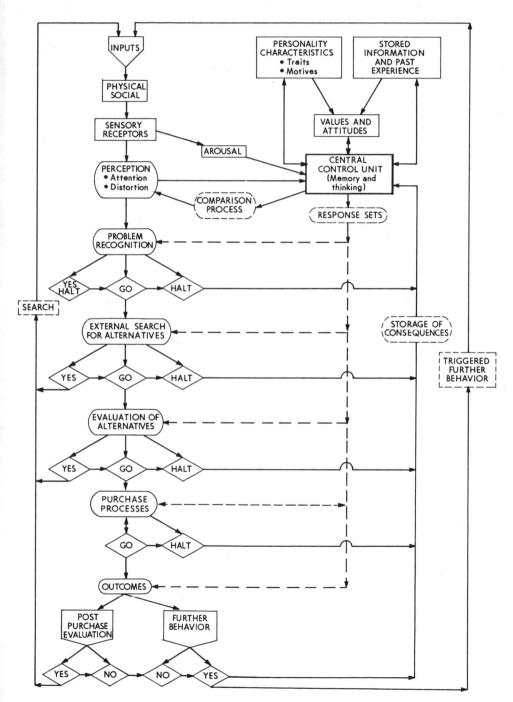

doubt that they chose the correct brand. This is especially likely if the purchase is financially burdensome and several favorable alternatives were rejected. The husband and wife now would be especially sensitive to information that confirms their choice and thereby reduces the post-decision dissonance. Postpurchase evaluation obviously is most probable under true problem-solving behavior, and it would occur only rarely when a preferred brand or product is bought routinely.

The outcome also can change circumstances and thus trigger additional action. The purchase, for example, demands the outlay of a substantial sum of money, which may have to be procured through a loan of some type. This means that the husband and wife may now have to make a decision on the best type of financing. Many other examples could be given, of course; one is the possibility that matters essentially terminate at this point, with outcomes being stored in memory.

USING THE MODEL TO EXPLAIN CONSUMER BEHAVIOR

The discussion of the model and its components has, by necessity, been brief, and it is useful to trace two distinctly different buying situations: (1) the decision to remodel a kitchen (true problem-solving) and (2) purchase of a pound of coffee.

While most of the discussion thus far has centered on an individual consumer, it is clear that social influences are important. The outcomes from one person's actions can serve as inputs for others. The model, therefore, can easily be utilized to explain a family buying process as well as that of an individual.

REMODELING A KITCHEN

Let it be assumed that a family has purchased an attractive colonial home built around 1930. It is desirable in all respects except that the kitchen is badly out-of-date. A decision to remodel can easily necessitate the outlay of thousands of dollars, so this probably involves true problem-solving for most people.

Many things can now interact to arouse one or more of the family members to consider remodeling. The wife can quickly reach the point where inefficiency of design and inadequate storage become intolerable, to say nothing of her concern over its old-fashioned appearance. Here she perceives a need for greater efficiency as well as for the approval of others. These concerns easily might have been aroused by awareness that a friend has remodeled or even by reading an article in a magazine. When communicated to other family members, her concerns could, in turn, arouse their desires to act.

Once this stage is reached, family members probably will become increasingly sensitive to relevant stimuli from the environment (selective perception). They probably will notice others' kitchens, whereas previously they were ignored, and other examples of perceptual selectivity could be given. After considerable analysis, a decision may be reached that a problem indeed does exist but that action should be deferred until financial limitations become less stringent (shown in Figure 9 as "yes-halt" under problem recognition).

Assume, however, that better financial circumstances at a later point in time remove the barrier to action and a decision is made to "go." A search now begins in earnest for feasible alternatives. Should an architect be hired, a kitchen contractor, a remodeling firm, a handyman, or what? No doubt, information will be sought from many external sources such as friends and relatives (search). Search probably will continue even when the alternatives are specified until the pros and cons of each are determined. This search can extend over a considerable period of time.

The personality characteristics of various family members can be influential in shaping the outcome. The wife, for instance, may be very other-minded—that is, much of what she does is undertaken with an eye toward the reactions of others. This trait will predispose her to base decisions at least in part on the responses of those she talks with. The husband, on the other hand, may prefer distinctly modern styles. This attitude clearly will affect the kinds of choices made later.

Each action undertaken along the way also will be stored in the memory of each family member. Stored knowledge of architect's fees and procedures conceivably could be useful in later years when further remodeling is done.

Assume that an architect is hired—the major decision at early stages of the remodeling process. Once the contract is signed, however, post-decision doubts can quickly set in, especially once the probable costs become known. The husband might have regrets, especially when he views other uses for the same funds, and he will be sensitive to ways of reducing his dissonance. One valuable way is to discuss the decision with others and to receive their support. Another may be to study remodeling magazines in the effort to convince himself that this action is worthwhile.

Hiring the architect also has the significant outcome of triggering considerable further behavior. Anyone who has remodeled knows of the many decisions that must be made about cabinet styles, floor coverings, wall coverings, electrical fixtures, and plumbing fixtures, to mention several. Each is a new decision necessitating the onset of problem-solving once again. Some might be made routinely, whereas others will require considerable search and analysis.

This decision process attains considerable complexity, perhaps more than is usually observed. Information is needed, and at many points there is opportunity for successful advertising and selling.

THE PURCHASE OF A POUND OF COFFEE

True problem-solving cannot be followed in every situation, because there simply are not enough hours in the day. Routines must be established to serve at least two purposes: (1) protect preference for a product or service and (2) avoid problem-solving. In the first situation, a housewife may feel that a particular brand suits her purposes well, and she will not consider others. In the second, she does not experience this degree of commitment but is brand loyal in order to avoid considering other alternatives.

Arousal to purchase a pound of coffee may take place in several ways. The housewife may feel tired and proceed to make a pot of coffee, only to discover that she is out of coffee. Here, an internal need was the trigger for arousal, but the information about the empty coffee can serves as a further incentive for action. She also may see an advertisement that arouses a desire for a cup of coffee, or a neighbor may suddenly stop in for a chat over coffee. In these instances, outside stimuli serve as the primary trigger.

A good cup of coffee is important to most housewives, and it is not unusual for distinct brand preferences to develop. If so, she probably will be unreceptive to advertisements for competing brands but, instead, will remain quite loyal to her preferred brand. The opportunity for successful persuasion by competing firms thus is small indeed. On the other hand, her loyalty may be such that it is quite permeable and susceptible to change through use of free coupons or other purchase incentives.

This housewife no doubt will make a note on her shopping list to replenish the coffee supply. Where brand preference is strong, there is no need to consider other alternatives. Hence, this stage of the decision-making process is bypassed, as is search for information on known alternatives. She no doubt will stay with her brand and experience little or no postdecision doubt. Her purchase and continued use thus are stored in memory and serve to strengthen her tendency to act in this way in the future.

IMPLICATIONS

Obviously, many other illustrations could have been given, but the purpose here was to present two at opposite ends of a continuum ranging from true problem-solving to habit. The marketing implications of each clearly differ, because in the first example the family is open to information and ideas. Salesmen and advertisements as well as other information sources will probably be consulted. There is indication that much can be done to persuade them to consider various alternatives throughout the remodeling decision. The housewife, however, does not consider any alternative other than her preferred brand of coffee, and it is unlikely that she will change her brand loyalty. She is, in other words, a poor target for marketing efforts by a competitor.

In both cases, much can be learned about how and why decisions are made. From this information, it then becomes apparent what, if anything, can be done to influence resulting action through skillful use of marketing efforts.

CONCLUSION AND OVERVIEW

This discussion completes the conceptual framework for this book. The readings that follow focus on various elements of the model. Gaps in the literature, however, prevent the desired degree of completeness, although several published contributions illuminate important topics and facets.

Part II covers the comparison process, beginning with the basic concepts of motivation, cognition, and learning. The discussion then proceeds to the influence of personality characteristics, perception, and attitude change. The subject of Part III is social influences, with special reference to the influence of large social groups versus face-to-face groupings. Part IV, in turn, focuses on the decision-making process, and various articles cover fundamental concepts and processes, behavior in the retail store, and the consequences of a decision. Finally, the book concludes with two articles on research into consumer decision making.

Frequent reference back to the model from time to time may help to clarify the way in which the articles are related. Unless this framework is grasped, the result will be the impression of a hodgepodge of unrelated articles. Furthermore, the model is useful in identifying gaps in the literature and stimulating needed research. This second point is most crucial; if only one reader is encouraged to inquire into previously unexplored areas, this book has been more than worthwhile.

Suggested additional AMA readings

Bross, Irwin D. J. *Design for Decision*, chap. 10. New York: The Free Press, 1953.

Brown, Judson S. *The Motivation of Behavior*, chap. 1. New York: McGraw-Hill Book Co., Inc., 1961.

Day, Ralph L. *Marketing Models, Quantitative and Behavioral*, pp. 3–8. Scranton, Pa.: International Textbook Co., 1964.

Engel, James F. "Psychology and the Business Sciences," *Quarterly Journal of Economics and Business*, Vol. 1 (1961), pp. 76–83.

Howard, John A. *Marketing Management Analysis and Planning*, chaps. 3–4. Rev. cd. Homewood, Ill.: Richard D. Irwin, Inc., 1963.

Jonassen, Christen T. "Contributions of Sociology to Marketing," *Journal of Marketing*, Vol. 24 (October, 1959), pp. 29–35.

Kotler, Philip. "The Use of Mathematical Models in Marketing," *Journal of Marketing*, Vol. 27 (October, 1963), pp. 31–41.

————. "Behavioral Models for Analyzing Buyers," *Journal of Marketing*, Vol. 29 (October, 1965), pp. 37–45.

Kuehn, Alfred A., and Day, Ralph L. "Probabilistic Models of Consumer Buying Behavior," *Journal of Marketing*, Vol. 28 (October, 1964), pp. 27–31.

Lazer, William. "The Role of Models in Marketing," *Journal of Marketing*, Vol. 26 (April, 1962), pp. 9–14.

Nicosia, Francesco. *Consumer Decision Processes*. Englewood Cliffs, N.J.: Prentice-Hall, Inc., 1966.

Part II

THE COMPARISON PROCESS

This section is concerned with the comparison process of the buyer behavior model, as is illustrated in Figure A. Of special importance are
arousal (motivation), the components of the control unit, perception,
and learning. Each of these is covered in this section, which consists of
four basic topics: (A) Basic Concepts, (B) Personality Characteristics,
(C) Perception, and (D) Attitude Change and Perception.

FIGURE A
THE COMPARISON PROCESS

A. Basic concepts

The first article stands as one of the most influential and widely quoted
contributions to the marketing literature. Although it was written several
years ago, Bayton clearly defined the meaning and significance of motivation, cognition, and learning. His was the first rigorous attempt to

assess the marketing significance of these fundamental concepts, and his thoughts still are highly relevant today. As such, this article serves as an excellent introduction to a difficult section.

2. MOTIVATION, COGNITION, LEARNING—
BASIC FACTORS IN CONSUMER BEHAVIOR*

James A. Bayton

MOTIVATION, COGNITION, LEARNING

The analysis of consumer behavior presented here is derived from diverse concepts of several schools of psychology—from psychoanalysis to reinforcement theory.

Human behavior can be grouped into three categories—motivation, cognition, and learning. Motivation refers to the drives, urges, wishes, or desires which initiate the sequence of events known as "behavior." Cognition is the area in which all of the mental phenomena (perception, memory, judging, thinking, etc.) are grouped. Learning refers to those changes in behavior which occur through time relative to external stimulus conditions.

Each broad area is pertinent to particular problems of consumer behavior. All three together are pertinent to a comprehensive understanding of consumer behavior.

MOTIVATION

HUMAN NEEDS

Behavior is initiated through needs. Some psychologists claim that words such as "motives," "needs," "urges," "wishes," and "drives" should not be used as synonyms; others are content to use them interchangeably. There is one virtue in the term "drive" in that it carries the connotation of a force pushing the individual into action.

Motivation arises out of tension-systems which create a state of disequilibrium for the individual. This triggers a sequence of psychological events directed toward the selection of a goal which the individual *anticipates* will bring about release from the tensions and the selection of patterns of action which he *anticipates* will bring him to the goal.

One problem in motivation theory is deriving a basic list of the human needs. Psychologists agree that needs fall into two general categories—those arising from tension-systems physiological in nature (biogenic needs such as hunger, thirst, and sex), and those based upon

Journal of Marketing, January, 1958, pp. 282–89.

tension-systems existing in the individual's subjective psychological state and in his relations with others (psychogenic needs).

Although there is not much disagreement as to the list of specific biogenic needs, there is considerable difference of opinion as to the list of specific psychogenic needs. However, the various lists of psychogenic needs can be grouped into three broad categories:

1. *Affectional needs*—the needs to form and maintain warm, harmonious, and emotionally satisfying relations with others.
2. *Ego-bolstering needs*—the needs to enhance or promote the personality; to achieve; to gain prestige and recognition; to satisfy the ego through domination of others.
3. *Ego-defensive needs*—the needs to protect the personality; to avoid physical and psychological harm; to avoid ridicule and "loss of face"; to prevent loss of prestige; to avoid or to obtain relief from anxiety.

One pitfall in the analysis of motivation is the assumption that a particular situation involves just one specific need. In most instances the individual is driven by a combination of needs. It seems likely that "love" brings into play a combination of affectional, ego-bolstering, and ego-defensive needs as well as biogenic needs. Within the combination some needs will be relatively strong, others relatively weak. The strongest need within the combination can be called the "prepotent" need. A given consumer product can be defined in terms of the specific need-combination involved and the relative strengths of these needs.

Another pitfall is the assumption that identical behaviors have identical motivational backgrounds. This pitfall is present whether we are thinking of two different individuals or the same individual at two different points in time. John and Harry can be different in the motivational patterns leading to the purchase of their suits. Each could have one motivational pattern influencing such a purchase at age twenty and another at age forty.

Ego-involvement

One important dimension of motivation is the degree of ego-involvement. The various specific need-patterns are not equal in significance to the individual. Some are superficial in meaning; others represent (for the individual) tremendous challenges to the very essence of existence. There is some evidence that one of the positive correlates of degree of ego-involvement is the amount of cognitive activity (judging, thinking, etc.) involved. This means that consumer goods which tap low degrees of ego-involvement will be purchased with a relatively lower degree of conscious decision-making activity than goods which tap higher degrees of ego-involvement. Such a factor must be considered when decisions are made on advertising and marketing tactics.

At times the ego-involvement factor is a source of conflict between client and researcher. This can occur when research reveals that the product taps a low degree of ego-involvement within consumers. The result is difficult for a client to accept; because *he* is ego-involved and, therefore, cognitively active about his product, consumers must certainly be also. It is hard for such a client to believe that consumers simply do not engage in a great deal of cognitive activity when they make purchases within his product class. One way to ease this particular client-researcher conflict would be for the researcher to point out this implication of the ego-involvement dimension.

"TRUE" AND RATIONALIZED MOTIVES

A particular difficulty in the study of motivation is the possibility that there can be a difference between "true" motives and rationalized motives. Individuals sometimes are unaware of the exact nature of drives initiating their behavior patterns. When this occurs, they attempt to account for their behavior through "rationalization" by assigning motivations to their behavior which are acceptable to their personality structures. They may do this with no awareness that they are rationalizing. There can be other instances, however, in which individuals are keenly aware of their motivations, but feel it would be harmful or socially unacceptable to reveal them. When this is the case, they deliberately conceal their motivations.

These possibilities create a problem for the researcher. Must he assume that every behavior pattern is based upon unconscious motivation? If not, what criteria are to be used in deciding whether to be alert to unconscious motivation for this behavior pattern and not that one? What is the relative importance of unconscious motives, if present, and rationalized motives? Should rationalized motives be ignored? After all, rationalized motives have a certain validity for the individual—they are the "real" motives insofar as he is aware of the situation.

The situation is even more complicated than this—what about the dissembler? When the individual actually is dissembling, the researcher must attempt to determine the true motives. But, how shall we determine whether we are faced with a situation where the respondent is rationalizing or dissembling? In a given case, did a projective technique reveal an unconscious motive or the true motive of a dissembler? Conceptually, rationalized motives and dissembled motives are not equal in psychological implication; but it is rare, if ever, that one finds attempts to segregate the two in consumer research directed toward the analysis of motivation. This failure is understandable, to some extent, because of the lack of valid criteria upon which to base the distinction.

COGNITION

NEED-AROUSAL

Motivation, thus, refers to a state of need-arousal—a condition exerting "push" on the individual to engage in those activities which he anticipates will have the highest probability of bringing him gratification of a particular need-pattern. Whether gratification actually will be attained or not is a matter of future events. Central to the psychological activities which now must be considered in the sequence are the complex of "mental" operations and forces known as the cognitive processes. We can view these cognitive processes as being *purposive* in that they serve the individual in his attempts to achieve satisfaction of his needs. These cognitive processes are *regulatory* in that they determine in large measure the direction and particular steps taken in his attempt to attain satisfaction of the initiating needs.

THE EGO-SUPEREGO CONCEPT

The ego-superego concept is pertinent to a discussion of cognitive activities which have been triggered by needs. Discussions of the ego-superego concept usually come under the heading of motivation as an aspect of personality. It is our feeling that motivation and the consequences of motivation should be kept systematically "clean." In the broadest sense, ego and superego are mental entities in that they involve memory, perceiving, judging, and thinking.

The ego. The ego is the "executive," determining how the individual shall seek satisfaction of his needs. Through perception, memory, judging, and thinking the ego attempts to integrate the needs, on the one hand, and the conditions of the external world, on the other, in such manner that needs can be satisfied without danger or harm to the individual. Often this means that gratification must be postponed until a situation has developed, or has been encountered, which does not contain harm or danger. The turnpike driver who does not exceed the speed limit because he sees signs saying there are radar checks is under the influence of the ego. So is the driver who sees no cars on a straight stretch and takes the opportunity to drive at excessive speed.

The superego. The superego involves the ego-ideal and conscience. The ego-ideal represents the positive standards of ethical and moral conduct the individual has developed for himself. Conscience is, in a sense, the "judge," evaluating the ethics and morality of behavior and, through guilt-feelings, administering punishment when these are violated. If a driver obeys the speed limit because he would feel guilty in doing otherwise, he is under the influence of the superego. (The first driver above is under the influence of the ego because he is avoiding a fine, not guilt feelings.)

SPECIFIC EXAMPLES

Credit is a form of economic behavior based to some extent upon ego-superego considerations. It is generally felt that one cause of consumer-credit expansion has been a shift away from the superego's role in attitudes toward credit. The past ego-ideal was to build savings; debt was immoral—something to feel guilty about, to avoid, to hide. These two superego influences restrained the use of credit. For some cultural reason, credit and debt have shifted away from superego dominance and are now more under the control of the ego—the primary concern now seems to be how much of it can be used without risking financial danger.

The purchasing of specific consumer goods can be considered from the point of view of these two influences. Certain goods (necessities, perhaps) carry little superego influence, and the individual is psychologically free to try to maximize the probability of obtaining satisfaction of his needs while minimizing the probability of encountering harm in so doing. Other goods, however, tap the superego. When a product represents an aspect of the ego-ideal there is a strong positive force to possess it. Conversely, when a product involves violation of the conscience, a strong negative force is generated against its purchase.

Let us assume that, when the need-push asserts itself, a variety of goal-objects come into awareness as potential sources of gratification. In consumer behavior these goal-objects may be different brand names. The fact that a particular set of goal-objects come into awareness indicates the generic character of this stage in the cognitive process—a class of goal-objects is seen as containing the possible satisfier. What the class of goal-objects and the specific goal-objects within the class "promise" in terms of gratification are known as "expectations."

There are, then, two orders of expectation: generic expectancies, and object-expectancies. Suppose the needs were such that the individual "thought" of brands of frozen orange juice. Some of the generic expectations for frozen orange juice are a certain taste, quality, source of vitamin C, protection against colds, and ease of preparation. The particular brands carry expectations specifically associated with one brand as against another. The expectation might be that brand A has a more refreshing taste than brand B.

In many instances, cognitive competition occurs between two or more generic categories before it does between goal-objects within a generic category. Much consumer-behavior research is directed toward the investigation of generic categories—tires, automobiles, appliances, etc. But perhaps not enough attention has been given to the psychological analysis of cognitive competition between generic categories. An example of a problem being studied is the competition between television viewing, movie going, and magazine reading. For a particular producer, cognitive competition within the pertinent generic category is usually of more concern than cognitive competition between his generic category and others. The producer usually wants only an intensive analysis of consumer psychology with respect to the particular generic category of which his product is a member.

Let us now assume that under need-push four alternative goal-objects (brands A, B, C, and D) came into awareness. Why these particular brands and not others? Why are brands E and F absent? An obvious reason for brand E's absence might be that the individual had never been exposed to the fact that brand E exists. He had been exposed to brand F, however. Why is it absent? The problem here is one of memory—a key cognitive process. The producers of brands E and F obviously are faced with different problems.

Two sets of circumstances contain the independent variables that determine whether a given item will be remembered. One is the nature of the experience resulting from actual consumption or utilization of the goal-object. This will be discussed later when we come to the reinforcement theory of learning. The other is the circumstances present on what might be called vicarious exposures to the goal-object—vicarious in that at the time of exposure actual consumption or utilization of the goal-object does not occur. The most obvious example would be an advertisement of the goal-object. Of course, the essential purpose of an advertisement is to expose the individual to the goal-object in such a manner that at some subsequent time it will be remembered readily. The search for the most effective methods of doing this by manipulation of the physical aspects of the advertisement and the appeals used in it is a continuing effort in consumer-behavior research. Finally, for many consumers these two sets of circumstances will be jointly operative. Experiences with the goal-object and subsequent vicarious exposures can coalesce to heighten the memory potential for an item.

MAKING A CHOICE

With, say, four brands in awareness, the individual must now make a choice. What psychological factors underlie this choice? The four brands could be in awareness due to the memory factor because they are immediately present in the environment; or some because they are in the environment, and the others because of memory.

The first problem is the extent to which the items are differentiated. The various goal-objects have attributes which permit the individual to differentiate between them. The brand name is one attribute; package another; design still another. These differentiating attributes (from the point of view of the consumer's perceptions) can be called signs or cues. All such signs are not equally important in consumer decisions. Certain of them are depended upon much more than others. For example, in a study of how housewives select fresh oranges, the critical or key signs were thickness of skin, color of skin, firmness of the orange, and presence or absence of "spots" on the skin.

The signs have expectancies associated with them. Package (a sign) can carry the expectancy of quality. Thin-skin oranges carry the expectancy of juice; spots carry the expectancy of poor taste quality and insufficient amount of juice. Often sign-expectancies determined through consumer research are irrelevant or invalid. Signs are irrelevant when they do not represent a critical differentiating attribute of a goal-object. Certain discolorations on oranges have nothing to do with their intrinsic quality. Expectancies are invalid when they refer to qualities that do not in fact exist in association with a particular sign.

The different goal-objects in awareness can be assessed in terms of the extent to which they arouse similar expectancies. This phenomenon of similarity of expectations within a set of different goal-objects is known as generalization. One goal-object (brand A, perhaps), because of its associated expectancies, can be assumed to have maximum appeal within the set of alternative goal-objects. The alternates then can be ordered in terms of how their associated expectancies approximate those of brand A. Is this ordering and the psychological distances between the items of the nature of:

Brand A	Brand A
Brand B	

or

	Brand B
Brand C	Brand C

These differences in ordering and psychological distance are referred to as generalization gradients. In the first case, the expectancies associated with brand B are quite similar to those for brand A, but are not quite as powerful in appeal. Brand C has relatively little of this. In the second case, the generalization gradient is of a different form, showing that brand B offers relatively little psychological competition to brand A. (There will also be generalization gradients with respect to cognitive competition between generic categories.) In addition to the individual producer being concerned about the memory potential of his particular brand, he needs to determine the nature of the generalization gradient for his product and the products of his competitors. Mere ordering is not enough—the "psychological distances" between positions must be determined, also, and the factor determining these distances is similarity of expectancy.

The discussion above was concerned with cognitive processes as they relate to mental representation of goal-objects under the instigation of need-arousal. The items brought into awareness, the differentiating sign-expectancies, and the generalization gradient are the central factors in the particular cognitive field aroused under a given "need-push." One important dimension has not yet been mentioned—instrumental acts. These are acts necessary in obtaining the goal-object and the acts involved in consuming or utilizing it. Examples are: "going downtown" to get to a department store, squeezing the orange to get its juice, ease of entry into service stations, and the operations involved in do-it-yourself house painting.

Instrumental acts can have positive or negative value for the individual. One who makes fewer shopping trips to downtown stores because of traffic and parking conditions displays an instrumental act with negative value. Frozen foods are products for which much of the appeal lies in the area of instrumental acts. The development of automatic transmissions and of power-steering in automobiles are examples of product changes concerned with instrumental acts. The point is that concentration upon cognitive reactions to the goal-object, *per se,* could be masking critical aspects of the situation based upon cognitive reactions to the instrumental acts involved in obtaining or utilizing the goal-object.

LEARNING

GOAL-OBJECT

Starting with need-arousal, continuing under the influence of cognitive processes, and engaging in the necessary action, the individual arrives at consumption or utilization of a goal-object. Using our consumer-behavior illustration, let us say that the consumer bought brand A and is now in the process of consuming or utilizing it. We have now arrived at one of the most critical aspects of the entire psychological sequence. It is with use of the goal-object that degree of gratification of the initial needs will occur.

REINFORCEMENT

When consumption or utilization of the goal-object leads to gratification of the initiating needs there is "reinforcement." If at some later date the same needs are aroused, the individual will tend to repeat the process of selecting and getting to the same goal-object. If brand A yields a high degree of gratification, then at some subsequent time, when the same needs arise, the consumer will have an increased tendency to select brand A once again. Each succeeding time that brand A brings gratification, further reinforcement occurs, thus further increasing the likelihood that in the future, with the given needs, brand A will be selected.

This type of behavioral change—increasing likelihood that an act will be repeated—is learning; and reinforcement is necessary for learning to take place. Continued reinforcements will influence the cognitive processes. Memory of the goal-object will be increasingly enhanced; particular sign-expectancies will be more and more firmly established; and the generalization gradient will be changed in that the psychological distance on this gradient between brand A and the competing brands will be increased.

HABIT

One of the most important consequences of continued reinforcement is the influence this has on the extent to which cognitive processes enter the picture at the times of subsequent need-arousal. With continued reinforcement, the amount of cognitive activity decreases; the individual engages less and less in decision-making mental activities. This can continue until, upon need-arousal, the goal-obtaining activities are practically automatic. At this stage there is a habit.

Note this use of the term "habit." One frequently hears that a person does certain things by "*force* of habit," that habit is an initiator of behavioral sequences. Actually habits are not initiating forces in themselves; habits are repeated response patterns accompanied by a minimum of cognitive activity. There must be some condition of need-arousal before the habit-type response occurs. This has serious implications in the field of consumer behavior. The promotional and marketing problems faced by a competitor of brand A will be of one type if purchase behavior for brand A is habitual, of another if this is not true. If the purchase is largely a habit, there is little cognitive activity available for the competitor to "work on."

Frequency of repeating a response is not a valid criterion for determining whether or not a habit exists. An act repeated once a week can be just as much a habit as one repeated several times a day. The frequency of a response is but an index of the frequency with which the particular need-patterns are aroused. Frequency of response also is often used as a measure of the *strength* of a habit. The test of the strength of a habit is the extent to which an individual will persist in an act after it has ceased providing need gratification. The greater this persistence, the stronger was the habit in the first place.

PROBLEM—CONCEPT—RESEARCH

The above views integrate concepts in contemporary psychology which seem necessary for a comprehensive explanation of human behavior, and apply these concepts to the analysis of consumer behavior. Each psychological process touched upon contains areas for further analysis and specification.

Some type of comprehensive theory of human behavior is necessary as a *working tool* to avoid a lack of discipline in attacking problems in consumer behavior. Too frequently a client with a practical problem approaches a researcher with an indication that all that is needed is a certain methodology—depth interviewing, scaling, or projective devices, for example.

The first step should be to take the practical problem and translate it into its pertinent conceptual entities. This phase of the problem raises the question of motivations. Here is a question involving relevance and validity of sign-expectancies. There is a question dealing with a generalization gradient, etc. Once the pertinent conceptual entities have been identified, and only then, we arrive at the stage of hypothesis formulation. Within each conceptual entity, a relationship between independent and dependent variables is established as a hypothesis to be tested.

Often the relation between conceptual entities must be investigated. For example, what is the effect of continuing reinforcement on a specific generalization gradient? Within the same research project, one psychological entity can be a dependent variable at one phase of the research and an independent variable at another. At one time we might be concerned with establishing the factors associated with differential memory of sign-expectancies. At another time we could be concerned with the influence of remembered sign-expectancies upon subsequent purchase-behavior.

Discipline requires that one turn to methodology only when the pertinent conceptual entities have been identified and the relationships between independent and dependent variables have been expressed in the form of hypotheses. Fundamentally this sequence in the analysis of a problem serves to delimit the methodological possibilities. In any event, the methodologies demanded are those which will produce unambiguous tests of each particular hypothesis put forth. Finally, the results must be translated into the terms of the original practical problem.

We have used the term "discipline" in this phase of our discussion. The researcher must discipline himself to follow the above steps. Some find this a difficult thing to do and inevitably their data become ambiguous. They must resort to improvisation in order to make sense of the results *after* the project is completed. A research project is truly a work of art when the conceptual analysis, the determination of the hypotheses, and the methodologies have been developed in such an "air-tight" sequence that practically all that is necessary is to let the facts speak for themselves.

B. The influence of personality characteristics

Two articles are reprinted in this section. The Evans reading represents an early attempt to assess the relevance of personality characteristics as a predictor of purchase action. While his findings are by no means definitive, he served to stimulate interest in this important area. Much research has followed this early contribution.

Gottlieb, on a somewhat different tack, focuses on personality differences between buyers and nonbuyers. He does not necessarily use standardized personality tests as Evans did, but he tests realistic hypotheses about possible psychological differences. His results are intriguing, and he suggests meaningful managerial applications from his findings and from his method of analysis.

3. CORRELATES OF AUTOMOBILE SHOPPING BEHAVIOR*

Franklin B. Evans

In most American families the purchase of a new automobile is a major event. Automobile shopping behavior may take at least three forms:

1. Both the brand of car and the dealer are selected in advance. Shopping then consists of going to only one dealer.
2. Only the brand is preselected. Two or more dealers of this brand are visited in order to secure the "best deal."
3. Neither the brand nor the dealer is chosen in advance. The purchase is consummated only after comparison shopping of both brands and prices.

This article presents a discriminatory analysis of the extremes of shopping behavior: (1) *nonshoppers*—20 randomly selected individuals who visited only one dealer before buying a new car; and (2) *shoppers*—20 randomly selected individuals who visited dealers of different makes before buying a new car.

These shoppers and nonshoppers were selected in mid-1958 from a larger random sample of Ford and Chevrolet owners in a middle-class Chicago suburban area, Park Forest.[1] The shoppers and nonshoppers each represented approximately one-sixth of the larger random sample.

To control or limit the effects of other intervening variables, this sample was further restricted. Each group of 20 shoppers and nonshoppers consisted only of white males who had owned a car previously and who had purchased a new car in either 1955, 1956, or 1957. Each group also contained 10 Ford and 10 Chevrolet owners.

The cars actually purchased by the two contrasted groups indicate the similarities of the external factors involved in the purchase decision. Each group was equally split between six-cylinder and eight-cylinder models. Chevrolet accounted for seven of the nonshoppers' six-cylinder models and for six of the shoppers'. Body styles chosen were also quite similar; two- and four-door sedans were in the majority. The only noticeable difference was that the shoppers purchased six station wagons, compared with two for the nonshoppers. As a group, the shoppers' cars had 18 radios, 15 automatic transmissions, and 15 two-tone paint jobs; the nonshoppers had 15 radios, 12 automatic transmissions, and 14 two-tone paint jobs. These similarities suggest that shopping was not done simply to find particular features or combinations of them.

Journal of Marketing, October, 1962, pp. 74–77.
[1]Franklin B. Evans, "Psychological and Objective Factors in the Prediction of Brand Choice," *Journal of Business*, Vol. 32 (October, 1959), pp. 340–69.

Initial differences between the two groups were indicated by their answers to the question, "What make of car do you think you'll buy next?" Nine of the shoppers answered "Don't know" to this question, compared with only four of the nonshoppers. Table 1 shows the range of answers.

It would appear that shoppers are conscious of their behavior patterns and intend to maintain them.

TABLE 1
FUTURE AUTOMOBILE PURCHASE PLANS

"Will buy next?"	Shoppers (N = 20)	Nonshoppers (N = 20)
Don't know	9	4
Ford or Chevrolet	5	15
Other brand	6	1

PERSONALITY CORRELATES OF SHOPPERS AND NONSHOPPERS

PERSONALITY NEEDS

The respondents in this study took a paper-and-pencil psychological test which purports to measure inner personality needs.[2] The pattern of needs defines the personality and allows something meaningful about the person to be communicated to others. The needs treated as psychological variables were:[3]

1. *Achievement:* To do one's best, to accomplish something of great significance.
2. *Deference:* To find out what others think, to accept the leadership of others.
3. *Exhibition:* To say witty and clever things, to talk about personal achievements.
4. *Autonomy:* To be able to come and go as desired, to say what one thinks about things.
5. *Affiliation:* To be loyal to friends, to make as many friends as possible.
6. *Intraception:* To analyze one's motives and feelings, to analyze the behavior of others.
7. *Dominance:* To be a leader in the groups to which one belongs, to tell others how to do their jobs.
8. *Abasement:* To feel guilty when one does something wrong, to feel inferior to others in most respects.

[2]For details of the test, see same reference as footnote 1, pp. 344–46.
[3]Allen L. Edwards, *Personal Preference Schedule Manual* (New York: Psychological Corporation, 1957), p. 14.

9. *Change:* To do new and different things, to participate in new fads and fashions.
10. *Aggression:* To attack contrary points of view, to get revenge for insults.

TEST SCORES

The group means for each of the personality needs for shoppers and nonshoppers are given in Table 2. Shoppers had higher scores than nonshoppers for achievement, affiliation, intraception, dominance, change, and aggression. The shopping personality syndrome is supported by the high scores for the needs of achievement, dominance, intraception, and change. By contrast, nonshoppers scored higher than the shoppers on the needs for deference, autonomy, abasement, and exhibition. The first three of these fit the hypothesis for a nonshopping personality.

The personality profiles of the two groups show considerable differences between shoppers and nonshoppers. (The ranking of personality needs shows greater differences than one would expect from chance occurrence alone. Rank-order correlation coefficient = .60. We accept the null hypothesis at the .05 level of significance—2-tail test.)

TABLE 2
AVERAGE PERSONALITY NEED SCORES OF SHOPPERS
AND NONSHOPPERS

	Shoppers (N = 20)		Nonshoppers (N = 20)	
	Score	Rank	Score	Rank
Achievement	13.05	2	12.75	1
Deference	8.95	8	10.85	4
Exhibition	9.20	7	10.80	5
Autonomy	8.00	9	10.20	6
Affiliation	11.00	5	9.40	8
Intraception	11.20	4	10.90	3
Dominance	13.20	1	11.90	2
Abasement	7.45	10	8.00	10
Change	11.35	3	10.00	7
Aggression	9.95	6	9.20	9

The greatest differences were for change—shoppers ranked this need third most important and nonshoppers ranked it seventh—and for deference—shoppers ranked this eighth and nonshoppers ranked it fourth. Also, shoppers ranked aggression and affiliation three ranks higher than nonshoppers, and they placed autonomy three ranks lower.

LINEAR DISCRIMINANT FUNCTION

To test for discrimination between shoppers and nonshoppers, using all the personality need scores (ten independent variables) at one time, a linear discriminant function was computed.

The purpose of the function was to weight the personality need scores of the two groups, so as to provide maximum linear separation between them. That is, a model was used that computed predicted scores by linear equations and found the "best" coefficients for these equations in achieving discrimination.[4] The multivariate problem is thus reduced to a univariate one.

The weights for the ten psychological need variables for this discriminant function are shown in Table 3.

TABLE 3
LINEAR DISCRIMINANT FUNCTION OF PERSONALITY
NEEDS FOR SHOPPERS AND NONSHOPPERS*

Variable	Weight	Shoppers (N = 20)	Nonshoppers (N = 20)
Achievement	$+ 1.0000 X_1$	13.05	12.75
Deference	$- 1.9928 X_2$	8.95	10.85
Exhibition	$- .6027 X_3$	9.20	10.80
Autonomy	$- 2.8751 X_4$	8.00	10.20
Affiliation	$+ 2.4717 X_5$	11.00	9.40
Intraception	$+ .7791 X_6$	11.20	10.90
Dominance	$+ 1.6182 X_7$	13.20	11.90
Abasement	$- 1.2875 X_8$	7.45	8.00
Change	$+ 2.5882 X_9$	11.35	10.00
Aggression	$+ 2.6620 X_{10}$	9.95	9.20
		$+ 70.2148$	$+ 46.3481$

*$Y_1 = \Sigma$ weights times group means.

To test whether this function really discriminated between shoppers and nonshoppers, an analysis of variance was performed. The multiple correlation coefficient (R) of this discriminant function is .6558, and its square (R^2) is .4301. The resulting F ratio with 10 and 29 degrees of freedom is 2.189. This is significant at the 5% level.

This discriminant function misclassified nine of the 40 cases from which it was developed. It correctly classified 77.3% of the sample. A completely random basis of classification, such as flipping a coin, would misclassify approximately 50% of the sample. Thus, the personality need scores improved prediction by slightly better than 50%.

OBJECTIVE CHARACTERISTICS OF SHOPPERS
AND NONSHOPPERS

THE VARIABLES

The selection of Park Forest as the area of study restricted the ranges

[4] R. A. Fisher, "The Use of Multiple Measurements in Taxonomic Problems," *Annals of Eugenics*, Vol. 7 (1936–37), pp. 179–88. See also footnote 1, pp. 368–69.

of the demographic variables. The ages and incomes of the survey respondents, for example, were of much narrower range than would be found in sampling larger and less homogeneous areas.

Seven objective variables were selected from the interview data to represent factors which could be causally related to the behavior studied. The variables used were:

1. Home ownership—owners versus renters.
2. Family size—zero to two children at home versus three or more.
3. Church attendance—less than versus more than once a month.
4. Age—age of owner.
5. Education—formal education of owner.
6. Job tenure—worked for present firm less than five years versus more than five years.
7. Family yearly income—current year estimate.

These objective variables describe several different aspects of the respondents' lives. Family size, home ownership, and frequency of church attendance may reflect personality and family values. Age, education, job tenure, and income are not necessarily associated with any specific shopping behavior patterns.

Examination of the intercorrelation of these seven objective factors indicates that they are "relatively independent" measures. The highest intercorrelations are between home ownership and three or more children living at home (+ .55) and age and job tenure (+ .50). The others range from − .42 (age and income) to + .35 (job tenure and income).

GROUP SCORES OF THE OBJECTIVE VARIABLES

The average scores of shoppers and nonshoppers are shown in Table 4.

The shoppers were older than the nonshoppers, better educated, more likely to rent than own a home, and more frequent churchgoers. The non-

TABLE 4
AVERAGE SCORES OF OBJECTIVE VARIABLES FOR
SHOPPERS AND NONSHOPPERS

Variable	Range	Shoppers (N = 20)	Nonshoppers (N = 20)
Own—rent	1 (Rent)−0 (Own)	.55	.40
Three or more children at home	1 (Yes)−0 (No)	.20	.45
Attend church more than once a month	1 (No)−0 (Yes)	.50	.40
Age	1 (19)−9 (54)	5.45	4.75
Education	1 (College)− 0 (Less than College)	.95	.75
Five or more years with same firm	1 (Yes)−0 (No)	.45	.80
Income (midpoints)	1 ($3750)−6 ($16,250)	2.85	3.60

shoppers were younger, had more children at home, had worked longer for the same firm and had a higher income. The lower income of the shoppers' group suggests the importance of economic determinants of behavior.

The greater home ownership and number of children at home for the nonshopper suggests less involvement with automobiles than with home centered activities.

LINEAR DISCRIMINANT FUNCTION

Similar to the personality need analysis, a linear discriminant function was computed for these seven objective variables. This is shown in Table 5.

TABLE 5
LINEAR DISCRIMINANT FUNCTION OF OBJECTIVE
VARIABLES FOR SHOPPERS AND NONSHOPPERS*

Variable	Weight	Group Means	
		Shoppers ($N = 20$)	Nonshoppers ($N = 20$)
Own–rent	$- 1.0000\,X_1$	.55	.40
Three or more children ...	$- 1.4493\,X_2$	.20	.45
Attend church oftener than once a month	$+ .1143\,X_3$	.50	.40
Age	$- .1029\,X_4$	5.45	4.75
Education	$+ 1.9811\,X_5$	.95	.75
Five or more years w/same firm	$- 1.0005\,X_6$	.45	.80
Income	$- .4403\,X_7$	2.85	3.60
		$- 1.1165$	$- 2.3950$

*$Y_1 = \Sigma$ weights times group means.

This discriminant function misclassifies eight of the 40 cases from which it was calculated. Thus, it does a slightly better job of correctly placing the owners than the function that used the personality need scores for independent variables.

The multiple correlation coefficient (R) of this function is .5741 and its square (R^2) is .3296. Analysis of variance of this function shows it to be statistically significant at almost the 5% level ($F\ 7,32 = 2.248$).

CONCLUSIONS

Both the objective and psychological variables used in this study show that shoppers and nonshoppers differed in many important ways. However, it should be remembered that the two groups in this study represented extremes of the shopping distribution. Further studies of the other parts of the market are needed before one can draw any rigorous conclusions about segmenting the market by shopping behavior.

4. SEGMENTATION BY PERSONALITY TYPES*

Morris J. Gottlieb

Every practitioner of marketing research has at one time or another been approached by a sales or advertising executive with a problem stated in terms such as these—"Look," the executive will say, "It's really quite simple. All I want to do is to talk to the people who are buying my product and ask them why they buy it. Then, I want to get the people who are not buying it and ask them why they're *not* buying it."

Really, this is a very reasonable request. It has only three false premises:

1. That it's really quite simple. It practically never is.
2. That you can find out why by asking.
3. That it would necessarily be helpful to know why.

Nevertheless, the request generally stems from a genuine need to know and it is the market researcher's job to find out enough of why people do or do not buy one product rather than another or one brand rather than another to help management do a better marketing job.

One of the modest but important trends in modern marketing research has been to transform these "why" questions into "who" questions. The general idea is that if you know in sufficiently meaningful terms *who* is and *who* is not buying the product or who is and who is not a *potential* customer you really know why as well.

I'd really like to be able to say that I am going to expound the strategy of market segmentation by personality types, but it will be helpful to think of this segmentation as a research strategy rather than a marketing strategy. Hopefully, it will yield results which would suggest market segmentation strategies.

Rather than attempting to outline a general technique, I shall restrict myself to illustrating some cases where the concept seemed to be useful and discuss some of the limitations as well as the possibilities of this approach.

The first product is a proprietary medicine. It is an antacid and analgesic or pain killer which is sold mainly through drug stores and does not require a prescription. Let's call it Brominex. There are many directly competitive products in the proprietary field. However, the product class boundaries tend to become rather vague—extending from home remedies such as bicarbonate of soda or even water or orange juice on

*From *Advancing Marketing Efficiency*, American Marketing Association, December, 1958, pp. 148–58.

the one hand to analgesics such as aspirin on the other. In addition, many products in this category are prescribed by doctors.

For the purposes of this discussion, the product class was defined as proprietary products which are primarily combinations of antacids and analgesics. The bulk of this market is divided among seven or eight well-known products.

Our hope is that if we can find out how users of antacid-analgesics differ from non-users or how frequent users differ from infrequent users we can learn enough to help us locate the potential Brominex user and to reach him successfully.

At first thought it might seem a very simple matter to define the market for this type of product as simply the people who have upset stomachs and headaches. But it might be of use to know whether any particular type of person tends to have these symptoms. A little introspection will probably convince you of the difficulty of trying to pin down these symptoms. There is actually a considerable element of discretion in judging at what point you have an upset stomach or a headache bad enough to make you use an analgesic.

One person will choose to put up with any amount of pain or discomfort rather than take anything. Another will take something at the slightest suggestion of anything wrong, or as a preventive measure. Another will choose to see a doctor who may prescribe something else.

It is precisely in this kind of a situation that the "who" question is interesting. By understanding the differences between users and non-users—or between frequent and infrequent users—of a completely discretionary product we can understand more precisely what needs the product class is satisfying and hopefully how the marketing of our product can be effectively geared to this need.

Now, most of the trick in getting useful answers to the "who" question is to ask it the right way. The more thought given to outlining the various dimensions along which to compare users and non-users the more useful the answers will be.

It is generally stated that at this stage of an investigation depth interviewing is of the most use. However, the older I get, the more it is brought home to me that depth interviewing is at best a supplement to and not a substitute for deep thinking.

The only method is to learn the subject thoroughly, to observe carefully with an open mind, to listen to the experts in the field—whether there are any real experts or not. Past experience will suggest many possibilities. Finally, it helps to be insightful, incisive, and wise.

In the Brominex problem, we started by getting some medical counsel. Doctors told us that middle aged men are the most frequent sufferers from this kind of condition.

One could further anticipate that frequent users of such products would be common among the lower income groups and groups with a lower educational level because of cultural and economic factors. In any event, one always tries segmenting the market by age, sex, and income whenever there is an adequate sample and in this case there was one.

This analysis showed that age and sex were dominant factors in use, and that use tends to be greater at the lower educational levels in each of the age and sex groups. However, since use is not *completely* universal in the higher usage groups nor completely absent in the lower usage groups, one feels that *other* factors must be operating as well.

It seems a fairly sound principle to examine any factors which reflect group or other cultural influences before turning to an examination of individual characteristics distinguishing users and non-users.

One might suspect that geographic factors would influence usage. However, while usage *is* higher in the South—among white as well as non-white—it turns out upon analysis that this is almost entirely a reflection of income and education. Similarly, greater usage among non-white in the North also reflects income and educational factors. In fact, since education is an important factor in use, one would expect any cultural factors—such as differing ethnic origin—to be cancelled out by education, and in fact this seems to be the case.

Now, one form of education that bears directly on use of this kind of product is based on contact with doctors. One would suspect that people who have more contact with doctors tend to use these products less, since doctors tend to focus on the cause of these symptoms and would be inclined to counsel changes in diet or some form of medical treatment, rather than on the use of proprietary products. However, this study showed that exposure to doctors had no effect on usage for two different reasons:

1. Since there was no accurate way of determining who had the symptoms more frequently, the two factors—existence of symptoms leading to increased usage, and exposure to doctors presumably leading to decreased usage—tended to be confounded and to cancel each other out.
2. Examination of some medical histories showed that doctors rarely discussed the use of this type of product with their patients, so that it would be quite possible that while the doctors might have counseled the patient against the use of such products had the subject come up, the subject rarely came up.

At this point it would seem natural to consider some of the social pressures that might be operating to influence usage of this type of product. However, the social class position information was found to add relatively little to education data.

Now, the use of this type of product is generally a pretty personal affair, so that one suspects that there is a great deal of room for individual personality variables to affect the use of antacid-analgesics.

Given one's cultural background and susceptibility to the relevant symptoms, one suspects that attitudes towards one's own health would affect the decision to use a proprietary medicine. It is significant that use tends to be higher among hypochondriacs—or at least among people who show a greater than average concern with their health. Thus, in the accompanying chart, people who expect a great deal of illness tend to use antacid-analgesics more frequently.

USAGE RELATED TO HEALTH ATTITUDES

| Age | *Average Annual Dosage* | | | | | |
| | *35 or under* | | *36–50* | | *Over 50* | |
Health Attitude	Poor	Good	Poor	Good	Poor	Good
Low educational level	4.1	3.9	14.2	12.2	13.5	5.8
High educational level	3.2	3.4	15.7	10.8	11.5	4.9

This chart is about men. Note that for every age group and for each educational level, usage is greater among people with a *poor* opinion of their health than among those with a good opinion of their health— with only one exception.

The questions I'd like to answer here are:

1. How do you decide which attitude or temperament variables to examine?
2. Of what earthly use is the information?

Answer the first question by saying—deep thinking. But the fact is that while this finding of the relation between hypochondria and antacid-analgesic usage seems just what you'd expect after you see it, it was called to our attention rather dramatically by some depth interviews which were really intensive case histories. In some 20 case histories it was obvious that the more frequent users were all marked hypochondriacs and the non-users were people who were aggressive in their assertions that they enjoyed perfect health.

Back in the early days of marketing research—three or four years ago —there would have been many people in the marketing research business who would have been content to take the results of these 20 interviews and form conclusions. But enough of us feel the need for a sample large enough to permit an analysis of the relation between different factors.

The answer to the second question is that to be effective, the advertising message must take into account the health attitudes of the potential user. One would expect to communicate one way with a person who hated to admit that he was ill and was only seeking relief for a well localized symptom, and another way with a person who complained about various aches and pains and was possibly seeking to allay non-specific anxieties.

Another personality variable which appears to differentiate users of this product class is what one might call "compulsiveness." This is measured by the extent of agreement or disagreement with such statements as:

I like to set up a schedule for my activities and then stick to it.
I never seem to be able to throw things away.
Most people don't keep themselves as clean as they should.
I make decisions only after a great deal of thought.

The following chart shows the effect of compulsiveness—as measured by agreement with the first of these statements on antacid-analgesic usage.

USAGE RELATED TO COMPULSIVENESS

| Age | Average Annual Dosage | | | | | |
| | 35 or under | | 36–50 | | Over 50 | |
	Compulsive	Non-compulsive	Compulsive	Non-compulsive	Compulsive	Non-compulsive
Low education	6.5	4.2	14.5	9.9	9.2	10.0
High education	3.5	2.8	13.9	12.9	8.2	4.5

The significance of this factor is illustrated by the fact that our client had been having considerable success with an advertising campaign based on a principal theme which was in itself ineffective. However, the advertising presented Brominex in the context of a routine or schedule or regimen. It seemed to be this element of imposed orderly routine which was appealing to the compulsive tendencies of the users of this product class. Incidentally, establishing this conjecture required a secondary analysis to show that compulsives were more attracted by the advertisement in question than non-compulsives.

Still another area which was relevant in the examination of this product class was the attitude toward discipline and punishment. Some people tend to be punitive or puritanical, others permissive. People who tend to be more self-punitive rather than hedonistic in their outlook might want a medicine that gives relief to taste bad in order to do them good. The analysis of this factor is interesting because it illustrates an ever present pitfall in considerations of this sort. Our first conclusion was that *punitiveness* is positively associated with usage. Here, punitiveness is measured by agreement with such statements as:

People learn a great deal from suffering.
Discipline is the single most important factor in building children's character.

However, it can be seen from the following chart that if one shows the appropriate regard for the basic variables of age and education, the

USAGE RELATED TO PUNITIVENESS

Age	35 or under		36 to 50		Over 50	
	Punitive	Non-punitive	Punitive	Non-punitive	Punitive	Non-punitive
Low education	6.4	4.5	12.7	17.7	7.4	9.1
High education	3.1	3.9	13.6	15.5	4.7	5.1

opposite is the case. Within any age-education cell, punitive people use less than non-punitive ones. What misled us at the outset was the compound effect that:

1. Lower education groups tend to have more punitive attitudes.
2. Lower education groups tend to use more antacid-analgesics.

The fallacious conclusion that antacid-analgesic users tend to have more punitive attitudes was avoided by observing that *within* a given age-education stratum, usage is *negatively* rather than positively associated with punitiveness. In other words, it is *not* necessary or desirable that the product should taste bad.

Now let's try to make the transition from research strategy to marketing strategy. On the basis of these findings one would expect the most successful product in this class to be a lower class product which made extensive claims,[1] advertised regular use, and tasted good. Actually the *single* dominant product in the field was one used widely by the higher status groups, which advertised very specific use and made fewer broad claims than other products. It was a product which had higher approval by doctors and hospitals than most others. It didn't taste particularly good but was in the process of correcting this defect; it was not our client's product.

The reason for the unexpected success of this leading product was simple. Instead of competing with other products for the most profitable segments of the antacid-analgesic market, that contrary product had captured the less prominent—but still highly significant minority segments—where it had no competitor.

Incidentally this was a pleasant by-product of the study. Our client had been developing a different type of analgesic beamed toward this segment. The study confirmed his hunch that there was room for a competitive product here.

So, answering the *why* question with a *who* question had these positive results:

1. It pointed to an important segment which offered potential for a new product which our client was developing to supplement his present major product.

[1] It would have to cure many things to satisfy the hypochondriac.

2. It enabled him to direct the advertising for his present major product more effectively since he knew whom he was speaking to.

Now let's examine some of the limitations and difficulties of this approach of segmentation by personality types.

It is interesting that the difference in usage between the various personality groups is not very large. Thus, it is not as large as the difference between age or sex groups or between social class groups.

This phenomenon occurs rather frequently. One might think that it was a function of scales or tests to characterize these groups. It is true that where one is dealing with a scalable characteristic and where it is possible to pick out the extremes, the differences between these extremes are a little larger, but even then the differences are often small.

It is probably not possible to address oneself to a clearly delineated compulsive group. *What one should do is to address himself to the compulsive in all of us.*

Social and personality variables operate in a kind of residual area left by the product considerations. The residual nature of these variables becomes even more pronounced for large ticket items where product or price considerations are more important.

For conspicuous consumption items, social class considerations are likely to outweigh personality factors. To illustrate this another product generally consumed in public has implications of social status. This is a liquor product somewhat like a liqueur or cordial but used more widely than products of that type are generally. Let's call it *Bayou Rum.*

Since this is a drink that would often be served in company, it is not surprising that it has a very definite social position. A broad cut at the subject by such variables as income and education shows that usage is greater *towards* but not *at* the upper end of the scale.

BAYOU RUM USAGE BY EDUCATION

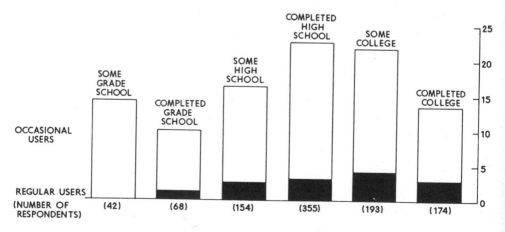

This impression is reinforced by our looking at the relation between objective social class as measured by occupation and status orientation as measured by the person's assignment of himself to a social class.

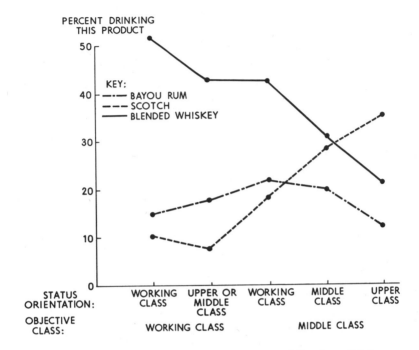

BAYOU RUM USAGE BY SOCIAL CLASS

Here it is clear that our product is really a middle class drink.

The social position is spelled out even more clearly by relating usage to social mobility. Its use is by far the greatest among stable members of the middle class.

BAYOU RUM USAGE

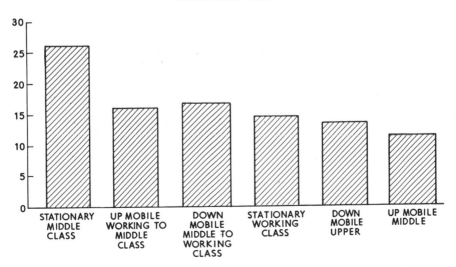

How does one know whether he should be looking at social characteristics, at personality or temperament traits? Which traits are likely to be important? How deep should one go into motivations?

A passage from a recent very interesting book on Motivational Research by Harry Henry puts the matter interestingly. It says, "This sort of case-history makes fascinating reading, for a time. But sooner or later the profit-conscious business-man is bound to ask himself what guidance this gives him for the formulation of manufacturing, marketing, or advertising policies. And it is for this reason that, . . ., constructive and useful Motivation Research is concerned only with getting *sufficiently* below the surface to do the necessary job."

I don't think that anyone can disagree with this statement any more than anyone can use it for practical guidance. It is patently uneconomical to get more information or more depth than one needs. But I don't know of anyone who can be certain that he has enough information unless he has too much—at least in the sense of being able to select and reject, or who can be sure he's thought enough about something until he's thought too much.

Many of us in the marketing research profession pride ourselves on the desire to focus research on a specific marketing decision. True, this makes for efficient research. But I wonder if there isn't failure to understand all aspects of a problem. In fact, it is only when the researcher knows much more about a situation that he can profitably communicate an airtight case to management.

Finally, no matter how skillfully such an analysis has been conducted, the road to marketing strategy is still tortuous. What starts out as a good idea based on sound research may lead to a poor strategy.

As we get more sophisticated in developing research which produces ideas leading to marketing strategies, we will have to start tackling seriously the tremendously difficult problem of testing these strategies—of measuring advertising and marketing success and relating it to the specific components of the strategies developed.

C. Perception

Perception is the study of the process by which an individual sizes up and makes sense out of stimuli received by his sensory receptors. As such, it is of vital significance in the analysis of buyer behavior; yet, it has been largely ignored until rather recently. In part, this is because the study of perception has only recently matured in the related behavioral sciences.

Each of the two articles included here focuses on somewhat different aspects of perception. Engel reviews the literature on selective perception, and assesses findings on the influence of needs and attitudes. Levy takes a somewhat different tack and develops the manner in which meaning is attributed to various products and services that are viewed, in his opinion, as symbols. He stresses that this meaning is complex, and he thereby clarifies the manner in which the personality characteristics and past information stored in one's control unit profoundly affect the way in which stimuli are evaluated. Levy's article is rich with managerial significance.

5. THE INFLUENCE OF NEEDS AND ATTITUDES ON THE PERCEPTION OF PERSUASION*

James F. Engel

My purpose is to review and interpret the literature of psychology and communications pertaining to what is loosely called "selective perception." The topic has been defined to encompass the evidence on the manner in which an individual's needs and attitudes affect his reactions to persuasive communication.

This paper will discuss the nature of selective perception, a summary of the findings of a literature survey, a discussion of the implications of these findings, and a statement of directions for future research.

THE NATURE OF PERCEPTION

An unequivocal definition of perception is sidestepped by most authorities. Generally, the concept refers to the process by which a stimulus and a response are related. The nature of this assumed relationship can best be grasped by a diagram.

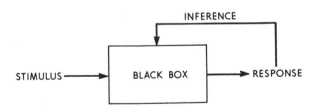

An individual is exposed to a stimulus of some sort which he receives through his five senses to taste, touch, smell, sight, and hearing. Some-

*From *Toward Scientific Marketing*, American Marketing Association, December, 1963, pp. 18–29.

thing happens in his unseen mental mechanisms, or "black box," to give meaning to these inputs, and this reaction is translated into an output—either overt behavior or some other response. To explain this process an inference is necessary to what happened within the black box, and the literature of psychology abounds with theories of this type.

Much of contemporary perception theory is built on the assumption that each stimulus or information input is somehow checked against stored categories of meaning. Many of these categories function quite predictably from individual to individual. For example, a yellow pencil is usually perceived as a yellow pencil because of its distance and angle from the perceiver, its relationship to its surroundings, and common individual experience with pencils among other reasons. Other times, however, the response is unpredictable and appears to depend upon unique individual predispositions such as physical needs, psychological needs, and attitudes. In the latter instance the person is said to perceive selectively.

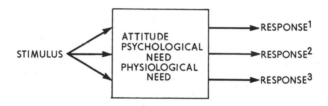

Each of these factors (attitude, psychological need, or physiological need) can become dominant and affect the response, and it is also probable that they somehow work in combination. It will become apparent, however, that little is known about how and why they work in this manner, and this is an important limitation to be elaborated upon later.

SUMMARY OF EVIDENCE

Let us now proceed to a summary of the findings of the review of literature. The discussion will be organized under the three headings used above: (1) physiological influence; (2) psychological influence; and (3) attitudes.

Physiological influence

The typical experiment designed to isolate the influence of physiological or bodily needs on perception usually encompasses experimental manipulation of need. A typical experimental design may include deprivation of a subject for a period of time followed by momentary exposure to some kind of ambiguous stimuli which will permit responses consistent with a state of need. In one important study, for instance, Atkinson and McClelland deprived a group of subjects of food for varying periods of time up to 24 hours.[1] Some subjects were led to believe they viewed the projection of slides on a screen, but nothing appeared. Even in the absence of real stimuli, subjects replied that they saw food objects, and this tendency increased reliably as hours of food deprivation increased.

Numerous other experimenters have found similar results, leading Jenkin to conclude that properly designed stimulus objects will induce selective perception in keeping with a state of bodily need.[2]

PSYCHOLOGICAL INFLUENCE

Literally hundreds of experimental reports in the literature affirm that psychological needs and personal values can affect perception. For example, Bruner and Goodman determined in their now classic 1947 study that children from low socio-economic backgrounds tend to over-estimate the size of coins when adjusting a patch of light to correspond with various types.[3] Similar tendencies were not exhibited by wealthy children. Supposedly, then, the variable of social class mirrors a need for money which is reflected in perceptual reactions. Other experimenters have found conflicting results, but most authorities feel that the evidence favors the interpretation that value and need, working through perceptual mechanisms, are determinants of size judgments.

Another important series of experiments has been undertaken to assess the role of personal values on thresholds for value-related words. The common hypothesis seems to be that individuals are sensitive to words reflecting values which are important to them, and hence the perceptual threshold or reaction time will be lower for these words. Early studies verified this hypothesis but neglected to control for the possibility that individuals will be more familiar with value-related words and should be expected to react quickly for this reason alone. Later studies have determined that value appears to influence reactions only on words which are infrequent in usage. Perhaps it is acceptable to conclude that the selective influence of values on perception appears to have been demonstrated, but ambiguities of evidence still remain due to methodological difficulties.

Other published studies indicate that there appears to be little doubt that psychological influences in perception are pervasive. The value and size judgment experiments are mentioned here primarily to point up a problem in interpreting the psychological literature. Note that word familiarity, if uncontrolled, will in itself dictate findings consistent

---

[1]D. C. McClelland and J. W. Atkinson, "The Projective Expression of Needs: 1. The Effect of Different Intensities of the Hunger Drive on Perception," *Journal of Psychology*, Vol. 25 (1949), pp. 205–22.

[2]Noel Jenkin, "Affective Processes in Perception," *Psychological Bulletin*, Vol. 54 (1957), pp. 100–27.

[3]J. S. Bruner and Cecile C. Goodman, "Value and Need as Organizing Factors in Perception," *Journal of Abnormal and Social Psychology*, Vol. 42 (1947), pp. 33–44.

with the hypothesis in the value studies. Therefore, artifacts of the research design can be responsible for results, and the variables under analysis are obscured. The history of psychological experimentation shows a tortuous process in arriving at generalizations which withstand methodological criticism. Perhaps the best conclusion to draw is the fallacy of accepting any study at face value without awareness of its predecessors and its followers. This precaution has sometimes been violated by those who would have us believe that the behavioral sciences are some sort of salvation for marketing theory and practice. All too frequently, this is far from being true.

Before leaving this series of studies, let us raise the question as to whether or not individuals can unconsciously screen stimuli and distort their response. The evidence on this issue is complicated, and a controversy was generated by the finding that GSR (skin response) shows elevation upon exposure to unacceptable stimuli such as swear words. The presumption is that GSR reflects unconscious reaction.

Critics have since claimed that the common definition of threshold (the division point between perception and non-perception) which relies on correct reactions 50 percent of the time does not rule out conscious perception below the threshold. It is claimed that some information is gathered from the stimulus even though an incorrect verbal response is given, and there is supporting evidence for this point of view. Once again methodological difficulties have introduced uncertainty, so the most that can be claimed is that unconscious perceptual screening has neither been proved nor disproved convincingly. Perhaps it is sufficient to state that advertisers have enough problems without worrying about unconscious perceptual activity until more convincing evidence is available.

THE INFLUENCE OF ATTITUDES

No specific attention has thus far been directed toward studies documenting the role of motivational influences on reactions to persuasion. The primary reason is that experiments conducted for this purpose largely focus on attitudes.

It appears on the basis of an extensive volume of evidence that three generalizations are warranted. All other things being equal:

1. Persuasion which contradicts or otherwise is inconsistent with the predispositions of those for whom it is intended is likely to provoke a reaction of selective exposure whereby non-acceptable messages are avoided.
2. Once exposed to the message, the individual may perceive and interpret it in a manner consistent with his predispositions toward that topic, and appeals which deviate substantially from these predispositions are likely to be distorted or otherwise interpreted in a manner not intended.

3. Recipients of persuasive communication messages will tend selectively to recall appeals in a manner consistent with existing predispositions toward the topic. Unacceptable appeals are likely to be forgotten.

The data relative to these generalizations are extensive, and they warrant careful study by all involved in advertising or selling. It does appear, as Bauer points out, that a communication tends to trigger a response representing substantially what the individual was likely to do in any event.[4]

IMPLICATIONS OF FINDINGS

A full appreciation of the implications of the evidence on motivational influences in perception, of course, requires a more extensive appreciation of methodological problems and the chain of evidence which has been generated over time on each topic. By necessity, these points have been referred to here only briefly.

In general, it seems safe to state that motivational factors such as needs, values, and attitudes can and do influence perception. Probably it goes without saying that this evidence should put to an end all beliefs that consumers can be appealed to in any manner without knowledge of their psychological makeup. A market can be segmented along any of these variables, so a real service has been performed by the psychologist in isolating factors which *can induce* selective reactions to persuasion.

Do we now know enough, however, to state clearly what is likely to happen when, say, a consumer is exposed to an advertisement? Can we predict his reaction and thereby provide a firm basis for decision making? The answer unfortunately must be "no" at this time. Perhaps one could state that it may be rewarding to attempt to assess reactions to promotional appeals when subjects are experimentally placed under states of need deprivation, for example, or when distinct attitudinal differences exist. Laboratory experimentation along these lines may give an insight into the manner in which motivational states direct responses to an appeal, but such efforts can only be tentative and perhaps speculative. Prediction of response, our ultimate objective, still remains for the future.

It is important that we see the reasons for this somewhat negative conclusion. In exposing our consumer to the advertisement, what is the stimulus? Is it the product feature, the use of color, or what? Then, what is his response? He might purchase the product, show an elevated skin response, react with a look of boredom, or perhaps give no visible response. The point is that the stimulus used and the resulting response

---

[4]Raymond A. Bauer, "The Communicator and the Audience," *Journal of Conflict Resolution*, Vol. 2 (1958), pp. 66–77.

must be specified with great precision, and this strikes at the heart of many methodological criticisms appearing in the psychological literature such as those referred to earlier. The evidence by and large must remain tentative for predictive purposes until greater precision is attained in research methodology. Broadbent puts it this way:

> The classical type of perception experiment is eminently suitable for fields in which all subjects behave similarly, in which the subjects possess an accurate vocabulary for describing their experience and in which a fairly brief experience is followed by an interval in which it may be described. But these are severe limitations, particularly the last: the closer we come to the problems of everyday life, the harder it is to stay within them.[5]

Perhaps even more important is the question of why his response or lack of response occurred. No unifying theory of perceptual processes has yet emerged. Perception has been conceived as covering a practically limitless list of variables such as needs, wishes, and rationalizations. We appear to have gone too far and have included nearly everything under this concept, thereby obscuring the mechanisms involved. In other words, it is necessary to attempt to uncover more specifically *what the individual does with information received from the environment* before the evidence will attain much predictive usefulness. New insights may then be derived into the relationship between inputs and outputs.

To sum up, a large and valuable step has thus far been taken—the isolation of key motivational influences in perception. Hurdles yet remain, however, before these findings attain real practical significance.

DIRECTIONS FOR FUTURE RESEARCH

A revolution is now underway in thinking and experimentation on perception, and there are two key incidents to report: (1) experimentation on higher mental processes and (2) dissonance theory.

EXPERIMENTATION ON HIGHER MENTAL PROCESSES

Broadbent and others are exploring some exciting new frontiers. Primary attention is being directed to the mechanisms which seem to influence perception. Broadbent in particular departs somewhat from stimulus-response methods and considers the translation of perceptual input into output in view of a whole group of possible stimuli.[6] He clearly distinguishes between the arrival of this information to one's senses and the uses made of the information by the individual. Starting with the assumption that perception is a neural rather than a sensory process, he has postulated the existence of limits on capacity and has isolated important principles which seem to explain why some informa-

---

[5]D. E. Broadbent, *Perception and Communication* (New York: Pergamon Press, 1958), pp. 7–8.
[6]*Ibid.*

tion is accepted and other information is discarded. Evidence thus far appears to support the existence of a filtering mechanism between the sensory receptors and central mental mechanisms as well as immediate and long-term memory centers, both of which perform very different functions.

Chomsky and others at MIT are pursuing a much broader line of inquiry. They are attempting to develop a theory of the mind which will explain perceptual behavior and other mental processes such as learning. Computer simulation models are being utilized as analogies with little or no reliance on stimulus-response models.

Inquiries of this type are tentative at the moment, but the writer is optimistic that a meaningful theory of perception is not far in the future. This work bears close watching by marketing men, because it may contain some of the missing keys to successful prediction of promotional response.

DISSONANCE THEORY

A second promising development, the theory of cognitive dissonance, seems to offer some rich insights into the role of attitudes in reactions to persuasion. Cognitive dissonance refers to a state of anxiety arising from non-fitting cognitions (that is, knowledges, opinions or beliefs) regarding some topic or event. The heavy smoker may very well experience dissonance when he hears claims that smoking may cause cancer. Attempts will no doubt be made to remove this conflict by stopping smoking, by seeking out new evidence to downgrade the claimed relationship between smoking and cancer, or by avoiding exposure to new information causing dissonance.

The evidence on cognitive dissonance to date is tentative, largely because three criteria must be met before dissonance can be demonstrated: (1) the individual must be committed to a point of view; (2) the undertaking of dissonance-causing action must be done as a result of free will (volition), because to offer a reward, for example, may induce behavior to receive the reward without any voluntary commitment to dissonance-causing action; and (3) the issue or behavior must be of some importance to the individual or dissonance will not arise. Nonetheless, the implications of dissonance are worth exploring, because a potentially useful basis is provided upon which to explore the perception of persuasive messages.

Reconsideration of selective processes. Hovland has pointed out that attitude change can be produced in the laboratory when subjects have no particular point of view on a topic and when issues often assume little importance.[7] Yet he notes that studies conducted in the field usually involve deep-seated issues such as racial prejudice and political prefer-

---

[7]C. I. Hovland, "Reconciling Conflicting Results Derived from Experimental and Survey Studies of Atttiude Change," *American Psychologist*, Vol. 14 (1959), pp. 8–17.

ences. When this is true, selective exposure, perception, and retention usually result. Notice that the three criteria of dissonance studies appear to be met: (1) commitment to a point of view; (2) opportunity for exposure to contradictory information under volition; and (3) issue importance. The upshot seems to be that individuals can avoid dissonance caused by contradictory information through selective exposure, selective perception, and selective retention.

It thus appears even more definite that the possibility of selective exposure, perception, and retention of promotional messages cannot be dismissed, especially if the target of these efforts is committed to another product through brand loyalty. If this commitment is present, it seems reasonable to expect that a kind of defense mechanism will be activated through dissonance processes to screen out unwanted promotion and to screen in messages which reinforce preferences.

The difficulty of creating dissonance through advertising also raises the question of the relative efficacy of voluntary versus involuntary exposure. Can involuntary exposure, for example, through television advertisements, arouse dissonance and possibly motivate the viewer to undertake purchasing action? The answer can be yes under most circumstances *only* if the viewer watches the advertisements and voluntarily considers contradictory information, but it is doubtful that true volition accompanies the viewing of many commercials. No doubt selective exposure would occur if the individual had the means more readily available. The fallacy of assuming that advertising exposure infers favorable advertising results becomes abundantly obvious. Dissonance theory may thus present a useful perspective to discover the psychological nature of voluntary and involuntary exposure.

The discussion thus far assumes the existence of brand preferences. Evidence seems to indicate that consumers regularly develop smoothly working routines for purposes of buying efficiency and embrace certain brands for this purpose. Continued satisfied use of a product or of several brands which offer comparable satisfactions only reinforces this loyalty and renders the consumer a progressively less accessible promotional target. Furthermore, this situation is likely to become accentuated as the consumer is faced with more new products and more competing advertising messages. A point is simply reached where continued exposure can become overwhelming. This prediction does not paint a pretty picture for the advertiser of tomorrow, but it may be a fatal mistake to assume otherwise.

Seeking consonant information. A series of studies in the dissonance literature tentatively supports the hypothesis that a person experiencing dissonance will seek out information to restore a neutral state. It no doubt is fairly common to expect that advertising functions at times to reach dissonant consumers. Perhaps the consumer has experienced negative results with a product or service and finds his commitment badly shaken. Such a situation presents an ideal promotional opportunity; the full informational and persuasive powers of advertising would be exerted. The problem, of course, is that such an opportunity represents only individual incidents that are almost impossible to isolate and capitalize upon in a mass market.

Also notice the possible role of advertising to confirm brand loyalty in existing consumers. The writer has explored the implications of advertising to new owners of automobiles as have others. While the evidence is contradictory, it may be that new purchasers of many products look to advertisements for reassurance following purchase. Additional investigation into this topic is clearly warranted.

The role of "forcing methods." Let us turn to quite a different aspect of dissonance theory. Several studies demonstrate the possibility that attitude change can follow commitment to dissonant behavior under conditions of volition. The implications of this finding are intriguing. Quite an assortment of promotional gimmicks is available, such as price offers and premiums, to induce a consumer to try a given product or service. Often such direct action or forcing methods are used on the assumption that trial of a product may weaken or destroy preference for a competing brand. It is more probable, however, that nothing will result, because the consumer was not induced to try the product under true volition. As several studies have demonstrated, she may reason that the offer is too great to pass up for one purchase while existing preferences remain unshaken. Additional research is needed to verify or refute this hypothesis.

SUMMARY

The role of brand loyalty seems to be a central one in the selective perception of advertising. It is recommended that advertisers seriously consider continuing analysis of the strength of brand preferences both of existing consumers and of those buying competing products. Attitude scaling devices and other methodology are available for this purpose. A good indication should thus be provided of the chances of holding one's present market and of making inroads into a competitor's market share. If existing consumers are found to lack commitment to the product, in all probability they are vulnerable to competitive efforts. It is then essential to analyze all phases of the marketing mix with an eye toward remedial efforts.

Additional evidence obviously is required if these suggestions are to have much practical significance. First, it must be determined whether or not brand loyalty represents psychological commitment or merely is an habitual response generated by inertia. Also, it is not known if dissonance resistance arising from commitment can vary from product to product, although one would expect the commitment to a convenience good to be less psychologically secure than to a major purchase item.

Furthermore, dissonance has not been examined over time. What will happen, for example, under the cross-fire of competitive advertising over a period of months? Finally, selective exposure, perception, and retention may represent boredom with advertising and not dissonance. These possibilities might be investigated profitably by directing research toward those who were not exposed or who did not react favorably to promotion.

CONCLUSIONS

A full appreciation of this complex subject necessitates a thoughtful analysis of the evidence. Nevertheless, it should be apparent that a number of key variables which can influence reactions to persuasion have been documented in the psychological literature. No doubt there will always be skeptics saying that most of these variables have been known for years to marketing practitioners and that explorations in the behavioral sciences should be abandoned in favor of the "mainstream of marketing" as it has long been known. There, of course, is one fundamental truth in such a statement: it is totally unwarranted to deny that a valid body of knowledge called marketing exists and to propose that existing literature be abandoned, as some have done recently. On the other hand, long embraced notions must be subjected to experimentation and analysis to assess their validity if progress is to be made. *To the extent that the psychologist has clarified experimentally the variables underlying promotional response, existing marketing knowledge has been expanded and enriched.*

Again it must be stated that for various reasons little predictive use can *now* be made of the findings on perception of promotional messages. I am optimistic that inquiry into higher mental processes ultimately will yield a general theory relating many of the variables discussed in this paper. For now, however, dissonance theory provides one useful meeting ground for psychologists and marketing men in that it represents a welcome step, albeit a small and tentative one, past the listing of variables stage. If nothing else, a heretofore non-existent perspective is provided upon which to base well-oriented research into the promotional task.

It should be clear that psychology has not provided definitive solutions to overcoming selective perception of persuasion, and much is yet to be learned. It is high time that we cease making sweeping and unsupported statements about the great untapped reservoir of knowledge in the behavioral sciences, because such claims usually dissolve upon careful analysis. Critical and knowledgeable analysis of the psychological literature will continue to be rewarding, but improvement in methods and theory is not the psychologist's task alone. As useful developments are reported, it is our role to interpret and apply them whenever there is the smallest hint of managerial significance. With this effort a body of valid experimental evidence should result which moves beyond our present knowledge of perceptual processes. The net result cannot help but be a gain in the efficiency of promotional efforts.

6. SYMBOLS BY WHICH WE BUY*

Sidney J. Levy

The science and practice of marketing have recently been infused with new life. There are many reasons for this. One of the core reasons is that behavior in the marketplace has become increasingly elaborated. The great multiplicity of goods, the burgeoning of new products, and their eager fruition in the consumers' homes, have moved our society to a point where practical considerations in the purchase of goods are often not given the central attention that was true in the past. The modern marketplace—exemplified so dramatically in the vast supermarket, whether called food, drug, or furniture store—reminds us daily of the marketing revolution that has come about.

In these new settings, with their astonishing arrays of merchandise, their frozen, prepackaged, precooked foods; their plastic containers; their polyethylene gadgets; and their intellectual appliances that can thoughtfully govern their own behavior—what kind of consumer is conjured into being? It is hardly an economic man—especially since there is a lot of evidence that he does not buy economically; is often vague about the actual price he pays for something; has few standards for judging the quality of what he buys; and often winds up not using it anyway! This is not just a joke. The point I am making is that nowadays when people shop, they buy relatively lavishly. They still talk about price and quality and durability, since these are regarded as sensible traditional values. At the same time, they know that other factors influence them, and they believe these to be legitimate influences. This point is worth some emphasis since there are many who disapprove of the fact that purchases may be made on grounds they think are insubstantial. The fact that people don't buy their furniture to last 20 years may be deplored as a sign of the lightheadedness of our times; on the other hand, such massive, stoutly made furniture may be dismissed from the home at the behest of other values in comfortable living and changing tastes.

Not only do people not want furniture such as grandmother used to cherish; they also know that practical considerations can hardly determine their choice between Post or Kellogg, between Camels or Luckies, between Buick or Oldsmobile, between Arpege or Chanel. They know that package color and television commercials, newspaper and magazine

*From *Advancing Marketing Efficiency,* American Marketing Association, December, 1958, pp. 409–16.

ads incline them toward one preference or another—and when they can't really tell the difference among competitive brands of the same product, they don't believe that any of them should necessarily go out of business for being unable to distinguish his product.

At the heart of all this is the fact that the consumer is not as functionally oriented as he used to be, if he ever really was. The esthetic preferences that were there have changed somewhat—we no longer go in for stained glass lamps and antimacassars, although the latter were probably more attractive than transparent couch covers; and the diversity of choices that are now possible in the ways people can spend their money makes for a diversity of reasons for the choices. When people talk about the things they buy and why they buy them, they show a variety of logics. They refer to convenience, inadvertence, family pressures, other social pressures, complex economic reasonings, advertising, pretty colors, a wide range of feelings and wishes. They are trying to satisfy many aims and circumstances. The pleasure they gain from buying objects is ever more playful—less the question, do I need this? more the ideas, do I want it? do I like it? Answering these questions takes the definition of goods into new realms—at least new in the sense that they are studied more nowadays. The things people buy are seen to have personal and social meanings in addition to their functions. Modern goods are recognized as psychological things, as symbolic of personal attributes and goals, as symbolic of social patterns and strivings. In this sense, all commercial objects have a symbolic character, and making a purchase involves an assessment—implicit or explicit—of this symbolism, to decide whether or not it fits. Energy (and money) will be given when the symbols are appropriate ones, and denied or given parsimoniously when they are not. What determines their appropriateness?

A symbol is appropriate—and the product will be used and enjoyed when it joins with, meshes with, adds to, reinforces, the way the consumer thinks about himself. In the broadest sense, each person aims to enhance his sense of self, to behave in ways that are consistent with a set of ideas he has about the kind of person he is or wants to be. Prescott Lecky has written an interesting essay on how people behave in consistence with their self-concepts.[1] The variety of goods available permits more ways of living than was ever the case. Because of their symbolic nature, consumer goods can be chosen with less conflict or indecision than would otherwise be the case. Buridan's ass starved to death equidistant between two piles of attractive hay; he wouldn't have had the problem if one pile had been a bit more asinine—let's say—than the other. Our choices are made easier—either more routine, or more impulsive, seemingly—because one object is symbolically more harmonious to our goals, feelings, and self-definitions than is another. The difference may not be a large one, nor a very important one, in the manufacture or adver-

---

[1] Prescott Lecky, *Self-consistency* (New York: Island Press, 1945).

tising of the products; but it may be big enough to dictate a constant direction of preference in the indulgence of one's point of view. There is then more well with the world when the bathroom tissue is pastel blue, the car a large one, the newspaper a tabloid size, the trousers with pleats, and so on. It becomes increasingly fashionable to be a connoisseur or gourmet of *some* kind, to consume with one or another standard of discrimination at work.

Research helps to identify the kinds of symbols utilized in the market, and the intensity with which they operate as determinants of purchases. Because some people don't like the idea that such things as feelings and symbols are influential in situations which they feel should be more purely utilitarian, they dislike research that investigates such ideas and meanings. Sometimes they even blame the research for having caused the phenomena, as though a microscope were responsible for the goodness or badness of the bacteria it examines.

In several years of research into the symbolic nature of products, of brands, of institutions and media of communication, much has been shown of the way consumers are able to gauge subtly and grossly the symbolic language of these objects, and to translate them into meanings for themselves. They understand that darker colors are symbolic of more "respectable" products, that pastel colors mean softness, youthfulness, femininity; that yellows and brown are manly, that red is exciting and provocative. They "know" that science means technical merits and an interest in quality and probably less enjoyment; that theatrical references imply glamour and the suspension of staid criteria. They think that Winston Churchill would be good testimony for cigars, whiskey, and books; and if they are very average consumers they are apt to miss (or ignore) the point of a Springmaid sheet ad altogether.

One of the most basic dimensions of symbolism is gender. Almost all societies make some differential disposition of the sexes, deciding who will do what; which objects will be reserved to men and which to women. They usually find it hard to evade thinking of inanimate things as male or female. Through such personalization, vessels tend to become feminine —and motherly if they are big enough. Men are challenged by the virgin forest which must be raped of its resources; they fall in love with their ships and cars, giving them women's names. And such places and objects are reserved for men, relatively speaking.

In America there has been complaint that some of this differentiation is fading, that women get more like men, and men shift to meet them, in a movement toward homogeneous togetherness. No doubt hunting and agricultural societies make sharper distinction between what is masculine and what is feminine. Still, products and behaviors tend to be more one or the other, and in minutely graded ways. Probably all cigarette brands could be placed on a continuum of degrees of gender, as one of their complex symbolic patternings. The same is true for musical compositions, and the recorded interpretations of any one of them, of cheeses and the brand versions of each kind.

These sexual definitions may seem absurd at times, and often are of modest influence in one or another choice. But they are at work and form a natural part of, for instance, the housewife's logic (and teaching) as she makes her selections in the food store and serves her family. She sums it up by thinking of what will please her husband's preference, what a growing boy should have, what is just right for a girl's delicate tastes. Since smoothness is generally understood to be more feminine, as foods go, it seems fitting that girls should prefer smooth peanut butter and boys the chunky. While the overlap is great, a cultivated society teaches such a discrimination, and the children, being attentive to their proper sex roles, learn it early. Families work busily at such indoctrination of symbolic appropriateness. One little 6-year-old boy protested in an interview how he had never liked peanut butter, but that his mother and sister had always insisted that he did, and now he loved it. Apparently a violent bias in favor of peanut butter is suitable to little boys, and may be taken as representing something of the rowdy boyishness of childhood, as against more restrained and orderly foods.

Similarly, in a recent study of a pair of cheese advertisements for a certain cheese, one wedge of it was shown in a setting of brown wooden cutting board, dark bread, and a glimpse of a chess game. The cheese wedge was depicted standing erect on its smallest base. Although no people were shown, consumers interpreted the ad as part of a masculine scene, men playing a game, being served a snack. The same cheese was also shown in a setting with lighter colors, a suggestion of a floral bowl, with the wedge lying flat on one of its longer sides. This was interpreted by consumers as a feminine scene, probably with ladies lunching in the vicinity. Each ad worked to convey a symbolic impression of the product, to modify or enhance the beliefs already held about it. Symbols of gender are among the most readily recognized. Most people are usually quite alert to whether something is addressed to them as a man or as a woman. Similarly symbols of age are familiar. Teenagers are quite sensitive to communications which imply childishness. Presented with a layout showing a family going on a picnic, their reaction is apt to be, "Kid stuff." They are trying to break away from the family bosom. While they might actually enjoy a family picnic, the scene symbolizes restraint, being unable to get away to be with people their own age. Clothing is quite carefully graded in people's eyes; we normally judge within a few years' span whether some garment is fitted to the age of the wearer. Women are particularly astute (and cruel) in this, but men also observe when a pin-striped suit is too mature for one wearer, or when an outfit is too young for a man who should be acting his age.

Symbols of social participation are among the most dramatic factors in marketing. Most goods say something about the social world of the people who consume them. Debate goes on now whether automobiles are still related to people's social wishes or strivings, because some motivation research brought this rather well-known fact to the fore, and because some advertising has taken rather self-conscious account of it. This hardly changes the fact that cars say prominent things about their owners, and are likely to continue to do so. Like it or not, there are social class groupings formed by the ways people live, the attitudes they have, the acceptance and exclusiveness of their associations. The things they own are partly chosen to attest to their social positions, in one way or another. The possession of mink is hardly a matter of winter warmth alone, as all women know who wear mink with slacks while strolling at a beach resort. The social stature of mink—and its downgrading—leads us to marvel that it is now sold at Sears. But then, Sears has upgraded itself and become more middle class too. Shopping at Sears is symbolic of a certain chic among many middle class people who used to regard it as much more working class. Now they boast that Sears is especially suitable for certain kinds of merchandise, and their candor in saying they shop there is not matter-of-fact but is laughing, as if to point out that it is an amusing quirk in one's social behavior.

Membership in one social class or another tends to affect one's general outlook, modes of communication, concreteness of thinking and understanding.[2] Advertising often says different things to people of different social levels. A perfume ad showing an anthropological mask and swirling colors is likely to be incomprehensible to many working class women, whereas New Yorker readers will at least pretend they grasp the symbolism. On the other hand, working class women will accept a crowded, dark, screaming sale advertisement as meaning urgency and potential interest, while higher status women will ignore it as signaling inferiority. Sometimes, the symbolism becomes confined to a social class subgroup: even some upper middle class people aren't sure what is being said in various modern liquor ads with their groups of sinister men, their red shoes, and handsome males riding sidesaddle. Even while suspecting the symbolic language may be gibberish, they have some undercurrent of anxiety about not being part of the ingroup who use these "nonsense syllables" to tell each other about vodka. Since, as Susanne Langer discusses so well, symbolizing is a natural human function, it is not reserved to such formal categories as gender, age, and social status.[3] Any given complex of acts, gestures, movements, pictures, words, will signify much to the consumer. From commercials and ads, from television shows and editorial materials, the viewer or reader concludes about the meanings being offered. These meanings may correspond to the advertiser's inten-

---

[2]Leonard Schatzman and Anselm Strauss, "Social Class and Modes of Communication," *The American Journal of Sociology*, Vol. LX, No. 4 (January, 1955).

[3]Susanne K. Langer, *Philosophy in a New Key* (New York: The New American Library of World Literature, Inc., 1942).

tion—although often they are separate from, in addition to, or even contrary to his aim. A striking instance of such contradictory communication was an advertisement with a headline claiming the product was worth the 1¢ more that it cost when compared to its competitors. Housewives interpreted this claim as a sign of cheapness; they needed only to see the 1¢ in the headline to believe it was "one of those penny deals." Merely the idea of talking about 1¢ suggested cheapening, even to those readers who understood literally what was said. The literal aim had been to refer to the greater worth of the product; the symbolic means used were poor.

As consumers, we buy our way through a welter of symbols reflecting taste patterns, and the multitudes of human qualities we want to attach to ourselves. Just to refer to some of these symbolic poles brings images to our minds of "what that's like." The Ivy League cluster of symbols organizes purchases in one direction; being a suburbanite is a broad identification, but it starts one's purchasing ideas moving in certain lines. Name your own suburb, and they leap into rather sharp focus. Neighbors are quite acute judges of the symbolic significance of how money is spent; they are quick to interpret the appropriateness of your spending pattern for the community, the kind of people you are, making reasonable or unreasonable deductions from books, liquor, power mowers, cars, and the gifts your children give at birthday parties.

Some objects we buy symbolize such personal qualities as self-control, others expose our self-indulgence. We reason in these directions about people who drink and smoke or who don't—and such reasoning will play a role in our choices of doing one or the other. A hard mattress is readily justified on pragmatic grounds of health, sound sleep, and the like; but people recognize the austere self-denial at work that will also strengthen the character. Then again, soft drinks may quench thirst, but people know that they are also buying an indulgent moment, a bit of ease, a lowering of adult restraints.

An outstanding dimension of symbolic guidance to consumers is that of conventionality versus self-expression. Some purchases are very conventional—a quart of milk, for instance. Others are conventional, but allow room for individuality—dishes, cups, silverware, let's say. Books become quite personal purchases, by and large. So, no one thinks much if you have milk on your table; (at least, they reason only generally about children)—it's different when you order a glass of milk at a businessmen's lunch. They also expect dishes, but may admire the taste demonstrated by the pattern. They will respect you personally for *Dr. Zhivago* on the coffee table, and perhaps raise an eyebrow at *Lolita*.

A whole treatise could be written on the symbolic dimension of formality-informality. A great many of our decisions to buy take into account the degree of formal or informal implication of the object. Housewives are constantly gauging the place of hot dogs, the gifts they are giving, the tablecloth they plan to use, with an eye to how informal things are or they want them to be. The movement toward informality has been a fundamental one in recent years, governing the emphasis on casualness in clothes, backyard and buffet meals, staying at motels, and bright colors —with some current overtone of reaction to this and seeking of contrast again in the direction of more graciousness in living, a new interest in the elegance of a black car, a wish for homes with dining rooms, and greater individual privacy.

As this indicates, among all the symbols around us, bidding for our buying attention and energy, there are general trends that seem to fit the spirit of the time more aptly. Every so often there comes along a new symbol, one which makes a leap from the past into the present and has power because it captures the spirit of the present and makes other ongoing symbols old-fashioned. The Pepsi-Cola girl was a symbol of this sort. She had precursors, of course, but she distinctly and prominently sig- nified a modern phantasy and established an advertising style, one some- what removed from the Clabber girl.

I have touched on only a few of the varieties of symbols encountered in the identification of goods in the marketplace, especially as these be- come part of the individual identities of consumers. The topic is as ramified as our daily lives and behaviors, and everyone handles symbols of these sorts with relatively little strain. Nevertheless, the interactions that go on around the symbols by which we buy are likely to involve the difficulties of all communications, and warrant study. Talking about symbols often involves discussion of much that is obvious or easily appar- ent—and most of us think we say what we mean. But much marketing and advertising thinking goes on with little actual regard given to the kinds of symbolic meanings that are so intrinsic to consumer viewpoints. Greater attention to these modes of thought will give marketing manage- ment and research increased vitality, adding to their own practical and symbolic merits.

D. Attitude change and perception

Discussion of the comparison process concludes with a rigorous analysis of whether or not it is possible to change attitudes and values with persuasive communications. In his sophisticated review of this difficult problem area, Maloney develops a number of research-based propositions and advances some meaningful conclusions for those con- cerned with the use of persuasive communication. As might be expected, the problems encountered are many, but Maloney points the way to some intriguing solutions.

Wells and Chinsky, on the other hand, attempt much less and merely present the findings of a relatively simple set of experiments on repetition of communication messages. As such, their findings cannot be generalized. Yet, they have indicated the possible way in which repetition can serve to change predispositions and thereby have advanced some highly important hypotheses for research under full-scale field conditions. For this reason, their conclusions are worthy of careful analysis and reflection.

7. IS ADVERTISING BELIEVABILITY REALLY IMPORTANT?*

John C. Maloney

The use of presently available advertising testing methods has encouraged an oversimplified view of the ways in which advertising works.

Many of these methods suggest that X% of an advertising audience noted an advertisement while Y% did not; that X% understood it while Y% did not; or that X% "believed it" while Y% did not. Thus, a single advertisement's performance is often seen as a series of "jumps" over a number of successive hurdles, with belief of the advertisement being the last of these.

Although such assumptions may be true in general, they may be dangerously misleading in their particulars. Research in recent years has clearly demonstrated that noting, understanding, and believing are *not* either-or, or go or no-go occurrences.

More importantly, it is now apparent that *no advertisement is likely to be completely "believable" when its purpose is to change people's minds. Moreover, an advertisement need not be believed completely to be effective.*

These views are based on three years of background research; a continuing program of communication research conducted by the Leo Burnett Company, and from a survey of hundreds of books and articles concerning all phases of persuasive communications.[1]

COMPETITION BETWEEN PERSUASIVE MESSAGES AND OLD BELIEFS

Advertising believability *does* represent the net effect of advertising upon the mind of the reader, listener, or viewer. Few advertisers, advertising researchers, or psychologists would disagree with the statement that an advertisement is "believed" when it leaves the consumer with that attitude, belief, or intention toward the product which the advertiser

---

Journal of Marketing, October, 1963, pp. 1–8.

[1]For a description of one of the author's own studies in this area see John C. Maloney, "Curiosity vs. Disbelief in Advertising," *Journal of Advertising Research,* Vol. 2 (June, 1962), pp. 2–8.

intended that he or she should have after exposure to the advertisement.

However, *believability is not an inherent property of the advertisement itself.* It is not a mystic something that some advertisements have and others do not have. Believability depends upon the *interaction* of each advertisement with the consumer's attitudes and memories accumulated from prior experience.

Each person's predispositions to note, understand, and accept or reject certain messages is *learned.* Different people have different expectations about the trustworthiness of various kinds of advertising; they have developed different kinds of knowledge and different types of feelings about the products or brands being advertised. This means that an advertisement completely believable to one person may not be at all believable to another.

In other words, we must specify *believable to whom* when we consider the "believability" of an advertisement.

We must also take the advertiser's intentions into account in a very explicit way. What was it that was to be believed? What *specific* attitudes or beliefs should be left in the consumer's mind if the advertisement is believed? It is important to know which understandings or feelings toward the product amount to belief, and which amount to disbelief after exposure to the advertisement.

DECODING, APPERCEPTION, AND "SEEING IN THE LIGHT OF PAST EXPERIENCE"

A great deal has been learned in recent years about how people "make sense out of new information by viewing it in the light of past experience." Communications researchers often refer to this very general process as message *decoding;* psychologists may use the general term *apperception.* Either term refers to the process by which advertising messages interact with people's pre-existing memories, attitudes, and beliefs.

One thing is certainly apparent: "Reminder messages" can be believed very easily. If a message is aimed at the reinforcement of already existing beliefs, it will be easily accepted. To use the psychologist's terms, such a message easily finds a place in the "cognitive structure" of what people think they know, and in the "affective structure" of how they feel about a product or service.

However, when the message is not intended as a "reminder" message, but rather as a *persuasive* message aimed at *changing* people's minds about something, we have a different story. The persuasive message is sure to run into a conflict or competition with the pre-existing beliefs which the message seeks to change. Since these pre-existing beliefs make up part of the past-experience mechanism used to decode the persuasive message; these old beliefs have a clearcut advantage over the newer beliefs called for by the message.

Decoding, apperception, and the competition between new information and old beliefs have been studied intensively from many different points of view. The clinical psychologist has studied these phenomena as part of the *ego-defense* mechanisms involved in personality formation and change. The same phenomena are crucial to the *trial-and-check* phases of most of the newer learning theories and perception theories (whereby new information "inputs" are compared with old information "memories"). These same processes are also central to a whole range of new *homeostatic* or *balance* theories of attitude change.[2]

In whatever context the conflict between new information and old beliefs is studied, the implications are the same. All such research leads to this conclusion: *By its very nature persuasion calls for the communication of messages that will NOT be believed easily.*

This conclusion is supported by hundreds of actual studies of mass communication effects. Thus, one reviewer of dozens of communication research studies concludes that mass media are much more likely to maintain, rather than to change, people's states of mind.[3] This basic fact is attributed to three aspects of apperception, commonly referred to as factors of "perceptual defense."[4]

1. Selective attention
2. Selective perception
3. Selective recall

SELECTIVE ATTENTION AND BELIEF OF ADVERTISEMENTS

Selective attention is a general term which has this implication for advertisers: *People tend to select out for attention those advertisements which are quickly recognizable as being in accord with interests or beliefs which they already hold; and they are much less likely to pay attention to other advertisements.*

Other elements of attention relate to the intensity of the advertisement's sight or sound stimuli, and the intrigue or "affective value" of the advertisement itself.[5]

The selective attention phenomenon accounts for the fact that users

---

[2]The newer balance theories of attitude change are particularly relevant to the basic processes described here; see Robert B. Zajonc, "The Concepts of Balance, Congruity, and Dissonance," *Public Opinion Quarterly*, Vol. 24 (Summer, 1960), pp. 280–96. For a review of the literature on trial-and-check phases of perception and learning Theory, see Charles M. Solley and Gardner Murphy, *Development of the Perceptual World* (New York: Basic Books, Inc., 1960), pp. 220–37.

[3]Joseph T. Klapper, *The Effects of Mass Communication* (Glencoe, Ill.: The Free Press, 1960), p. 8.

[4]For a discussion of these perceptual defense factors in a broader context of mass media audience expectations, see Raymond A. Bauer, "The Initiative of the Audience," *Journal of Advertising Research*, Vol. 3 (June, 1963), pp. 2–7.

[5]Daniel E. Berlyne, *Conflict Arousal and Curiosity* (New York: McGraw-Hill Book Co., Inc., 1960), pp. 73 ff.

of an advertised product are more likely than nonusers to note an advertisement for the product in question. The same phenomenon probably accounts for the fact that readership "noting scores" are typically much higher for advertising for high-interest products than for advertising which features products of low interest.

Since the advertiser finds it easiest to arrest the consumer's attention by using illustrations or sounds of considerable general interest, he is sometimes tempted to resort to featuring interesting but irrelevant material in an advertisement. If the product itself is not relevant to an active consumer interest, this tactic will solve the problems imposed by selective attention; but mere noting is not believing, and such action may easily impair ultimate belief in the advertisement.

SELECTIVE PERCEPTION AND BELIEF OF ADVERTISEMENTS

If an advertisement arrests the consumer's attention, it will have some effect upon the beliefs of the consumer, if only to confirm or strengthen already existing beliefs. However, there is no assurance that beliefs concerning the advertised product will be affected in the intended way.

Thus, people may fail to believe the persuasive message because of the way in which they *selectively perceive* the meaning of the message in accordance with old beliefs. More specifically, selective perception can lead to the misunderstanding of a message because of *misindexing* or *message distortion*.

THE PROBLEM OF MISINDEXING

Any particular communication may seem relevant to many different kinds of beliefs; it might be "viewed in the light of" many different past experiences. The question of *which* attitudes will be influenced by a given advertisement depends upon the way in which the reader, listener, or viewer classifies or categorizes the tentative meaning of the advertising message as he or she begins to decode it.

This kind of classification of messages has been variously referred to by communications researchers and psychologists as "cognitive tuning" or "message indexing."[6]

Belief in advertising messages is commonly impaired by three kinds of misindexing. The reader, listener, or viewer may "get hung up on the advertisement itself" and never get around to thinking about the advertised product or service. The mind may be led astray by some "borrowed attention" device in the advertisement. The advertisement may stir up thoughts about competing products or more general issues than the advertiser had in mind.

The first of these kinds of misindexing is graphically described by

[6]Percy H. Tannenbaum, "The Indexing Process in Communication," *Public Opinion Quarterly*, Vol. 3 (Summer, 1955), pp. 292–302.

Alfred Politz: "Imagine a room with a large window that looks out on a beautiful countryside. On the wall opposite the window are three mirrors. The first mirror is uneven, spotted, and dirty looking. The second mirror is clean and neat, and in addition is framed by a beautiful ornamental engraving. The third mirror has no frames or ornament, and is nothing but a plain, but perfectly flawless mirror. Now, an observer (critic or client) is taken into the room and his guide points to the first mirror and says, 'What do you see?' The observer says, 'I see a bad mirror.' His guide points to the second mirror and asks again, 'What do you see?' The observer says, 'I see a beautiful mirror.' Finally, his guide points to the third mirror and says, 'What do you see?' The observer says, 'I see a beautiful scene out of an open window.' "[7]

Just as many supposedly fine mirrors are much too gaudy and distract attention from that which they are supposed to reflect, many advertisements have a comparable defect. The "addy" advertisement may attract attention, but it often distracts from the message about the product or service. People tend to react to such advertisements as *ads*. They may think them very bad, very good, very pretty, or very novel; but they never quite get around to reacting to what it is the ad is *"saying"* about the product.

The second common type of misindexing of advertising relates to the hazards of using attention-getting devices not appropriate to consumers' attitudes toward the product being advertised. In such instances the reader, listener, or viewer is not likely to respond to the advertisement as a message about the product or the service being advertised. The advertisement is more likely to stimulate thoughts about the subject from which attention was "borrowed."

Some advertisers argue that the main illustration in a print advertisement need not be appropriate to the reader's way of looking at the product in question. "After all," they contend, "the picture is just to 'stop' the reader. Once I pull him into the ad, he will get my message from the copy."

However, people are *not obliged* to understand the intended advertising message once they are "pulled into the ad." The reader can "get into the ad," reflect upon the personal meaning of the borrowed-attention device, and "get out of the ad" without ever having any compunction about reading the body copy or understanding the intended meaning of the advertisement.

Attention-getting devices should start the reader's stream of consciousness toward, not away from, the intended meaning of the message.

The third manner in which advertisements are commonly misindexed is by "me-tooism." Some advertisers apparently cannot resist the temptation to emulate claims made by their more successful competitors, or to

---

[7]Alfred Politz, "The Dilemma of Creative Advertising," *Journal of Marketing*, Vol. 25 (October, 1960), pp. 1–6, at pp. 4–5.

imitate the advertising styles of such competitors, even though these claims or styles may have become fixed in people's minds as the "hall-marks" for competing brands.

Television commercials have an advantage over printed advertise-ments in this regard. The most noticeable features of a printed advertise-ment must quickly stir the reader's recollections or expectations about the product if the message is to be properly indexed. But the television commercial can have greater influence on the viewer's "stream of con-sciouness" than that.

The commercial can begin with a human interest drama and lead gradually into the advertising message, so long as the "tie-in" is accom-plished in a way that is remindful of the viewer's own experiences with the product. Repeated tests have shown that failure to relate the "story line" to typical ways in which the consumer sees the product often lead to strong recall of the commercial, but without any "stirring up" of atti-tudes toward the product itself.

AIDS TO PROPER INDEXING

Evidence accumulated from the Leo Burnett Company's studies of over 50 television commercials reflects upon the extreme importance of the advertiser's ability to *empathize* with consumers' memories of or expectations about the advertised product. Commercials which show the product in unusual positions or unfamiliar settings are not conducive to proper indexing.

But the liberal use of "product experience cues" does clearly seem to enhance the chances of proper indexing. A "product experience cue" is a sight or sound stimulus exactly like those experienced by the con-sumer when he or she buys, serves, eats, rides in, or otherwise experiences the product himself or herself.

At the same time "across-message cues"—elements that are common to consumers' exposures to printed advertisements *and* commercials *and* package designs *and* other representations of the product—can also go a long way toward "pulling together" all of the consumers' impressions of a product. Unique and consistently used trademarks, slogans, and type faces are examples of such "across-message cues."

Without the use of such common-to-all-messages aids to proper index-ing, the cumulative effects of a product's advertising are impaired; and each commercial, each advertisement, and each display piece is likely to "trigger" separate and unrelated associations in the consumer's mind.[8]

THE PROBLEM OF DISTORTION

Suppose that an advertisement has arrested attention of the intended audience and has been properly indexed. Is the advertiser now *assured*

[8]For a selective review of the literature on empathy see Kenneth Gompertz, "The Relation of Empathy to Effective Communication," *Journalism Quarterly*, Vol. 37 (1960), pp. 533–46.

that his message will be believed? Of course not. The old beliefs already lodged in people's minds still have ample opportunity to resist the change called for by the advertising message.

People see meanings which they *expect* to see. If the message meaning does not "fall into place" with old beliefs, an uncomfortable "imbalance" is created, and feelings of curiosity or doubt are likely to ensue. Such imbalance—often referred to as *cognitive dissonance*—can be resolved in one of two ways: *by changing old beliefs to conform to the message; or through distortion of the meanings of the message so that the message more easily fits in with old beliefs.*[9]

The advertising message may be distorted by being *leveled* or *sharpened.*

An advertising message is *leveled* when people distort the meaning, by overlooking something in the advertising message which is out of phase with pre-existing beliefs.

A message is most likely to be leveled when it presents information which is *generally* in accord with what the reader, listener, or viewer would expect, but when at the same time it contains information just a little out of the ordinary. Under these circumstances the person quickly characterizes the advertisement as something quite familiar ("something I already know all about") and overlooks the new details in the message.

The advertiser who wishes to avoid the risk of nonbelief due to leveling should ask himself what it is in his message that deviates from what the consumer feels that he already knows about the product or service. He should make this portion of his message stand out *sharply,* and not bury it in the midst of many other familiar-to-the-consumer ideas about his product or service.

The advertising message is *sharpened* when people "read into the message" additional or unintended meanings in order to make the message conform to pre-existing beliefs.

The message is quite likely to be sharpened if it represents a departure from long-standing advertising themes for the product. Thus, out of any 100 respondents to an advertisement for a product of the Campbell Soup Company, a few respondents may be expected to report that the advertisement contained pictures of the Campbell Kids, whether or not the Campbell Kids actually were pictured. Because of many repeated past experiences, many people have come to expect Campbell advertisements to picture the Campbell Kids.

Strangely enough, while the believability of advertising often is adversely affected by people's tendencies to think the advertising says something different from what it actually does say, *sharpening can and often does work to the advertiser's advantage.*

Virtually all "reminder advertising" depends on people's tendencies

---

[9]Leo Festinger, *A Theory of Cognitive Dissonance* (Evanston, Ill.: Row, Peterson and Co., 1957). Also see Jack W. Brehm and Arthur R. Cohen, *Explorations in Cognitive Dissonance* (New York: John Wiley & Sons, Inc., 1962).

to sharpen messages. If the advertiser knows that the attitudes which people already have for his product are quite favorable, and if his main intention is to reinforce such attitudes—rather than to create new attitudes or change old ones—he needs only to provide the consumer with a pleasant reminder of the product.

If the advertiser can count on the favorability of the consumer's attitudes to lead to a favorable kind of "filling in," it may be well to create an implicit advertising message, leaving room for the consumer to decide for himself why the product or service is to be preferred.

On the other hand, *if the advertiser wants to change people's attitudes or create new attitudes, he should be very explicit,* with a detailed explanation of the product or service benefits and the reasons underlying these benefits.[10]

SELECTIVE RECALL AND BELIEF OF ADVERTISEMENTS

Belief of an advertising message shortly after the consumer is exposed to the advertisement is often misleading. With the passage of time, belief may either increase or fade away. Both an increase of belief with passage of time (often referred to as positive *sleeper effect*) and a decrease in belief are forms of *selective recall.*

POSITIVE SLEEPER EFFECT

Positive sleeper effect is most likely to occur when an advertising message is initially discredited as having come from an insincere advertiser or advertising spokesman but later becomes "the best information I have to go on" in making a buying decision.

There is good reason to believe that much "at-home disbelief" of advertising changes to 'in-the-store belief" when an actual buying decision must be made. However, the evidence on this point is not conclusive; and it may be that the repetitive nature of advertising precludes any chance for a sleeper effect to operate.[11]

The fading of belief with the passage of time might be viewed in very general terms as mere forgetting of the advertising message, but this is an oversimplification. Actually the fading of belief can be attributed to *"overcrowding the active file space"* in the reader, listener, or viewer's mind (known technically as *retroactive inhibition*), or to *failure to reinforce tentative beliefs.*

"OVERCROWDING THE ACTIVE FILE SPACE"

The consumer is usually much less interested in a product or service than the advertiser. People can ordinarily retain only a limited amount

[10]Herbert I. Abelson, *Persuasion* (New York: Springer Publishing Co., 1959), pp. 10–13.

[11]Martin Weinberger, "Does the 'Sleeper Effect' Apply to Advertising?" *Journal of Marketing,* Vol. 25 (October, 1961), pp. 65–67.

of information about a product, service, or brand in their "active file memories." In trying to fill his advertisements with more and more information about his product or service, the advertiser can easily diminish his chances of leaving a clear, unitary impression of his product or service in the consumer's mind.

However, the problem of "active file space" is complicated somewhat in the case of infrequently purchased items which involve greater than average purchase risk. Automobile purchases are an example. The minority of consumers who are in-the-market automobile buyers at any one time act somewhat like businessmen who set up a special, temporary "mental file" for information related to a special project. Typically they will notice and remember many more advertising messages about automobiles than less interested persons would ever notice or remember.

In this regard, advertisers for major-purchase items face a dilemma. They can create advertising which provides a little bit of information to a lot of potentially interested people, or they can provide a lot of information to a few very actively interested people.

If they elect the former alternative, advertisements will be simple and uncluttered—with every element in the advertisement making a single idea easy to believe. If they elect the latter alternative, advertisements are likely to have a very "busy" look—with seven, eight, or nine separate selling points for the product. Either type of advertisement might be very "believable"; but the two types are likely to be believable in different ways to different audiences.

Thus, competitors' selling messages, the advertiser's own irrelevant claims, or many other factors may crowd out basic attitudes toward a product from the consumer's conscious memory. But this is only one cause for the fade of belief over time.

Failure to reinforce tentative belief

Many advertising messages are believed on a pending-further-evidence ("I'll believe it when I see it") basis.

Tentative beliefs of this sort may be crystallized by first-hand experience with the product itself; or such beliefs may be "shored up" by comments or examples offered by a consumer's friends or associates. However, such tentative belief or attitude imbalance represents an unsatisfactory state of affairs for the consumer; and such beliefs will give way to older modes of thinking if not reinforced.

The advertiser can cope with these problems in a variety of ways:

By frequent exposure to the consumer of the same or similar advertising messages.

By use of advertising messages with highly compatible messages in point-of-purchase materials, package designs, direct mail, etc.

By use of advertising messages which can easily be confirmed by those who have already used the product—that is, those to whom the consumer might turn for advice or example once he or she becomes tentatively convinced of the product's merits.

SPECIAL ROLE OF ADVERTISING IN GRADUAL FORMATION OF BELIEFS

In the past 25 years social scientists, particularly sociologists, have conducted numerous "diffusion research" studies to determine the way in which new ideas, opinions, and preferences "catch on" and spread throughout groups of people. A good deal has been learned from such studies about the ways in which "brand loyalty" develops for everything from political issues and candidates to consumer products.

One of the major findings, often confirmed and reconfirmed by such research, is that people's beliefs in new ideas develop gradually. The obvious implication is that new products usually are not accepted or adopted by people suddenly. People gradually *become aware* of new products . . . *become interested* in them or curious about them . . . *mentally evaluate* them in terms of their own needs or interests . . . and finally *try* them and *adopt* or reject them.

These or similar stages of belief formation have been variously described as the "product adoption process," the marketing communications spectrum," "the staircase of persuasion," and by other terms.[12]

ADVERTISING AND THE ADOPTION PROCESS

The influence of advertising is found at each step in the adoption process—from making people *aware* of the product initially, to making them more willing to buy it again after they have already bought it and used it. *However, advertising usually has its greatest effects prior to use of the product.* Advertising may make someone buy a "bad" product once, but not more than once.[13]

The implications seem clear. *No single advertisement is likely to produce absolute "belief" in a product. Rather, each advertisement is likely to make its most significant contribution by "nudging" the consumer onto and along the path of the adoption process.*

This is especially true for infrequently purchased products with high purchase risk. It should be noted that the duration of the gradual product adoption process may vary from a matter of seconds for an inexpensive product (such as a potato peeler) to many months for products which involve considerable purchase risk. For many products, it may be better to work gradually toward belief of favorable attitudes toward a product or service one step at a time.

---

[12]H. F. Lionberger, *Adoption of New Ideas and Practices* (Ames: Iowa State University Press, 1960).

[13]Steuart Henderson Britt, *The Spenders* (New York: McGraw-Hill Book Co., Inc., 1962), at p. 106.

Automobile advertisers have used this approach effectively. "Teasers" may be used prior to new model introductions each year. No pictures of the car are shown, and no specific facts are presented; and the sole purpose of such advertising is to intrigue consumers. Teaser advertisements may be followed by more detailed illustrations of the car, after new-model introductions, to stimulate further interest. These advertisements may be followed, later in the model year, with detailed facts about the car for aware, interested, fact-seeking buyers. In turn, these advertisements are backed up by dealers' local advertising to provide the try-it-here, buy-it-now impetus to actual trial or purchase.

"OPINION LEADERS" AND THE "TWO-STEP FLOW"

As indicated above, many tentative beliefs of advertising crystallize *only* after the advertising message is given support from the example or advice of consumers' friends or acquaintances. However, many studies have shown that certain people are more likely to be "opinion leaders," acting with a minimum need for support or word-of-mouth confirmation from others, while others are more likely to be "opinion followers."[14]

The "opinion leaders" within any consumer group have been found to be more likely to expose themselves directly to advertising and to other mass media information sources than other people. Thus, they may by advice or example pass along the influence of advertising to less interested or less well-informed segments of the population.

This process has been described as the "two-step flow" of advertising influence—from advertising to the "opinion leaders," and from the "opinion leaders" to others.[15] The consumer goods manufacturer who advertises to the "retail trade" which sells his goods provides an example of trying to capitalize on this "two-step flow."

The "opinion leadership" and "two-step flow" concepts have been widely popularized, but not always accurately. While it is true that advertising believability *can* be enhanced a good deal by word-of-mouth support of "opinion leaders," it should be noted that:

Opinion leadership is typically very informal in its operation. The two-step flow of information is most likely to occur via subtle comment or example, without opinion leader or opinion follower being especially conscious of what is happening.

Opinion leadership is not a matter of social leadership. Opinions about most products or brands do not flow from upper class to lower class. Opinion leaders are found at all social strata, as people "take their cues" about new products or brands from neighbors, friends, fellow workers, or others with whom they have social contacts.

---

[14]Elihu Katz and Paul F. Lazarsfeld, *Personal Influence: The Part Played by People in the Flow of Mass Communications* (Glencoe, Ill.: The Free Press, 1955).

[15]Elihu Katz, "The Two-Step Flow of Communication: An Up-to-Date Report on an Hypothesis," *Public Opinion Quarterly*, Vol. 21 (Spring, 1957), pp. 61–78.

There are different opinion leaders for each product class. Although the opinion leader has been characterized in many general ways (for example, in terms of his or her gregariousness, social and geographic mobility, and so on) the main characteristic of an opinion leader is greater-than-average interest in or heavier-than-average use of the type of product or service in question.

The very first people to adopt a new product will not necessarily be the opinion leaders for that product. Such "innovators" are often an extremely interested minority, with specialized and largely unshared interests in the product class. Widespread belief of an advertising message or adoption of the product will likely require that the message or product "catch on" with a larger minority who have many contacts with the slow-to-believe or slow-to-adopt majority.

The advertiser may gain very little advantage from any attempt to cater to the opinion leader or to reinforce the two-step flow of beliefs. If his product can be accepted with a minimum of financial or social risk—if people typically make up their own minds about such products— the advertiser should ignore the opinion leader and short-circuit the "two-step flow."

CURIOSITY VERSUS DISBELIEF

In the light of the foregoing discussion, one thing is very clear. *Advertising is most likely to be believed when its purpose is to reinforce already existing attitudes toward the product.*

While such "reminder" advertising is usually very believable, "it is *minding* them in the first place" (creating a new attitude or changing an old one) that causes problems.

When the advertiser's task involves *persuasion*—that is, a change, rather than a mere reinforcement of attitudes—belief is likely to come slowly. A single advertisement will rarely account for a change from complete nonbelief or disbelief to complete belief in the merits of a product or service.

Therefore, it may be more important for advertisers to forget about the "believability" of single advertisements and to turn attention to the individual advertisement's potential for contributing to a cumulative influence upon consumers' beliefs. *There is an important difference between the expectation that a single advertisement should be believed in an absolute sense and the expectation that it should contribute to a gradual, eventual belief.*

If asked about his reaction to a given advertisement, a consumer may say, "I don't believe it." Such responses can be very misleading. The consumer may be reflecting *actual disbelief* of the message, or he may be reflecting a *curious nonbelief* of the sort that implies, "It sounds too good to be true."

The author's own research has shown that the latter sort of response, although it may seem negative in a superficial sense, is actually conducive to "nudging" the consumer along the path of the product adoption process.[16]

TEN CONCLUSIONS

Here are ten important conclusions to be drawn:

1. Different consumers bring different beliefs, interests, and attitudes to an advertisement; and an advertisement which is believable to some people will not be believable to others. To evaluate the belief of advertising, one must know *who* should believe and *what* should be believed in terms of the advertiser's intentions.

2. Consumers' already existing beliefs or attitudes relate to many separate stages of believing advertisements. As a preliminary to belief, the consumer must focus attention upon the advertisement once he is exposed to it. In doing this, he makes a very general "what-this-is-all-about" judgment of the advertisement. At this early stage, the advertisement loses any chances of being believed unless it somehow relates to previously developed beliefs, interests, or attitudes.

3. Once the consumer focuses attention on an advertisement, the advertising message must find its way to the consumer's already existing attitudes *toward the product* without being side-tracked. Too often the advertising message is "misindexed" at this stage because: (a) it is too "addy" and simply reminds the consumer of advertising rather than the product; (b) it is too remindful of competitors' products or services; or (c) it starts a chain of thoughts about irrelevant attention-getting devices in the advertising.

4. Once the advertisement is seen as being germane to the consumer's way of looking at the product or service, the main impediment to belief is unconscious distortion of the intended meaning of the advertising message. In order to make the meaning of the message fit in with his old attitudes, the consumer may "level" the message, overlooking parts of the message with which he disagrees; or he may "sharpen" the message, adding certain meanings to the advertisement which the advertiser had not really intended. In either case, the distortion of the message meaning precludes any chance of belief. ("Sharpening" *sometimes* works to the advertiser's advantage *if* the consumer's attitudes toward the product are already favorable.)

5. If the consumer focuses attention on the advertisement, indexes it properly, and does not distort its meaning, he may believe the advertising message only temporarily. There are two main reasons that much apparent belief of advertising fails to hold up over time. One is the simple fact that consumers cannot or will not remember all the things about

---

[16]Same reference as in footnote 1, at p. 3.

a product that advertisers might like them to remember. Second, much belief of advertising is tentative belief, not sufficiently well supported by the consumer's earlier experiences or previously developed attitudes. Such tentative belief will fade unless there is early support from future experiences with the product, repeated exposure to similar advertising, or word-of-mouth advertising.

6. No single advertisement is likely to be believed completely if belief requires the consumer to change his mind about the product. Unless the consumer is already "sold" on a product, complete belief in new products, involving "adoption" of them, may take months or even years.

7. Advertising is especially effective for making people aware of, interested in, *or curious about* new or improved products; and thus advertising is a very effective aid to developing *tentative belief* in a product. While advertising also helps to induce trial of the product, complete belief in the product's merits usually requires that the selling messages be supported by sales personnel, and the comments or example of family members or acquaintances.

8. Within the groups of people to whom consumers look for example and guidance in making product or brand choices, there is a minority of people who are especially interested in the product class. These "opinion leaders" often relay advertising messages to others or reinforce the "believability" of these messages for others—by example or by word of mouth. Thus, there often tends to be a "two-step flow" of advertising influence—from the advertising to "opinion leaders," and from "opinion "leaders" to "opinion followers."

It is sometimes to the advertiser's advantage to cater to the "opinion leaders" and to capitalize upon the "two-step flow" of advertising influence. Sometimes, however, the advertiser is better off to ignore the potential "opinion leaders" and to short-circuit the "two-step flow" of advertising. The latter course of action is no doubt best when the consumer feels little risk in believing in the product or service, that is, when he can make a brand choice without feeling any need to depend upon the guidance of others.

9. The advertiser must always be concerned about having his message noticed; and consumers should be able to recognize easily that the message relates to the advertised product in a way that is relevant to their own needs or interests. However, the advertiser need not be too concerned about advertising messages which "sound too good to be true" *if* the consumer has a real opportunity to find out that they *are* true.

10. Finally, the advertiser must remember that the most persuasive advertising messages are those which are most congruent with the consumer's experiences, both past and future. And it is not just the consumer's experience of seeing, hearing, or reading advertisements that matters.

One-at-a-time advertising exposures do not account for belief by themselves. ALL BELIEVABLE ADVERTISING IS, TO SOME DEGREE, "REMINDER ADVERTISING."

8. EFFECTS OF COMPETING MESSAGES: A LABORATORY SIMULATION*

William D. Wells and Jack M. Chinsky

Many of the choices consumers make are based in part upon the net effect of competing communications. For example, a housewife's choice of a cake-mix in the supermarket on Saturday may well have been influenced by the cake-mix advertisements she saw during the preceding week. While advertising is obviously not the only influence on such a choice, it does seem safe to assume that competing advertising messages often have some bearing—sometimes a most important bearing—on choices among competing brands.

The advertiser can enhance his place in this competition in several ways. If his budget is large enough, he can broadcast more messages than anybody else and dominate the stream of messages the consumer receives. If his budget does not enable him to dominate the whole message stream, he can sometimes arrange to increase his share of certain important parts of it, like the parts that occur just before the heaviest shopping days. He can space his messages evenly through time, if he thinks that is good strategy, or he can broadcast his messages in "flights" or "bursts."

This paper reports a series of experiments attempting to simulate such influences on choice. In each experiment the choice-maker received streams of competing messages. In successive experiments, the messages were systematically varied in the degree to which they dominated the message stream, in proximity to the choice-point, and in degree of clustering. The results show quite conclusively that such tactics can change a message's effect.

SUBJECTS

Most of the subjects in these experiments were college students who volunteered to participate in "a study of perception and choice." In some of the experiments the subjects were fulfilling a course requirement, and in some they were paid for their time. In a few of the experiments, the subjects were adults obtained from a local employment service. Whether the subjects were males or females, fulfilling a course requirement or paid for their time, college or non-college adults, the results were the same.

---

*Journal of Marketing Research, Vol. II (May, 1965), pp. 141–45.

METHOD

The subject was seated in front of a keyboard containing two rows of numbers—1 through 5, and 6 through 10. He was fitted with earphones attached to a tape recorder and asked to read the following instructions:

This is an experiment in the way people make choices under conflicting directions. When the tape begins you will hear a series of twenty numbers and then a bell. When the bell rings, choose one of the numbers, press the corresponding key on the machine and pull the handle. This will register your choice. After a short pause you will hear another series of twenty numbers and another bell. You then make another choice. This sequence—numbers, bell, choice—will continue until you have made fifty choices.

The numbers are your directions as to what choice to make. They will contradict each other, so the directions will not be clear. Your job is to follow them as best you can even though they contradict each other and are confusing. Make a choice based on your interpretation of what the numbers are telling you to do.

When the bell rings, you must make your choice immediately. The next series of numbers will begin almost right away. Remember, follow the directions given by the numbers even though they seem to be all mixed up.

After the subject had read the instructions, the experimenter answered questions, and further instructed the subject to pay no attention to pauses or intonations of voice on the tape, to avoid thinking of the numbers as mathematical problems, and to avoid choosing numbers he had not heard.

The subject then heard the first series of numbers. They came at a rapid rate—about 2 per second. Since the series was twenty numbers long, it was well beyond the subject's memory span.

The subject made his first choice by pressing one of the buttons on the keyboard. Another series of twenty numbers began immediately. At the end of the second series, the subject made another choice. He heard a third series, made a third choice, and so on until the end of the experiment. A typical experiment required 50 choices of this kind. The object of the experiment was to find out how changes in these message streams influenced the choices subjects made.

At the conclusion of each experiment, the subject was interviewed by the experimenter to determine how the task had been interpreted and what choice-making procedure had been used.

RESULTS

EQUAL SHARES

The first experiment employed five numbers as messages: 2, 9, 3, 7, and 4. Before each choice, the subject heard a stream of twenty numbers

—2, 9, 3, 7, and 4 in random order four times each. The 58 subjects each made 50 choices, with the numbers in a different random order each time.

The purpose of this experiment was to find out whether subjects would tend to choose a particular number (such as "lucky 7") or a particular position on the keyboard. The results, in Table 1, show that they did not. Each number had a 20 percent share of each pre-choice message stream, and each was chosen almost exactly 20 percent of the time.

TABLE 1
SHARE OF CHOICES WHEN MESSAGE-NUMBERS HAD
EQUAL SHARES OF PRE-CHOICE MESSAGE STREAM

Message	Share of Messages	Share of Choices
2	20%	18%
9	20	20
3	20	19
7	20	22
4	20	21

UNEQUAL MESSAGE SHARES

The second experiment employed the same message-numbers as the first, but this time each number had a different share of the pre-choice message stream. In the set of twenty numbers heard before each choice, 2 appeared six times, 9 appeared five times, 3 appeared four times, 7 appeared three times and 4 appeared twice. As before, each subject made 50 choices, and the numbers were arranged in a different random order each time. This experiment was conducted in the same session and with the same 58 subjects as Experiment 1.

The purpose of this experiment was to find out whether a change in share of messages would produce a change in share of choice. The results, in Table 2, show that it most certainly did. In the aggregate data, corre-

TABLE 2
SHARE OF CHOICES WHEN MESSAGE-NUMBERS HAD
UNEQUAL SHARES OF EACH MESSAGE STREAM

Original Experiment				Replication		
Message	Share of Messages	Share of Choices		Message	Share of Messages	Share of Choices
2	30%	32%		1	30%	31%
9	25	25		4	25	27
3	20	20		6	20	18
7	15	14		2	15	12
4	10	9				

spondence between share of messages and share of choice was almost exact. Table 2 also shows the results of a replication experiment which employed a different set of 42 subjects and different message-numbers in different random orders. As in the original experiment the correspondence between share of messages and share of choices was very close.

In evaluating these data, it is important to remember that each pre-choice number series was well beyond the subject's memory span, and the subject made only one choice after each set of messages he heard. Subjects were not merely duplicating the stimuli they received.

Subjects were not just repeating the last number in each series. If a subject had been repeating the last number in each series, the number of agreements between number chosen and last number heard would have been 50. The actual number of agreements ranged from 5 to 34 with a median of 14.

The post-experiment interview shed some light on how the subjects interpreted the experiment and what they tried to do in making their responses. A few (about 15 percent) simply gave up. They regarded the experiment as an unsolvable mystery and chose numbers at random, without regard to the numbers they heard. A few (about 7 percent) interpreted the experiment as some sort of personality test. They tended to develop unique and often complex methods of choosing, *e.g.*, "I watched for doubles. If two two's or two seven's appeared together, I choose nines or fours." Most (about 78 percent) of the subjects interpreted the instructions as they had been intended and responded accordingly. A typical explanation from this group was this, "You wanted to see what I would choose if the numbers were repeated at different frequencies." Among this group each subject's response frequencies approximately matched the stimulus frequencies. Of the 58 subjects who participated in Experiment 2, 50 changed their responses in the anticipated direction. With a sign test, this proportion permits rejection of the null hypothesis at $p < .001$ [1].

DIMINISHING RETURNS

Experiments 1 and 2 demonstrated that the choice-making behavior of the subjects was highly sensitive to the perceived salience of each message in the pre-choice message stream. Experiment 3 was designed to determine whether this perceived salience would hold true even when one of the messages occupied a very large share of the messages the choice maker received.

The design of this experiment was similar to the design of Experiments 1 and 2, except that one of the message-numbers received a 50 percent share of each pre-choice message stream, while the remaining numbers received 20, 15, 10 and 5 percent shares. Fifty subjects participated in this experiment, and 50 subjects participated in the replication. As before, each subject received 20 message-numbers before each of the 50 choices he made. Also, as before, the number-messages were distributed at random through each pre-choice message stream.

The data in Table 3 show that a 50 percent share of the messages did not produce a 50 percent share of the choices. The most broadcast message-number was still the most chosen, but it was not chosen as often as it should have been considering how often it was heard. Evidently dominance of the message stream can be pushed to a point where it becomes inefficient.

TABLE 3

SHARE OF CHOICES WHEN ONE MESSAGE-NUMBER HAD
A 50 PERCENT SHARE OF EACH MESSAGE STREAM

Original Experiment			Replication		
Message	Share of Messages	Share of Choices	Message	Share of Messages	Share of Choices
1	50	36	6	50	40
4	20	20	3	20	19
6	15	15	2	15	18
2	10	10	4	10	10
3	5	19	1	5	13

MESSAGES NEAR CHOICE

It has long been assumed that messages delivered near the choice-point are likely to be more effective than messages delivered some distance from it. Political campaigns reach a crescendo just before election; advertising campaigns for seasonally purchased products are almost always seasonally timed. The third experiment investigated the effect of message position upon choice.

In general, the framework of this experiment was the same as the framework of Experiment 2, in which the different messages had 30, 25, 20, 15 and 10 percent shares of each pre-choice message stream. The same five message-numbers were used in the same relative proportions; and, as in Experiment 2, a series of twenty numbers preceded each choice.

This time, however, the number 7 was singled out for special treatment. In the first of three sub-experiments, the three 7's in each twenty-number message-series were all placed in the first ten numbers the subject heard. Their positions in the first ten were assigned at random; and, after the 7's had been placed, the positions of all the other numbers were assigned at random as before.

In the second sub-experiment, the 7's were all placed in the middle ten numbers of each twenty-number pre-choice series. In the third sub-experiment the three 7's were all placed in the last ten of the twenty numbers heard before each choice. Thus, the messages "in favor" of 7 were delivered during three different portions of each message sequence: at the beginning, toward the middle, and at the end—very near the point of choice.

In all three sub-experiments, the first twenty choices were used as a

"warm-up" period to produce a consistent frame of reference. The message-series preceding the first ten choices employed the message-shares
used in Experiment 1; the series preceding the second ten choices employed the message-shares used in Experiment 2.

Table 4 shows that changing the position of the 7's had a very clear
effect. When the 7's were in the early portion of the message series, a 15
percent share of the messages produced only a 9 percent share of the
choices. When the 7's were in the middle portion of the message series,
a 15 percent share of the messages produced a 13 percent share of the
choices. But when the three messages favoring 7 were delivered within
the last ten messages heard before the choice, a 15 percent share of the
messages produced a 21 percent share of the choices.

Table 4 also shows a replication in principle of the third sub-experiment. The replication employed different subjects and different message-
numbers in different random orders. In the replication, the number 6—
the number with the 20 percent share of messages—was the number
placed within the last ten messages before each choice. Under these
conditions, a 20 percent share of the messages produced a 30 percent
share of the choices.

TABLE 4

SHARE OF CHOICES WHEN MESSAGES "FAVORING" ONE NUMBER WERE PLACED AT
BEGINNING, MIDDLE AND END OF EACH PRE-CHOICE MESSAGE STREAM

	Original Experiment				Replication		
	Share of Mes-sages	*Share of Choices*				*Share of Mes-sages*	*Share of Choices*
Message		*7's at Begin-ning*	*7's in Middle*	*7's at End*	*Message*		*6's at End*
2	30	35	40	34	1	30	25
9	25	28	25	22	4	25	22
3	20	17	14	17	6	20	30
7	15	9	13	21	2	15	12
4	10	11	8	6	3	10	11

In this experiment, 70 percent of the 147 subjects changed their choice-
making behavior as a result of the changes in the message series. Again,
the proportion is so high that the null hypothesis can be rejected at
$p < .001$.

MESSAGES IN "FLIGHTS"

When a communicator has a certain number of messages at his command, he can decide whether their delivery should be spread-out or
massed. For example, if a political candidate has enough money to buy
three television spots per week during his campaign, he can buy three
each week, or he can "save up" his spots for three weeks and then in the

fourth week buy twelve. The argument in favor of even distribution of messages is that it places a reminder continually before the public eye. The argument in favor of "saving up" messages then massing them is that only messages above a certain critical mass may attract attention in the welter of competing messages. The fifth experiment investigated this question by delivering one of the message-numbers in "flights."

The design of the fifth experiment was quite similar to the design of the other four. The numbers 2, 9, 3, 7, and 4 were used again in the same proportions as in Experiment 2, and each of the subjects heard them in a number series before each of the 50 choices they made. This time, however, the 7's were withheld from the message-number series heard before the second ten choices, and the "saved up" messages were put into the series heard before the third ten choices at a double rate—six sevens instead of the normal three. Sevens were against withheld from the messages before the fourth ten choices, and put into the series heard before the fifth ten choices at a double rate. In choices 11 through 50, then, the 7's were delivered in "flights." They were withheld, then doubled; withheld, then doubled. This procedure alternately decreased by three then increased by three the number of pre-choice messages heard. Procedure for assigning other numbers remained the same.

Table 5 shows that "flighting" the 7's also had a clear impact upon choice. In accordance with instructions, subjects did not choose 7's when 7's were not heard; but when the 7's were restored, subjects chose them at greater than a double rate. Over the last 40 choices, "flighting" produced a 20 percent share of choices in return for a 15 percent share of messages.

Table 5 also shows a replication in principle of Experiment 5. In the replication, subjects, message-numbers and number arrangements were different, and the 20-share message was "flighted" instead of the 15-share message. Under these conditions, a 20 percent share of messages pro-

TABLE 5
SHARE OF CHOICES WHEN ONE MESSAGE-NUMBER WAS "FLIGHTED"

	Original experiment					Replication			
	7's Withheld from Message Stream		7's in Message Stream at Double Rate			6's Withheld from Message Stream		6's in Message Stream at Double Rate	
Message	Share of Messages	Share of Choices	Share of Messages	Share of Choices	Message	Share of Messages	Share of Choices	Share of Messages	Share of Choices
2	35	38	26	24	1	38	42	25	15
9	29	29	22	16	4	31	32	21	17
3	24	22	17	12	6	0	0	33	51
7	0	0	26	40	2	19	16	13	9
4	12	11	9	8	3	12	10	8	8

duced a 26 percent share of choices. In Experiment 5 and its replication, all 100 subjects changed their choice-making behavior as a result of flighting.

CONCLUSIONS

It goes without saying that these experiments omit many factors that influence the real choices real consumers make. They have nothing to say about message content, about the influence of already established preferences or attitudes, about distribution, packaging, shelf display or price. And of course, they have nothing to say about the product characteristics that produce or prevent a repeat sale. The only thing these experiments do say is that the perceived salience of a message can be enhanced by employing some of the tactics the advertiser normally has at his command.

Within this limited domain, however, the findings are clear. Perceived salience, as denoted by choice, can be increased by increasing a message's share of the total message stream. Up to a point an increase in share of messages produces a proportionate increase in perceived salience, but at some point further increases in share of messages become inefficient and do not produce commensurate returns.

Perceived salience of a message can also be increased by moving it toward the end of the message stream so that it is received near the time the choice is made. While this principle has long been recognized and used by advertisers of seasonal products, these experiments suggest that the principle also operates when the time span is very short.

Finally, these experiments suggest that the perceived salience of a message can be increased by issuing it in "flights" or "bursts." The effect on choice is not as great as the effect of getting and keeping a dominant share of the message stream continuously, but "flighting" does appear to be worth considering when a dominant share of messages cannot be sustained.

Further experiments, now in progress, are designed to develop these findings in two ways. In one set of experiments, the subjects see the number-messages on a motion picture screen. With this mode of presentation, it is possible to determine whether a three-second message is three times as effective as a one-second message, and whether a two-second message is more or less effective than a one-second message seen twice.

In another set of experiments the impoverished conditions of the original experiments are being enriched by giving the messages some content, by requiring the subjects to "pay" for what they choose, and by ensuring that different choices produce different degrees of satisfaction.

Both sets of experiments are attempts to move a little closer to the choice behavior of real consumers, using the present experiments as a base.

REFERENCE

S. Siegel. *Nonparametric Statistics.* New York: Mc-Graw-Hill Book Co., Inc., 1956.

Suggested additional AMA readings

Attitude Research at Sea. Chicago: American Marketing Association, 1965.

Bell, G. D. "Self Confidence and Persuasion in Car Buying," *Journal of Marketing Research,* Vol. 4 (1967), pp. 46–52.

Carey, James W. "Some Personality Correlates of Persuasibility," in *Toward Scientific Marketing* (ed. Stephen A. Greyser), pp. 30–43. Chicago: American Marketing Association, 1964.

Carrick, P. M., Jr. "Why Continued Advertising Is Necessary: A New Explanation," *Journal of Marketing,* Vol. 23 (April, 1959), pp. 386–98.

Claycamp, Henry J. "Characteristics of Owners of Thrift Deposits in Commercial Banks and Savings and Loan Associations," *Journal of Marketing Research,* Vol. 2 (1965), pp. 163–70.

Kassarjian, Harold H. "Social Character and Differential Preference for Mass Communication," *Journal of Marketing Research,* Vol. 2 (1965), pp. 146–53.

Myers, John. "Determinants of Private Brand Attitude," *Journal of Marketing Research,* Vol. 4 (1967), pp. 73–81.

Winick, C. "Major Concepts of Behavioral Science Applicable to Marketing Research," in *The Social Resonsibilities of Marketing* (ed. W. D. Stevens), pp. 222–32. Chicago: American Marketing Association, 1962.

Zielske, H. A. "The Remembering and Forgetting of Advertising," *Journal of Marketing,* Vol. 23 (January, 1959), pp. 239–43.

Part III

SOCIAL INFLUENCES ON BUYER BEHAVIOR

This section extends the discussion of the comparison process begun in Part II, but extends it to focus clearly on the role of social influences. This subject is of considerable importance, because much that is stored in the buyer's control unit has been profoundly shaped by the influence of others. Many people, for example, are quite other directed and, hence, have a personality trait of sensitivity to other people. Moreover, attitudes are not formed in a social vacuum; rather, much of their content is socially based. Many other examples could be given, but the readings in this part will provide the needed clarification. Four readings are presented under two basic headings: (A) The Influence of Large Social Groupings or Entities; and (B) The Influence of Face-to-Face Social Groupings.

A. The influence of large social groupings or entities

In this section, the focus is on the influence exerted by the larger social groupings often referred to as culture or subculture. Winick assesses in broad-brush fashion the contributions made to an understanding of the buyer by the discipline of cultural anthropology. The unique contribution of this discipline is a global view of a situation shown in the context of a larger background. Of special significance is the insight offered by the study of cross-cultural differences. The reader will quickly grasp the managerial significance of this interdisciplinary perspective.

Coleman narrows his inquiry to the important subculture referred to as social class. The late Pierre Martineau, Research Director at the *Chicago Tribune*, did much to popularize the significance of social class for marketing, and Coleman, a leading scholar in this field, assesses the numerous implications quite thoroughly and analytically. Perhaps social class is unique in that it has been among the most researched areas, and a great deal can now be said with some certainty. Few who are concerned with the marketing of consumer goods can fail to profit from Coleman's insights.

9. ANTHROPOLOGY'S CONTRIBUTIONS TO MARKETING*

Charles Winick

The relative slowness of anthropologists and marketers in finding common ground is surprising.[1] Anthropologists have served as colonial administrators, in foreign-aid programs, and in other situations requiring a special sensitivity to foreign cultures. They have also developed sales-training procedures which involve the analysis of the rate of speech of salesmen with potential customers, through devices which measure the rate of interaction between people talking.[2] Another specialized industrial situation in which anthropologists have worked involves the application of their knowledge of the field of anthropometry or measurement of the body, in the design of products like chairs and knobs.[3]

Other anthropologists have worked in applied fields such as: reactions to disaster, the operation of internment and relocation centers, mental health, medical care, labor–management relations,[4] the culture of a factory,[5] community organization, social work,[6] military government, the cultural change associated with economic development,[7] contact between cultures, the nature of small-town life, behavior in extreme situations, the study of culture at a distance,[8] the reconstruction of the themes of a culture, relations among minority groups, the social structure of a hospital,[9] American national character,[10] and television.[11]

*Journal of Marketing, July, 1961, pp. 53–60.
[1]John Gillin, "The Application of Anthropological Knowledge to Modern Mass Society," Human Organization, Vol. 15 (Winter, 1957), pp. 24–30.
[2]Eliot D. Chapple, "The Interaction Chronograph," Personnel, Vol. 25 (January, 1949), pp. 295–307.
[3]Earnest A. Hooton, A Survey in Seating (Cambridge: Harvard Department of Anthropology, 1945).
[4]Charles R. Walker, The Man on the Assembly Line (Cambridge: Harvard University Press, 1952).
[5]Eliot Jaques, The Changing Culture of a Factory (New York: Dryden Press, 1953).
[6]Franklin K. Patterson, Irving Lukoff, and Charles Winick, "Is Society the Patient," Journal of Educational Sociology, Vol. 30 (October, 1956), pp. 106–12.
[7]Almost every issue of Economic Development and Cultural Change carries relevant articles.
[8]Margaret Mead and Rhoda Metraux, The Study of Culture at a Distance (Chicago: University of Chicago Press, 1952).
[9]Charles Winick, "The Hospital as a Social System," New York State Nurse, Vol. 26 (January, 1954), pp. 9–13.
[10]David M. Potter, People of Plenty (Chicago: University of Chicago Press, 1954).
[11]Charles Winick, Taste and the Censor in Television (New York: Fund for the Republic, 1959).

Although anthropologists have published their findings on America in very accessible formats,[12] there has been little discussion of how their findings could be applied to marketing problems.[13] One advertising publication has published an article on the possibility of using anthropology in advertising.[14] The journal of applied anthropology, formerly called *Applied Anthropology* and now called *Human Organization*, almost never carries any material on marketing; and the national journal, *American Anthropologist*, also ignores the subject.

ANTHROPOLOGY, SOCIOLOGY, AND PSYCHOLOGY

Anthropology is usually defined as the study of man. Such a definition is so all-inclusive that the field is generally divided into four sub-fields: archeology, cultural anthropology, linguistics, and physical anthropology. Archeology is concerned with the historical reconstruction of cultures which no longer exist. Cultural anthropology examines all the behaviors of man which have been learned, including social, linguistic, technical, and familiar behaviors; often it is defined as the study of man and his works. Linguistics is the comparative study of the structure, interrelationships, and development of languages. Physical anthropology is concerned with human biology and the development of the human organism, with special interest in race differences.

When anthropology is employed in marketing, it is usually cultural anthropology which is relevant. Cultural anthropology began with the study of primitive cultures, and its comparative analyses documented the different ways in which cultures have solved their problems of living.

Cultural anthropology has much in common with psychology and sociology. All three are concerned with the examination of man in his cultural setting. They differ in the emphases which they place on different elements of the relationship between a person and his environment. It can be said that all human behavior essentially is a function of the interrelations of personality, the social system, and culture.

Oversimplifying, psychology is concerned with personality, sociology addresses itself to the social system, and anthropology explores the culture. The interdisciplinary field of social psychology may draw on all three of these fields, and there are integrated social psychology texts which do so.[15]

---

[12]Margaret Lantis, editor, "The U.S.A. as Anthropologists See It," *American Anthropologist,* Vol. 57 (December, 1955), pp. 1,113–1,380.

[13]Richard C. Sheldon, "How the Anthropologist Can Help the Marketing Practitioner," in W. David Robbins, ed., *Successful Marketing at Home and Abroad* (Chicago: American Marketing Association, 1958), pp. 209–304.

[14]Alan S. Marcus, "How Agencies Can Use Anthropology in Advertising," *Advertising Agency,* Vol. 49 (September 14, 1956), pp. 87–91.

[15]Steuart Henderson Britt, *Social Psychology of Modern Life* (rev. ed.; New York: Rinehart & Co., 1949). S. Stanfeld Sargent and Robert C. Williamson, *Social Psychology* (New York: The Ronald Press Co., 1958).

A sharper focus on the differences among these three social sciences may be obtained by speculating on how each of the three might look at a family.

The psychologist would be interested in the personal adjustment and emotional health of each member of the family. He would want to examine their attitudes, mutual perceptions, and motivational systems. Their happiness or lack of it would interest him.

The sociologist would be concerned primarily with the dimensions of role and status within the family and with the number of different kinds of families. He would examine how the social structure created various kinds of internal arrangements which made it possible for the family to exist. He would be interested in the norms of behavior and the stresses and strains shown by the deviations from the norm and resulting from role conflict. He would study class membership as well as the rates of various kinds of behavior, such as the birth rate.

The cultural anthropologist would examine the technological level which the culture had reached and the interrelations of technology with culture. He would scrutinize the procedures for inheritance of property and how kinship was reckoned and described, and how the spouses got to know each other. He would study the family's food and housing. He would be interested in the language level and dialects and in who talked to whom. He would be concerned with how the age of different members of the family affected their behavior, and with trends in illnesses. He would study how the culture "rubbed off" on the family unit. The anthropologist thus does not have information which it would be impossible for the sociologist or psychologist to obtain, but he has a special sensitivity to certain facets of social life.

The sociologist and psychologist bring a powerful and varied arsenal of concepts and approaches to the study of social life. In what ways is the anthropologist able to contribute insights and experience toward the science of "marketology," and to what extent may they not be immediately accessible, for example, to the sociologist?[16] The anthropologist is especially trained to have empathy with groups other than his own and to "tune in" on their patterns of culture. Inasmuch as his training has exposed him to a wide variety of cultures, he can take a global view of a situation and see it in the context of a larger background. His training makes him sensitive to cross-cultural differences which may be of crucial importance in many different situations, because his entire training is geared toward awareness of such differences.

Anthropology has less of the factionalism which characterizes psychology and sociology. This is not to suggest that all is serene in anthropology or that it has never been troubled by theoretical or methodological issues.

---

[16]Robert Bartels, "Sociologist and Marketologists," *Journal of Marketing*, Vol. 24 (October, 1959), pp. 37–40; Christen T. Jonassen, "Contributions of Sociology to Marketing," *Journal of Marketing*, Vol. 24 (October, 1959), pp. 29–35.

However, even though anthropologists may disagree on something like the exact value of the contribution of a particular anthropologist, they would generally agree on what the cultural anthropologist looks for, and there are standardized check lists on how to view a culture.[17] In contrast, a psychologist's allegiance to the Gestalt, behaviorist, psychoanalytic, learning-theory, or perception schools is likely to influence what he does with a given problem. A sociologist's commitment to the structure-function, historical, ecological, "middle range," environmental-determinism, or demographic schools would largely determine the emphases of his approach to a problem. Since such divergent schools are less likely to exist in cultural anthropology, it is probable that anthropological guidance on a given marketing problem would be relatively consistent.

WHAT THE ANTHROPOLOGIST KNOWS

The anthropologist is specifically trained to study national character, or the differences which distinguish one national group from another. He should be able to provide measures for distinguishing the subtle differences among a Swede, a Dane, and a Norwegian; or between a Frenchman and an Englishman; or a Brazilian and an Argentinian; or between a typical resident of Montreal and one of Toronto. The anthropologist is also a specialist in the study of subcultures. He would be able, in a city like New York, to differentiate the patterns of living of such disparate but rapidly homogenizing groups as Puerto Ricans, Negroes, Italo-Americans, Jews, Polish-Americans, and Irish-Americans.

Because almost any large community consists of a variety of subcultures, this awareness of subcultural trends can be especially useful. A more subtle area of special interest to anthropologists is the silent language of gesture, posture, food and drink preferences, and other nonverbal cues to behavior.[18]

Related to this is the anthropologist's professional interest in languages and symbols. He might, for example, be especially concerned about why a particular shape has special significance as a symbol in a society, or how the structure of a language or a regional speech pattern was related to how people think.[19]

Another area of concern to the anthropologist, because of its symbolic meanings, has to do with "rites de passage" or the central points in a person's life at which he may ritually be helped to go from one status to another, for example, birth, puberty, or marriage.[20]

[17]Royal Anthropological Institute, *Notes and Queries on Anthropology* (London: The Institute, 1956).

[18]Edward T. Hall, *The Silent Language* (New York: Doubleday & Co., 1959).

[19]Benjamin Lee Whorf, *Collected Papers on Metalinguistics* (Washington: Department of State Foreign Service Institute, 1952).

[20]Jan Wit, *Rites de Passage* (Amsterdam: De Windroos, 1959).

Taboos represent a continuing area of interest to the anthropologist.[21] Every culture has taboos or prohibitions about various things, such as the use of a given color, or of a given phrase or symbol. The anthropologist is aware of the larger values of a culture, which represent the substratum of custom which is taken for granted and the violation of which represents a taboo.

The anthropologist's method is primarily the exposure of his highly developed sensitivity to the area in which he is working, via observation and extended interviews with informants. Projective tests have also been widely used in anthropological studies. The anthropologist can bring a wealth of insight to marketing situations.

USE OF ANTHROPOLOGY IN MARKETING

There are at least three kinds of situations in which the knowledge of the anthropologist has been employed in marketing: specific knowledge; awareness of themes of a culture; sensitivity to taboos.

SPECIFIC KNOWLEDGE

Here are a few cases in which the specific knowledge of an anthropologist was applied to marketing situations.

A manufacturer of central heating equipment was planning to introduce central heating to an area which previously had used other heating. Since people generally grow up to accept a certain approach to heating which they take for granted, introduction of the new central heating posed marketing problems in coping with deeply imbedded consumer resistance to what would be a major innovation. An anthropologist was able to draw on his knowledge of the folklore and symbolism of heat and fire in order to suggest methods of presenting the new system, so as to make it as consonant as possible with the connotations of heat, even though the nature of the heating method had changed radically. There was considerable consumer resistance to the central heating, but it decreased substantially after the first year.

In addition to a marketing problem, the introduction of central heating also posed problems of public policy which the manufacturer had to overcome before he could obtain approval for the introduction of the heating equipment. The area was one which suffered from a declining birth rate, and officials were concerned about the extent to which central heating might cause the birth rate to decline further, because of their belief that heated bedrooms would cause a decline in sexual activity and ultimately in births.

The anthropologist was able to point to some cultures in which the birth rate had declined and some in which it had not done so after the introduction of central heating. The anthropologist's data made it possible for the manufacturer of the central-heating equipment to discuss

---

[21]Franz Steiner, *Taboo* (London: Cohen and West, Ltd., 1957).

its probable effects realistically with the appropriate officials.

Another field in which the anthropologist has specific knowledge that other social scientists are not likely to have is that of clothing and fashion. The only empirical study of the fashion cycle in women's clothing which has successfully been used for predictive purposes by clothing manufacturers was conducted by anthropologists.[22] In marketing situations, the anthropologist has often been able to combine his special knowledge of the needs of the body for clothing of various kinds at different ages, his sensitivity to what technology makes possible and his awareness of fashion.

For example, an anthropologist was consulted by a leading manufacturer of overalls for young children, a product which had remained unchanged for decades. He examined the product in the light of the special needs of children who wear overalls, the growing use of washing machines to launder the overalls, their relative frequency of laundering, and contemporary technology. He suggested that the overall straps have a series of sets of metal grippers instead of buttons, thus making it possible to use different sets of grippers as the child grew instead of tying or knotting the straps. Noting that straps often fall off the shoulders when children played, he suggested that the shirts which children wore under the overalls have either a loop for the straps to pass through or a synthetic fastener which faced matching material on the strap, so that the shoulder of the shirt could be pressed against the strap and remain attached to it until shoulder strap and shirt were pulled apart.

He also recommended that the seams of the overalls, previously single stitched, be double stitched like those of men's shirts, which have to withstand frequent launderings. The double-stitched overalls would be less likely to come apart as a result of frequent launderings in a washing machine. These recommendations were adopted, and within a few years substantially changed and expanded the nature of the overall market for young children. The children's parents were more pleased with the overalls because they lasted longer and looked better on the children, and they were far more functional than before.

The special knowledge of the anthropologist has been called into play where there are special subcultural groups to which the marketer wishes to address himself. One beer manufacturer wished to extend his market share among Negroes in a large eastern city in the United States. He was advised about reaching this group by an anthropologist who was familiar with the special subculture of Negroes, and who pointed to the profound effects of Negroes' caste membership on their purchasing behavior. The ambiguity of their role has led many Negroes to be especially aware of articles that have status connotations and of whether a brand symbolizes racial progress. Examination of the manufacturer's marketing program by the anthropologist led to several recommenda-

[22]Jane Richardson and Alfred L. Kroeber, *Three Centuries of Women's Dress Fashions* (Berkeley: University of California Press, 1940).

tions for change. The manufacturer began to help in the support of several major social events related to the arts in Negro communities, and to stress that the beer was a national brand with quality-control procedures. He changed the content of his advertising in the direction of enhancing its status and quality connotations. These changes were all directed toward improving the status connotations of the beer to Negroes.

Guidance on related problems with respect to the Puerto Rican and Jewish markets has also been used constructively. Since 35 to 40 percent of the population of the United States consists of minority subcultures, the anthropologist's contributions may be considerable.

Another situation had to do with the selection of specific symbols for various purposes. A major manufacturer of women's products was uncertain about whether to continue using the Fleur de Lis emblem on his package. Anthropological analysis of the symbol suggested that its association with French kings and other cultural connotations of maleness made it more masculine than feminine. The anthropologist's recommendations were confirmed by subsequent field testing.

In a related case, a manufacturer of women's cosmetics conducted an anthropological study of the comparative symbolism in our culture of women's eyes and mouth, which suggested that the eye tends to be experienced as a relatively protecting organ while the mouth tends to be experienced as more nurturing. This knowledge of the differences between the special meanings of eye and mouth could constructively be used in marketing the products, and especially in advertising. The advertising explicitly and implicitly mentioned the role of the eye in protection of the woman. It stressed the role of the mouth as the organ which both symbolically and literally gives love. This replaced the manufacturer's previous advertising, in which both eye and mouth were treated in the same way, as organs which could be made beautiful.

AWARENESS OF THEMES

The anthropologist has functioned in situations in which he can use his special understanding of themes of a culture, oftentimes taken for granted.

A major chain of candy shops was suffering a decline in sales. A marketing-research study had established that the brand was usually bought as a gift, either for others or as a gift for the purchaser. The chain was unable to develop any ways of using this finding that were not hackneyed. Anthropological guidance on the symbolism of gift-giving enabled the chain to develop merchandising, packaging, and advertising formats for the gift theme. Anthropological study of the connotations of the major holidays suggested themes for window displays, and advertising of the candy in conjunction with the holidays. The chain's marketing strategy was revised on the basis of the anthropological interpretation and clarification of the marketing-research study. Anthropologists are the only social scientists who have systematically studied gift-giving and gift-receiving.[23]

Another example of anthropological interpretation of a marketing-research study was provided by a shirt manufacturer. The study had established that women buy more than half of men's shirts in a particular price range. The anthropologist was able to interpret this finding in the light of several anthropological studies of the relations between husbands and wives in America. The manufacturer had been thinking of placing advertising for his men's shirts in selected women's magazines. The anthropologist was able to point to a number of studies of husband-wife relations which suggested growing resentment by men over the extent to which women had been borrowing and buying men's clothing, and which suggested that the proposed advertising campaign might not be propitious.

Another anthropologist's special sensitivity to the "rites de passage" helped a shoe manufacturer whose sales were declining because of aggressive foreign and domestic competition. The anthropologist was able to point to the extent to which shoes represent major symbols of our going from one stage of life to another, and to assist the manufacturer in developing methods for using the relationship between shoes and "rites de passage."[24]

A landmark along the road of an infant becoming a child usually is found between the ages of 4 and 6 when he can tie his own shoe laces. The manufacturer developed some pamphlets and other instructional material for parents on how to help children to learn to tie their shoe laces. Distribution by local retailers contributed toward making parents favorably aware of the brand's line for children in this age group.

The teenager signalizes her entrance into a new social world by her first high heels. Window displays and advertising which explicitly stressed the new social activities of the teenager wearing her high heels, and naming specific shoe models after teenage social events ("The Prom") contributed toward associating the manufacturer's name with the excitement of the new world symbolized by the high heels.

Older people see the wearing of special "old people's shoes" as the ultimate reminder that they are becoming old. The manufacturer was able to redesign his line for older people so that it retained its special health features but still looked as stylish as any adult shoe, and had no visible stigma of "old people's shoes."

SENSITIVITY TO TABOOS

Marketers may unwittingly violate a taboo, whether cultural, religious, or political, especially in selling overseas. Blue, for example, is the color for mourning in Iran and is not likely to be favorably received

---

[23]Marcel Mauss, *The Gift* (London: Cohen & West, Ltd., 1954).
[24]Charles Winick, "Status, Shoes, and the Life Cycle," *Boot and Shoe Recorder*, Vol. 156 (October 15, 1959), pp. 100–102.

on a commercial product. Green is the nationalist color of Egypt and Syria and is frowned on for use in packages. Showing pairs of anything on the Gold Coast of Africa is disapproved. White is the color of mourning in Japan and, therefore, not likely to be popular on a product. Brown and gray are disapproved colors in Nicaragua. Purple is generally disapproved in most Latin American markets because of its association with death. Feet are regarded as despicable in Thailand, where any object and package showing feet is likely to be unfavorably received.

The anthropologist can cast light on taboos and on their opposite: favored colors and symbols. The reason for the people in a country or an area liking or not liking a particular color or symbol may be a function of political, nationalist, religious, cultural, or other reasons.

SOME APPLICATIONS IN CANADA

Canada represents a special opportunity for the application of anthropology in marketing situations. Twenty-nine per cent of the country's entire population is in French-speaking Quebec, and over half of this number know no English. Canada thus offers a changing kind of bilingual and culture contact situation with major cross-cultural differences for anthropological analysis.

Both the farm community and the industrial community of Quebec have been studied by anthropologists.[25] The re-evaluation of the nature of Quebec family and community life sparked by Dean Phillipe Garigue of the University of Montreal and a team at Laval University has led to renewed interest in Quebec on the part of anthropologists. Their studies have produced considerable information on styles of life in Quebec which should be translatable into marketing data on pricing policies, colors, package size, flavor and taste of various food items, texture of fabrics, automobile symbolism, product scents, and related subjects.

SPECIFIC KNOWLEDGE

Perhaps the most frequent occasion for the anthropologist to demonstrate specific knowledge in Canada has to do with language. One laundry-soap company had point-of-sale material on its soap describing it as extra strong and the best one to use on especially dirty parts of wash ("les parts de sale"). After sales of the soap had declined, an anthropologist who was called in by the company pointed out that the phrase is comparable to the American slang phrase "private parts." This kind of mistake might have been avoided if anthropological guidance had been available before sales declined.

---

[25]Horace Miner, *St. Denis* (Chicago: University of Chicago Press, 1939); Everett C. Hughes, *French Canada in Transition* (Chicago: University of Chicago Press, 1943).

Some products do not sell well in Quebec because the English name may be almost unpronounceable to a French speaker, or the name of the product may be meaningless even when translated idiomatically. Even the English spoken in Montreal differs somewhat from the English spoken in Toronto, creating potential hazards for the marketers who may not know, for example, that a "tap" in a "flat" in Toronto is likely to be a "faucet" in a Montreal "apartment."

AWARENESS OF THEMES

A study done by an anthropologist for a food manufacturer demonstrated the relationship between the purchases of certain food items and the gradual decline of the wood-burning stove which used to be a staple of Quebec farm kitchens. The wood stove would almost always have a stew pot ("pot au feu") simmering all day. Various ingredients were put into the pot to provide flavor. With the introduction of gas and electric kitchen ranges, it not only became relatively expensive to keep the stew pot going but the simmering could not be sustained because the pot would tend to boil rather than simmer.

This change was accompanied by some radical adjustments in food consumption which were of great relevance to food marketing. The manufacturer was able to begin distribution of canned soups and stews which soon found a very large market and rapidly replaced the "pot au feu."

TABOOS

Alertness to taboos was illustrated by an anthropologist's suggestion to a manufacturer of canned fish for changing a series of advertisements which were appearing in Quebec magazines and newspapers. The same advertisement was run repeatedly. The advertisements showed a woman in shorts playing golf with her husband. The caption read that the woman would be able to be on the golf links all day and still prepare a delicious dinner that evening if she used the product. Every element in the advertisement represented a violation of some underlying theme of French Canadian life; the wife would not be likely to be playing golf with her husband, she would not wear shorts, and she would not be serving the particular kind of fish as a main course. In this case, the anthropologist was consulted *after* the series had been running for awhile.

THE MARKETER AS AN ANTHROPOLOGIST

A good case could be made for the thesis that marketing researchers do more anthropological research on modern cultures than do anthropologists. Marketing researchers are studying national character, subcultures, themes, and ways of life. The kind of information which marketing-research studies seek on how people live and what products they use represent first-rate material for the cultural anthropologist.

The questionnaire, panel, audit, sales analysis, and other methods of modern marketing differ in degree but not in kind from the trained observations of the anthropologists, but there is no reason why the two methods cannot complement each other. Greater communication between these two fields can and should lead to mutual enrichment of both.

10. THE SIGNIFICANCE OF SOCIAL STRATIFICATION IN SELLING*

Richard P. Coleman

Dating back to the late 1940's, advertisers and marketers have alternately flirted with and cooled on the notion that W. Lloyd Warner's social class concept[1] is an important analytic tool for their profession. The Warnerian idea that six social classes constitute the basic division of American Society has offered many attractions to marketing analysts when they have grown dissatisfied with simple income categories or census-type occupational categories and felt a need for more meaningful classifications, for categorizations of the citizenry which could prove more relevant to advertising and marketing problems. However, in the course of their attempts to apply the class concept, marketers have not always found it immediately and obviously relevant. Sometimes it has seemed to shed light on advertising and merchandising problems and at other times it hasn't—with the result that many analysts have gone away disenchanted, deciding that social classes are not much more useful than income categories and procedurally far more difficult to employ.

It is the thesis of this writer that the role of social class has too often been misunderstood or oversimplified, and that if the concept is applied in a more sophisticated and realistic fashion, it will shed light on a great many problems to which, at first glance, it has not seemed particularly relevant. What we propose to do here, then, is discuss and illustrate a few of these more subtle, more refined and (it must be acknowledged) more complicated ways of applying social class analyses to marketing and advertising problems. In other words, the purpose of this paper is to clarify *when* and *in what ways* social class concepts are significant in selling, and to suggest when they might not be as significant as other concepts, or at least need to be used in concert with other analytic categories.

---

*From *Marketing, A Maturing Discipline,* American Marketing Association, December, 1960.

[1]See W. Lloyd Warner, Marchia Meeker, Kenneth Eells, *Social Class in America* (Chicago: Science Research Associates, 1949).

THE WARNERIAN SOCIAL CLASSES

The six social classes which are referred to in this paper are those which W. Lloyd Warner and his associates have observed in their analyses of such diverse communities as Newburyport, Massachusetts,[2] Natchez, Mississippi,[3] Morris, Illinois,[4] Kansas City, Missouri,[5] and Chicago. These social classes are groups of people who are more or less equal to one another in prestige and community status; they are people who readily and regularly interact among themselves in both formal and informal ways; they form a "class" also to the extent that they share the same goals and ways of looking at life. It is this latter fact about social classes which makes them significant to marketers and advertisers.

Briefly characterized, the six classes are as follows, starting from the highest one and going down:[6]

1. The Upper-Upper or "Social Register" Class is composed of locally prominent families, usually with at least second or third generation wealth. Almost inevitably, this is the smallest of the six classes—with probably no more than one-half of one percent of the population able to claim membership in this class. The basic values of these people might be summarized in these phrases: living graciously, upholding the family reputation, reflecting the excellence of one's breeding, and displaying a sense of community responsibility.

2. The Lower-Upper or "Nouveau Riche" Class is made up of the more recently arrived and never-quite-accepted wealthy families. Included in this class are members of each city's "executive elite," as well as founders of large businesses and the newly well-to-do doctors and lawyers. At best only one and one-half percent of Americans rank at this level—so that all told, no more than 2 percent of the population can be counted as belonging to one layer or the other of our Upper Class. The goals of people at this particular level are a blend of the Upper-Upper pursuit of gracious living and the Upper-Middle Class's drive for success.

3. In the Upper-Middle Class are moderately successful professional men and women, owners of medium-sized businesses and "organization

---

[2]See W. Lloyd Warner and Paul Lunt, *The Social Life of a Modern Community* (New Haven: Yale University Press, 1941).

[3]See Allison Davis, Burleigh B. Gardner and Mary R. Gardner, *Deep South* (Chicago: University of Chicago Press, 1941).

[4]See W. Lloyd Warner and Associates, *Democracy in Jonesville* (New York: Harper & Bros., 1949).

[5]The writer's observation on the Kansas City social class system will be included in a forthcoming volume on middle age in Kansas City, currently being prepared for publication by the Committee on Human Development of the University of Chicago.

[6]Some of the phrases and ideas in this characterization have been borrowed from Joseph A. Kahl's excellent synthesizing textbook, *The American Class Structure* (New York: Rinehart & Co., Inc., 1957).

men" at the managerial level; also included are those younger people in their twenties or very early thirties who are expected to arrive at this occupational status level—and possibly higher—by their middle or late thirties (that is, they are today's "junior executives" and "apprentice professionals" who grew up in such families and/or went to the "better" colleges). Ten percent of Americans are part of this social class and the great majority of them are college educated.

The motivating concerns of people in this class are success at career (which is the husband's contribution to the family's status) and tastefully reflecting this success in social participation and home decor (which is the wife's primary responsibility). Cultivating charm and polish, plus a broad range of interests—either civic or cultural, or both—are also goals of the people in this class, just as in the Lower-Upper. For most marketing and advertising purposes, this class and the two above it can be linked together into a single category of "upper status people." The major differences between them—particularly between the Upper-Middle and the Lower-Upper—are in degree of "success" and the extent to which this has been translated into gracious living.

4. At the top of the "Average Man World" is the Lower-Middle Class. Approximately 30 percent or 35 percent of our citizenry can be considered members of this social class. For the most part they are drawn from the ranks of non-managerial office workers, small business owners, and those highly-paid blue-collar families who are concerned with being accepted and respected in white-collar dominated clubs, churches, and neighborhoods. The key word in understanding the motivations and goals of this class is Respectability, and a second important word is Striving. The men of this class are continually striving, within their limitations, to "do a good job" at their work, and both men and women are determined to be judged "respectable" in their personal behavior by their fellow citizens. Being "respectable" means that they live in well-maintained homes, neatly furnished, in neighborhoods which are more-or-less on the "right side of town." It also means that they will clothe themselves in coats, suits, and dresses from "nice stores" and save for a college education for their children.

5. At the lower half of the "Average Man World" is the Upper-Lower Class, sometimes referred to as "The Ordinary Working Class." Nearly 40 percent of all Americans are in this class, making it the biggest. The proto-typical member of this class is a semi-skilled worker on one of the nation's assembly lines. Many of these "Ordinary Working Class" people make very good money, but do not bother with using it to become "respectable" in a middle-class way. Whether they just "get by" at work, or moonlight to make extra, Upper-Lowers are oriented more toward enjoying life and living well from day to day than saving for the future or caring what the middle-class world thinks of them. They try to "keep in step with the times" (indeed, one might say the "times" are more

important than the "Joneses" to this class), because they want to be at least Modern, if not Middle-Class. That is, they try to take advantage of progress to live more comfortably and they work hard enough to keep themselves safely away from a slum level of existence.

6. The Lower-Lower Class of unskilled workers, unassimilated ethnics, and the sporadically employed comprises about 15 percent of the population, but this class has less than 7 or 8 percent of the purchasing power, and will not concern us further here. Apathy, fatalism, and a point of view which justifies "getting your kicks whenever you can" characterize the approach toward life, and toward spending money, found among the people of this class.

Now, we do not mean to imply by these characterizations that the members of each class are always homogeneous in behavior. To suggest such would be to exaggerate greatly the meaning of social classes. To properly understand them, it must be recognized that there is a considerable variation in the way individual members of a class realize these class goals and express these values.

For example, within the Upper-Middle and Lower-Upper Class, there is one group—called Upper Bohemians[7] by Russell Lynes—for whom cultural pursuits are more important than belonging to a "good" country club. As a result, the tastes in furniture, housing accommodations, and recreations exhibited by the men and women of this "issues-and-culture set"—leaning toward the avant garde and eclectic, as they do—are apt to be very different from those practiced by the more conventional, bourgeois members of these status levels. Nevertheless, to both the Upper Bohemians and the Upper Conventionals, displaying "good taste" is quite important, with the differences between them not so much a question of good-versus-bad taste as one of those whose form of good taste is preferred (though, to be sure, the Upper Bohemians are usually quite certain theirs is better).

Other sub-categories can be found in these higher classes and parallel kinds of sub-categories can be found in the Lower-Middle and Upper-Lower classes. Within the Upper-Lower Class, for example, there is a large number of people who are quite concerned with their respectability and spend much of their spare time in church trying to do something about it. Their respectability concerns are not quite like those of the Lower-Middle Class, however, for they seem to care more about The Almighty's view of them than of their fellow man's. Thus, the Upper-Lower Class might, for certain analytic purposes, be sub-divided into Church-Going and Tavern-Hopping segments, although this would by no means exhaust all possibilities of sub-categorization here.

All of this is by way of indicating that the millions of individuals who

---

[7]See Russell Lynes, *A Surfeit of Honey* (New York: Harper & Bros., 1957).

compose each social class are not necessarily similar or identical in their consumption patterns, even though they are of equal status socially and share a set of goals and points of view which are class-wide. Thus far, the literature on social class in both marketing journals and sociological publications has emphasized the similarities of people within classes and rarely pointed out these variations. This has been necessary, of course, in order to properly introduce the concept and educate social scientists and marketers to its utility, but it has led on occasion to naive misuse of the concept and ultimate disillusion. In my view, it has come time for us to advance into a more sophisticated application of social class to marketing problems, which involves awareness of the differences as well as similarities within each class.

SOCIAL CLASS VERSUS INCOME

Let us proceed now to stating the basic significance of this class concept for people in the selling field. In the first place, it explains why income categories or divisions of Americans are quite often irrelevant in analyzing product markets, consumers' shopping habits and store preferences, and media consumption. For example, if you take three families, all earning around $8,000 a year, but each from a different social class, a radical difference in their ways of spending money will be observed.

An Upper-Middle Class family in this income bracket, which in this case might be a young lawyer and his wife or perhaps a college professor, is apt to be found spending a relatively large share of its resources on housing (in a "prestige" neighborhood), on rather expensive pieces of furniture, on clothing from quality stores, and on cultural amusements or club memberships. Meanwhile, the Lower-Middle Class family—headed, we will say, by an insurance salesman or a fairly successful grocery store owner, perhaps even a Diesel engineer—probably has a better house, but in not so fancy a neighborhood; it is apt to have as full a wardrobe though not so expensive, and probably more furniture though none by name designers. These people almost certainly have a much bigger savings account in the bank.

Finally, the Working Class family—with a cross-country truck driver or a highly-paid welder as its chief wage-earner—is apt to have less house and less neighborhood than the Lower-Middle or Upper-Middle family; but it will have a bigger, later model car, plus more expensive appliances in its kitchen and a bigger TV set in its living room. This family will spend less on clothing and furniture, but more on food if the number of children is greater, as is likely. One further difference: the man of the house probably spends much more on sports, attending baseball games (for example), going hunting and bowling, and perhaps owning a boat of some description.

The wives in these three families will be quite noticeably different in the kind of department stores they patronize, in the magazines they read, and in the advertising to which they pay attention. The clothing and furniture they select for themselves and their families will differ accordingly, and also because they are seeking quite different goals. This has become very clear in studies Social Research, Inc., has done for the *Chicago Tribune* on the clothing tastes of Chicagoland women, for the Kroehler Company on the place of furniture in American homes, and for MacFadden Publications on the purchasing patterns and motivations of their romance magazines' Working Class readers.[8] (These have been contrasted in turn with the motivations of Middle Class women who read service magazines.)

The Upper-Middle Class wife—even of the struggling young lawyer— usually buys all her public-appearance clothes at specialty shops or in the specialty departments of her community's best department stores; she feels constrained to choose her wardrobe according to rather carefully prescribed standards of appropriateness. In furnishing her home, she thoughtfully considers whether a given piece or a combination of pieces will serve as adequate testament to her aesthetic sensitiveness, plus doing credit in turn to her husband's taste in wife-choosing. She pays careful attention to the dictates of the best shelter magazines, the "smart" interior decorators in town, the homes of other women in her class, and maybe that of the boss's wife.

The Lower-Middle Class woman is more single-mindedly concerned with furnishing her home so that it will be "pretty" in a way that suits her and hopefully might win praise from her friends and neighbors. She tries to get ideas from the medium-level shelter and service magazines and is perpetually depressed because her home isn't furnished as much like a dream house as she would like it to be. In this she is quite different from the Upper-Lower wife who is apt to care more about having a full array of expensive, gleaming white appliances in her kitchen than a doll's house of a living room. Where the Lower-Middle housewife usually has a definite style in mind which she's striving to follow, the Upper-Lower woman simply follows the lead of newspaper furniture advertising (and what she sees when window shopping) toward furniture which is "modern-looking," by which she means the "latest thing" that has hit the mass market.

A great many more examples of differences in consumption patterns by class levels could be given, but the principal ones have been well reported already—facetiously by Vance Packard and seriously by Pierre Martineau;[9] for further amplification on this point the latter source is

---

[8]This study has been published under the name *Workingman's Wife* (New York: Oceana Press, 1959) by Lee Rainwater, Richard P. Coleman, and Gerald Handel.

[9]See Pierre Martineau, *Motivation in Advertising* (New York: McGraw-Hill Book Co., 1957) and "Social Classes and Spending Behavior," *Journal of Marketing*, Vol. 23, No. 2 (October 1958), pp. 121–30.

recommended. The significance to merchandisers and advertisers of these findings about motivational differences between classes is fairly obvious, the major idea being that for many products, advertising appeals and merchandising techniques must be differentially geared to the points of view reflected in these three main social classes. Advertising of brands or goods aimed at a specific class must take into account the motivations of that class, and not try to sell everything as if it were an Upper-Class or Upper-Middle status symbol.

Up to now, we've been talking about product areas—clothing, furniture, and residential neighborhoods—where the relationship between social class and quality of goods purchased is highest. In these things the so-called "Quality Market" and the Upper-Middle (and higher) markets coincide. That is, the purchasers of highest quality clothing and highest quality furniture are more nearly from the Upper-Middle and Upper social classes than from the highest income categories, and so on it goes down the hierarchy. The correlation between price of goods purchased and social class is relatively quite high in these product areas while the correlation between price paid and annual income is lower than one might expect.

There is another group of products which are not linked in such a direct way with social class, but neither are they linked with income categories in any obvious relationship. The current car market provides an instructive example of this situation, for the nature of the market cannot be grasped by using one or the other concept exclusively. What is happening in today's car market can only be understood when income categories are placed into a social class framework.

THE "OVERPRIVILEGED" AS "QUALITY MARKET"

Within each social class group there are families and individuals whose incomes are above average for their class. The Upper-Lower family with an income above $7,000 a year—sometimes a product of both husband and wife working, and sometimes not—is an example of this. So, too, is the Lower-Middle Class business owner or salesman who makes more than $10,000 a year, but has no interest in either the concerts or country clubs of Upper-Middledom and hence is still Lower-Middle Class. The Upper-Middle Class couple with more than $25,000 a year at its disposal but no desire to play the "society game" of subscription balls or private schools is also in this category. These are what might be called the "overprivileged" segments of each class. They are not "overprivileged" in the absolute sense, of course; they are "overprivileged," however, relative to what is required or needed by families in their class. After they have met the basic expectations and standards of their group in the housing, food, furnishing, and clothing areas, they have quite a bit of money left over which is their equivalent of "discretionary income."

In much the same way, each class has its "underprivleged" members; in the Upper-Middle Class these are the younger couples who haven't made the managerial ranks yet, the college professors, the genteel professionals, and a few downwardly mobile people from high-status backgrounds who are trying to hang on to what fragments of status they have left—for the most part these people are below the $12,000-a-year mark and they can barely meet some of the basic requirements of Upper-Middle life, much less experience any of its little luxuries; in the Lower-Middle Class these are the poorly paid bank tellers, the rows of bookkeepers in railroad offices, the school teachers with considerably more status aspiration than income; and in the Upper-Lower Class it is almost any family earning less than $4,500 or $5,000 a year, at today's rates of pay in metropolitan areas.

In the middle of each class's income range are its "average" members, families who are neither underprivileged nor overprivileged by the standards of their class. You might think of this as the Upper-Middle Class family between $12,000 and $20,000 a year, the Lower-Middle family in the $7,000-$9,000 range, and the Upper-Lower family near $6,000 per annum. However, this word of caution is necessary: a lot of people in the middle income range of their class see themselves as underprivileged because they are aspiring to become one of the "overprivileged" in their class or to move on up the ladder to a higher class.

The relevance of all this to the car market is that when you look at this particular market today, you find it is the "average" members of each class, whether Upper-Middle, Lower-Middle, or Upper-Lower, who constitute the heart of the Low-Priced Three's audience; these are the people who are buying Fords and Chevrolets this year and last, and probably next. No longer is the Ford and Chevrolet market just a lower-middle income market, or (in class terms) a Lower-Middle or a Lower Class market. Rather, it is recruited from the middle income group *within each* social class. Indeed, the $15,000-a-year Upper-Middle "organization man" is apt to choose a Ford or Chevy from the Impala-Galaxie level or else a top-price station wagon once he ventures into this market, whereas the average-income Lower-Middle man will settle for a middle-series Bel Air or Fairlane 500, and the "average-income" Upper-Lower guy either splurges for an Impala or "sensibly" contents himself with the spartan Biscayne.

While this has been happening to the Low-Priced Three makes the heart of the medium-price car market has relocated in the "overprivileged" segments of each class. Today, rich blue-collar workers are joining prosperous Lower-Middle Class salesmen and well-to-do Upper-Middle Class business owners in buying Pontiacs, Buicks, Oldsmobiles, Chryslers, and even Cadillacs. In fact, what there is left of big-car lust in our society is found at peak strength among the "overprivileged" Upper-Lowers or else among men who have achieved higher status, but grew up as kids in the Upper-Lower class and have not forgotten their wide-eyed envy of the big car owner.

Finally, as you may have guessed by now, the compact car market's heart is to be found in the "underprivileged" segments of each class (here we are speaking of the market for a compact as a first car). The overwhelming majority of Rambler purchasers, Falcon buyers, and foreign economy car owners come from this socio-economic territory. Thus, it is not the really poor who are buying these cheapest, most economical cars—rather it is those who think of themselves as poor relative to their status aspirations and to their needs for a certain level of clothing, furniture, and housing which they could not afford if they bought a more expensive car.

The market for compacts as second cars is somewhat more complicated in its socio-economic geography, being located in the middle range of the Upper-Middle Class, and the "overprivileged" segment of the Lower-Middle. The "overprivileged" Upper-Middle may have one as a third car, but he prefers either a T-Bird, a foreign sports car, a Pontiac convertible, or a beat-up station wagon as his second car, while the "overprivileged" Upper-Lower is apt to go for a used standard if he wants a second car.

If marketers and advertisers had assumed that the market for compacts was going to be the lowest-income or lowest-status members of our society, they would have seriously miscalculated in their merchandising and advertising approach. Rambler, for one, did not make this mistake. American Motors advertised its cars as "bringing sense into the auto market" and thus enabled people who bought one to pride themselves on the high-minded rationality they had displayed. Rambler owners, as they drive down the street, are not ashamed that they couldn't afford better—instead, as the company has told them to be, they are proud that they did not yield, like their neighbors, to base emotional desires for a car bloated in size beyond necessity and loaded in gadgetry beyond reason. Compact car owners have their own form of snobbery— what might be called "sensibility snobbery"—with which to content themselves and justify their purchase.

This analysis of the car market is one example of what I mean by the sophisticated application of social class concepts to marketing and advertising problems. There are many products and many brands which, like cars, are more nearly symbols of high status class within class than symbols of higher status per se. A color television set is such a product, or at least it was two years ago when Social Research, Inc., studied its market. At the time color television manufacturers were puzzled because sales were thinly spread throughout the income scale, without any noticeable increase in concentration until an extremely high level was reached. Furthermore, they were unable to see any particular relationship between social class and color set ownership, since about as many Upper-Lower Class people owned them as did Upper-Middles. However, when the two factors of income and class were put together, in the manner described above, it became clear that the color television market was concentrated among high-income or "overprivileged" members of each social class. Other products which bear this complicated relationship to class and income are the more costly brands and larger sizes of home appliances. Fairly expensive recreational equipment like outboard motor boats also tend to be in this category.

In summary, today's market for quality goods and quality brands is not necessarily drawn from what has historically been described as the "Quality Market" of Upper-Middle and Upper Class people, nor even necessarily from the highest income categories. Rather, in many instances, it is drawn from those people within each social level who have the most discretionary income available for enjoying life's little extras above and beyond the requirements of their class. Every merchandiser and advertiser ought to take a good hard look at what he is selling and ask himself if it bears this particular relationship to the class and income picture. If his product does, and if his brand is one of the more expensive, then he should merchandise it not as if it were just for social climbers or for the upper classes, but rather as part of the Better Life, U.S.A. If, on the other hand, his brand is one of the least expensive, then he is not just selling to the poor, but rather to those in all classes who feel it is only sensible on their part to settle for a brand such as his and save the difference for other things which are more important in their statement of social class aspiration and identity.

SOCIAL CLASS ISN'T ALWAYS IMPORTANT

Now, to make the picture complete, it must be pointed out that Social Research, Inc., has found some products in which the income factor is all-important and the social class variable is relevant only to the extent that it is correlated with income. Perhaps the most perfect example of this is the market for air conditioners in Southwestern cities. There, everybody—except the sickly and the extremely old-fashioned—agree that air conditioning one's home is imperative if summer is to be survived with any degree of comfort. Consequently, the expensiveness of a family's air conditioning equipment—whether centrally installed, or window units to the number of four, three, two, or one—is directly correlated with family income. It is not merely a function of discretionary income—as in our example about purchase of medium-priced cars; it is instead almost completely a function of total annual income. If more Upper-Middles than Upper-Lowers are fully air-conditioned it is only because more of them can afford to be; it is not because Upper-Middles as a group are placing higher priority on the air-conditioned existence.

Undoubtedly air conditioners are not alone in being classless—so that one more thing the marketer who uses social class in a truly sophisticated way needs to understand is that there can be occasions when it is an irrelevant variable. Realizing this, he will not become disenchanted with social class when he finds a marketing problem where it does not shed light or where it does not seem pertinent. Of course, he will want to make sure that in advertising such a product there is indeed no need to take class into account. After all, some apparently classless products are properly sold to the market in a segmental approach, appealing first on one ground to one class, then on other grounds to another.

There are other products—and probably air conditioning is one of them and children's play clothes may be another—where this is not necessary. For such products some factor, such as physical comfort (in the one case) or simple durability (in the other), is so basic in the consumer's consideration that all other motivations pale into insignificance beside it. There are even products, like beer, where the democratic approach—that is, a tone of "let's-all-be-good-fellows-together" is exactly right and segmental appeals or snob stories are all wrong.

Another aspect to the sophisticated employment of social class refers back to the point made earlier that social class groups are not always homogeneous. It must be recognized that at times a product's market is formed by "highbrows" from the Upper-Upper Class on down to the Lower-Middle, or by "suburbanites" and suburban-minded people of all classes—in which case the social class variable may confuse a market analysis more than clarify it.

Particularly must merchandisers and market analysts beware of equating "Class" with "Brow"; for they are not synonymous. For example, the Upper-Middle Class and those above it are mainly middlebrow in taste (veering toward an all-American lower-middlebrow level of preferences in television shows and advertising messages) even though the majority of highbrows are found at this level. At times advertisers have made the mistake of assuming that the Upper-Middle Class should be appealed to in a highly sophisticated fashion—and though this is just fine if the product itself is likely to appeal primarily to the Manhattanized type of Upper-Middle, it is not correct if it is expected to sell to the kind of doctor in Dubuque who enjoys a visit to New York every now and then but would never want to live there.

In short, not only must the sophisticated marketer abandon social class in favor of income categories on occasion in his analysis and interpretation of a market, he must recognize that at times both income and class are superseded in importance by divisions of the public into brow levels, by divisions into "high mobiles" and "low mobiles," innovators and non-innovators, inner-directed and other-directed, urbanites, suburbanites, exurbanites, ruralites, and Floridians, or what have you. Usually, of course, fullest understanding of a market will require that social class be linked in with whichever sub-categorization proves pertinent from among those in the catalogue just recited, much as income and class were linked together for fullest comprehension of the car market.

As a final point, let it be noted that the way of life and the goals of people in each social class are in perpetual flux. Neither the "who" of each class nor "what motivates them" are constants to be assumed without continual re-evaluation. Right now, particularly, it is very clear that our society is changing. Every year the collar-color line is breaking down further. More blue-collar workers are becoming Middle Class as well as middle income and Modern, and a white-collar position is less and less a guarantee of Lower-Middle status. As a consequence of this, the Lower-Middle Class is perhaps somewhat more "materialistic" in outlook and slightly less "respectability" conscious than it was 25 years ago, or even 8. Meanwhile, for men and women to achieve Upper-Middle status without college backgrounds is becoming more and more difficult, so that this class is turning much more worldly-wise and well-read, much less conventionally bourgeois than it was in the Zenith of Babbitt's day.

In short, the form of our society and its division into social classes is not fixed as of Yankee City in 1931, Jonesville in 1944, Kansas City in 1952, or St. Louis in 1960. We won't be able to say exactly the same things about either the classes themselves or their relationships to specific markets by next year at this time. This fact about the American class structure, that it is not static, that it is in the process of change, is in itself important to merchandisers, to advertisers, to anyone in selling. Among other things, it means that undoubtedly they have played a part in past changes and can play a leading role in directing future changes. But of more direct concern here, to the marketing analyst it means that if he allows his stratification concept to become dated, his use of it will cease as of that moment to be sophisticated.

B. The influence of face-to-face social groupings

The emphasis shifts now to somewhat smaller groups, and the prime emphasis is on a more intimate personal interaction between individuals. In the first reading, Stafford reviews some of the pertinent literature on reference groups and then presents the results of an experiment on group influence in the choice of bread. This experiment is of special interest in that he used natural groups (as opposed to those assembled artificially in a laboratory for research) and found a considerable amount of social interaction of bread preferences. As such, his contribution should serve to generate further research.

King addresses himself to a related area—that of face-to-face dissemination of fashion trends. King attacks the long-standing assumption that certain society leaders first adopt a new fashion and then influence others lower on the social ladder to try it. This is sometimes called the "trickle down" theory. He reports findings that distinctly refute this theory. They suggest, instead, that social leaders are not necessarily the first to buy, and when they do they are no more likely to be opinion leaders than are others. Considerable research is now underway in the area of diffusion of innovations, and this article has done much to stimulate interest in this important area of research.

11. EFFECTS OF GROUP INFLUENCES ON CONSUMER BRAND PREFERENCES*

James E. Stafford

Most earlier marketing researchers described consumer brand preference behavior without attempting to uncover and analyze experimentally determinants of such brand preferences [2, 3]. With the advent of sophisticated mathematical models, however, renewed interest was shown in conducting experimental studies leading to an explanation of the process of brand preference behavior [4, 5, 8]. To date, the most important contributions of these studies have been their reliance on realism and their emphasis on brand loyalty as a probability process. For the most part, factors other than economic ones were not considered important, or at least they were de-emphasized. In recent years, however, marketing men generally have conceded that such social factors as acculturation, social class, ethnic groups and identification all play some role in consumer decision making. The question today is exactly how, in what way, and to what extent social factors influence consumer behavior.

A second thought which suggested this study revolves around the concept of group or interpersonal influence. From both a theoretical and empirical point of view, the literature of the behavioral sciences fully supports the idea that certain groups, and particularly certain individuals within the group, influence member behavior. While a great deal of marketing research has been conducted on various aspects of consumer behavior, there have been only a few analytical attempts [7, 9] to determine if such interpersonal interactions do, in fact, influence consumer behavior.

The lack of empirical research on determining whether small, informal,

Journal of Marketing Research, Vol. III (February, 1966), pp. 68–75.

Grateful acknowledgment is made to W. T. Tucker, University of Texas, for his valuable suggestions and constructive criticism, and to the Ford Foundation who partially supported this project.

social groups influence the purchasing behavior of their members led to this design of an experiment which would, first, indicate whether this influence exists and, second, describe and explain the process of group influence on one particular type of consumer behavior—brand preferences. The main objective was to explore in as much detail as possible if and how a consumer's brand preferences might be conditioned by intergroup communications and the perception of brand preferences of fellow group members.

The overall design of the experiment consisted of sociometrically selecting ten groups of women who were close friends, neighbors, or relatives; who might go shopping together; and who were given a common experimental task to perform. The assumption was that the resulting groups were "real" in some sense other than that of being arbitrarily brought together for the study. This did not mean that the groups had to have traditions of long standing, but they had to have real interaction among the individuals making up the group.

By analyzing first the relationship between the groups and their subsequent observed brand preference behavior, it was hoped that the influence of groups on the brand preferences of their members could be shown statistically. Second, by analyzing the interaction processes of each group, it was also hoped to illustrate that the degree of influence exerted varies according to the internal cohesiveness[1] of the group, and according to the type and strength of informal leadership exhibited.

REVIEW OF GROUP THEORY

During the past two decades there has been a resurgence of interest in individual-group relationships. This resurgence continued to build momentum until, today, the study of small groups has become a central area of theorization and experimentation for social psychologists. The major character of this trend, as contrasted with the individualistic emphasis, is the realization that group situations generate differential effects of significant consequence. Group interaction is seen as a major determinant in attitude formation and attitude change, as well as for other phenomena (satisfaction of social needs) of importance to the individual.

As is typical in the behavioral sciences, there is no one accepted definition of "groups." The most common definition revolves around the term "reference groups" which can include groups to which a person actually belongs, to which he aspires to belong, or dissociative groups to which he aspires *not* to belong. Thus, for one member a group may be a membership group while for another it is a reference group. Most social psychologists consider reference groups as a person's major source of values, norms, and perspectives.

---

[1]Cohesiveness refers to the attraction a group has for its members. The greater the attractiveness of the group, the more cohesive the group.

Reference groups influence behavior in two major ways. First, they influence *aspiration levels* and thus play a part in producing satisfaction or frustration. If the other members of a particular reference group (for example, neighbors) are wealthier, more famous, better gardeners, *etc.,* one may be dissatisfied with his own achievements and may strive to do as well as the others.

Second, reference groups influence *kinds* of behavior. They establish approved patterns of using one's wealth, of wearing one's prestige, of designing one's garden. They thus produce conformity as well as contentment (or discontentment). These two kinds of influence have, in general, a great deal in common. Both imply certain perceptions on the part of the individual, who attributes characteristics to the reference group which it may or may not actually have. Both involve psychological rewards and punishment.

Reference behavior itself is a cognitive process in which individuals evaluate their statuses, behavior, norms, and values by means of referents.[2] The four objects of evaluation—norms, values, statuses, and behavior—may be grouped into objective (statuses and behavior) and subjective (norms and values) categories. It is recognized that the contents of each category have important linkages with those of the other, but for purposes of analysis the distinction may be made.

Reference behavior is characterized by three general dimensions—knowledge, affectivity, and sanctions. These dimensions appear as interrelated variables which come into play in all forms of reference behavior.

For a phenomenon to be used, the individual must be aware (have knowledge) of its existence, and the degree and kind of knowledge serve as guides to his use of the referent. Through direct and indirect communication, members learn the norms and values of their informal groups and see how the normative structure is expressed in the status arrangements and corresponding behavior patterns.

The sanctions perceived by individuals constitute another dimension of reference behavior. The concept of referents indicates the existence of myriads of potential referents and, yet, the actual number of referents utilized by any one person is necessarily limited. When an individual perceives a potential referent, such as an informal social group, to be the source of positive sanctions (rewards) or negative sanctions (punishment or the withholding of anticipated rewards) which relate to himself, at that moment the informal group becomes an actual referent and is used in the evaluation of norms, values, statuses, and behavior.

The third dimension of reference behavior—affectivity—relates to the degree of identification a person has for a particular group. Recognition

---

[2]Referents are whatever individuals employ in evaluating their own statuses, behavior, norms, and values. In this paper the small, informal social group is the main referent being considered, although there are many other phenomena that one could use as referents.

of the importance of a person's degree of identification to a reference group is very valuable to an understanding of how groups influence the behavior of their members.

Because of the segmentation of life in an industrialized, mass society, important decisions faced by an individual can involve the perspectives of many referents without any perceived conflicts between them. In general, the more restricted the application of results of a process of evaluation, the more limited will be the number of referents mobilized in the process. If, for example, an individual was planning a small purchase (a gallon of milk), he would probably utilize very few referents to make a decision. On the other hand, if he were planning to purchase a new car, then he would probably evaluate his decision alternatives by considering a much larger number of referents. While determination of any rank order of influence potential is very difficult to accomplish, some mention can be made of two other concepts which have evolved out of group theory, and which are quantitatively measurable—group cohesion and group leadership.

Informal structuring tends to occur in all groups after a period of time during which the members have interacted with one another. Homans contended that "the usual outcome of interaction is the formation of interpersonal bonds of affect and respect [6]." The recipient of affect and respect was said to have social rank within the group. Differential social ranks provided the basis for informal structuring.

Were all members of a group to like and respect each other highly, no substructures would be said to exist. This condition would define complete, 100 percent positive cohesion. All social ranks would be equal. If, on the other hand, every member ignored every other one, each member would be considered a separate substructure, a one-man clique. This would define the state of zero cohesion. Internal social influence would be equal to zero. Much evidence exists to support the proposition that intergroup pressure to conform on matters of importance varies directly with cohesion. In a very cohesive group, a member will experience a great deal of pressure to conform. In a less cohesive group, pressure to conform is expected to vary directly with the amount of deviation from the group norms, at least up to a point.

The concept of "group leaders" developed from the evolution of role differentiation within the group. Except in very unusual circumstances, informal role differentiations are expected to occur in every group. As a result of this role differentiation process, each person in the group has a certain social rank or status. The more status an individual has, the greater his prestige; the greater one's prestige, the higher he is in the informal hierarchy and the more "social power" he possesses. Social power has been defined as the total amount of opinion change one person could induce another to make. The concept could, of course, be broadened to include the overt as well as the convert changes a member can effect in another member of the group. When a group member has social power over other members, he also usually has high status and is normally considered the group leader.

METHODOLOGY

OBJECTIVES AND HYPOTHESES

Considering the fertile field for research in consumer behavior offered by reference group theory, it seemed very pertinent to relate reference theory and consumer behavior in an empirical study. The first and foremost objective of the study, therefore, was to show statistically that small, informal groups do influence certain aspects of consumer behavior. In hypothesis form, the first objective was:

1. Small, informal social groups exert influence toward conformity on member brand preferences.

The second and third objectives were closely related to the first. In fact, they could be considered secondary objectives. Assuming support for the first goal, this part of the study attempted to determine how and to what degree informal groups influence member behavior. From a theoretical standpoint, group cohesion and group leadership played important roles in forming group opinions and behavior patterns. Specifically, then, Hypotheses 2 and 3 were:

2. The degree of influence exerted on a member by the group is directly related to the "cohesiveness" of that group.
3. Within a group, the "leader" is the most influential member with respect to member behavior patterns in purchase situations (brand preferences in this study).

RESEARCH DESIGN

The research design attempted to analyze the relationship among several variables (group influences and brand preferences) under controlled but "real-life" conditions. The broad steps of the research were as follows:

1. Specification and delineation of the first major variable of interest—small, informal groups. A two-stage, systematic random sample of ten housewives from one Census tract in Austin, Texas, was used as a representative basis to obtain ten informal groups. Each member of the original sample was asked to take a sociometric test, which was used to determine the interpersonal relationships of interest and to disclose the feelings which individuals have toward each other in respect to a group situation they are considering at that moment. Since consumer behavior was the broad topic of study, each woman was asked to nominate four friends, relatives or neighbors with whom "she likes to or would be willing to go shopping." The use of an activity criterion, rather than a

request for a general statement of friendship, was intended to reveal the specific basis on which a selection was made, as well as to uncover group interactions closely associated to some common activity like buying behavior. The end result of the sociometric test was ten groups of women who were friendly toward each other, who interacted, and who all were oriented toward one criterion—shopping behavior. The rest of the experiment dealt with how the influence of interpersonal relationships on a person's brand preferences could be observed.

2. A particular product, bread, was selected as a vehicle for the brand preference study because of ease of handling, frequent use, and financial considerations. Thin sliced white bread from a local bakery was packaged in identical clear unmarked cellophane bags. Large labels ($2'' \times 2''$) with the letters, "H," "L," "M," "P," were designated as "brands" to be placed on the bread. These four middle-alphabet consonants were chosen because, first, they were easy to remember and, second, they have about the same frequency of use in English. It was not assumed that these symbols (brands) were completely neutral because it is probable that no set of symbols could be neutral, equally pleasing, or have common meanings for all individuals.

3. The experiment itself was relatively simple. Called on at home twice a week (Tuesday and Friday) for eight weeks, each of the forty-two women in the study was given her choice of the four previously unknown brands of bread. The four brands were placed on a tray so the participant could easily see and choose the one she wanted. In order to control for position bias, the position of the brands on the tray was varied each day in Latin square design. The women were not aware that all of the brands were from the same bakery, or that the study was concerned with analyzing intergroup influences. Rather, they were told the purpose of the study was to discover how women go about choosing a brand of bread from several about which they knew nothing.

4. At the end of the test period, each woman was given a short questionnaire covering brand preferences and general opinions regarding the bread. The questionnaire also provided specific information for determining group cohesion, group leadership, and intergroup communication patterns.

5. Analysis of the data included determination of (a) group influences on brand choices and preferences; (b) influence of the degree of group cohesion on brand preferences; (c) influence of group leaders on brand choices of other group members, and (d) comparisons of actual brand choices with brand preferences.

RESULTS

By analyzing the similarities and differences of brand choice patterns within the entire sample and among the members of each group, it was expected to determine whether the group was in fact a source of influence on member brand preferences. On the assumption that the data were neither correlated nor binomial, two-way analysis of variance (F-test) was a valid tool to use to test the first hypothesis. If the study was properly designed to show that groups influence member brand preferences, then the statistical result should be a significant difference between the groups in the brands preferred. In other words, while within group brand preferences should be similar, the groups themselves should vary among one another with respect to brand preferences. The results are presented in Table 1.

TABLE 1
ANALYSIS OF VARIANCE SUMMARY FOR THE INFLUENCE
OF INFORMAL GROUPS ON BRAND PREFERENCES

Source of Variation	Sum of Squares	Degrees of Freedom	Variance Estimates by Pooling	F
Brands	22.90	3	7.60	.74
Groups	181.30	9	20.10	1.97*
Interaction	1,580.40	155	10.20	

*p = .05.

Statistically, the results of the analysis of variance test supported the first hypothesis. A significant difference was found between the groups with respect to preferred brands, while there was no significant difference between the brands themselves. Also, there was no significant interaction effect between brands and groups, thus disposing of one major source of statistical ambiguity. The first result, while explaining nothing of the determinants of group influence, did provide sufficient stimulus to carry on a more detailed analysis of the process of group influence.

While analysis of variance was a valuable and powerful tool in determining whether the groups did, in fact, influence member brand preferences, it provided no clues as to *how* this influence was initiated and whether this influence was exerted toward member conformity. Theoretically speaking, two factors—cohesiveness and informal leadership—have an important bearing on the effectiveness of internal group influences.

Essentially, group cohesiveness was measured by having each member of the group rate every other member of that group on a seven point bipolar scale which ranged from Best Friend (+ 3) to Hated (− 3), with Don't Know (0) as the center point. The algebraic sum of points given by all the group members was termed "Lib units [1]." The higher the mean Lib score for a group, the more cohesive (positive or negative) was the group.

Group leadership was defined operationally as the sum of three different sources of influence: attractiveness, expertness, and communications centrality. First, the attractiveness of each group member to every other group member was measured by taking the mean Lib score that person received on the group cohesion measurement. The individual who was most attractive or best liked by his group was considered to be a potential informal leader of the group. Second, expertness as a form of leadership was described rather arbitrarily as the woman in each group who had been a member of the first bread panel study conducted by Tucker [10]. Because of her previous experience on a similar study, it was believed that this individual might be considered an expert in this study, with her opinions being therefore more influential. Finally, the leader was defined as the individual in the central position of that group's communication network. Each woman was asked to tell how often (times per week) she called, was called by, or saw in person each of the other group members. By classifying this data, it was possible to describe rather accurately the communication patterns of each group. The women in the group with the highest frequency of communications (central position) was defined as the leader.

EFFECT OF COHESIVENESS ON BRAND PREFERENCES

The main function of this section of the study was to determine whether cohesiveness influenced the degree to which members would conform to each other's brand preferences. In other words, would members of more cohesive groups be more likely to prefer the same brand than members of less cohesive groups? A second consideration from a slightly different point of view from the above was: would members of more cohesive groups tend to be more or less brand loyal than members of less cohesive groups? Does increased cohesion lead to similarities in general behavior (brand loyalty) even though the loyalty may be expressed on different brands?

As shown in Table 2, there appeared at first to be no relationship between cohesiveness and similarity among member brand preferences.

TABLE 2

THE RELATIONSHIP BETWEEN COHESIVENESS AND
THE BEST LIKED BRAND OF EACH GROUP

Rank Order of Groups from Highest to Lowest in Cohesiveness	Cohesiveness in Mean Lib Scores	Percent Best Liked Brand Chosen by the Group
1	3.00	66.6%
2	2.50	65.6
3	2.00	30.9
4	1.90	50.0
5	1.40	25.3
6.5	1.10	28.2
6.5	1.10	29.7
8	1.00	43.7
9	0.90	50.0
10	0.65	34.2

The two groups highest in cohesiveness also had the highest percentage of mutually preferred brands. Groups 8 and 9, however, also exhibited high degree of internal similarity for the best liked brand. As a result, no concrete conclusions could be drawn from these data regarding the importance of cohesiveness in the effectiveness of group influence.

In an attempt to approach the determination of the influence of cohesiveness from a different direction, the collected data were reanalyzed and rearranged as shown in Table 3.

TABLE 3
COMPARISONS OF BEST LIKED BRANDS OF LEADERS AND
GROUPS TO GROUP COHESION

Rank Order of Groups from Highest to Lowest in Cohesiveness	Cohesiveness in Mean Lib Scores	Leader's Best Liked Brand	Percent Best Liked Brand Chosen by Leader	Entire Group's Best Liked Brand	Percent Best Liked Brand Chosen by Group (Leader Excluded)
1	3.0	H	68%	H	56%
2	2.5	M	100	M	48
3	2.0	H	43	H	31
4	1.9	P	83	P	50
5	1.4	H	43	H	25
6.5	1.1	M	37	P	28
6.5	1.1	L	40	H	29
8	1.0	P	43	H	28
9	0.9	M	100	M	50
10	0.6	P	43	M	34

Since it was known that group cohesion and leadership were closely related, Table 3 was revised to include not only the group's best liked brand but also that of the leader's. Notice that in the five most cohesive groups, the preferred brand of the group and the leader were the same. In the five less cohesive groups there was only one occurrence of preference similarity (Group 9).

No relationship was discovered between the degree of cohesiveness and the extent and strength of brand loyalty[3] in the group. In Table 4, for example, two groups ranked low in cohesiveness (8th and 9th) both had as many members brand loyal as the two top ranked groups. Also shown in the table was the fact that the average length of a brand loyalty run varied indiscriminately regardless of cohesiveness.

In this study, cohesiveness appeared to have its most important function in providing an agreeable environment in which informal leaders could effectively operate.

---

[3]Brand loyalty has been operationally defined as "three consecutive choices of the same brand."

TABLE 4
THE INFLUENCE OF GROUP COHESIVENESS ON THE
EXTENT OF STRENGTH OF BRAND LOYALTY

Rank Order of Groups from Highest to Lowest in Cohesiveness	Percent of Each Group Brand Loyal	Mean Length of Group's Brand Loyalty Runs
1	100%	8.0
2	100	10.5
3	50	4.0
4	80	7.0
5	60	2.6
6.5	100	5.2
6.5	40	2.6
8	100	9.7
9	100	6.0
10	60	3.6

EFFECT OF GROUP LEADERSHIP ON BRAND PREFERENCES

Group leadership, as previously mentioned, was measured in three ways: by attraction, expertness, and position centrality in the communications network. Since each was an independent measurement, it was possible that any or all of them would delineate a different group leader. Table 5 was the result of a cross tabulation of the measurements.

In six of the ten groups, the leader was the same individual regardless of the leadership measurement. In three of the other four groups it was impossible to obtain a meaningful measurement of individual attraction because (1) all of the members were related, or (2) all individuals in the group were liked by each other to about the same degree. The individual from each group ultimately selected as the leader for purposes of analysis was the member who had the highest average on the three measurements.

In order to substantiate the importance of informal leadership to effective group influence, one must refer back to Table 3. An important aspect of this table was that it indicated a definite relationship between how well the leader preferred his best liked brand and what brand was preferred (including the strength of this preference) by the other members of the group. In other words, regardless of the degree of cohesiveness, the more frequently the leader chose his best liked brand, the higher the likelihood that the rest of the group would prefer that brand more often than expected by chance. For example, in the group ranked ninth in cohesiveness, the leader selected one brand sixteen consecutive times; her fellow group members preferred the same brand 50 percent of the time when it was expected by chance only 25 percent of the time.

Table 6 indicates this relationship even more clearly. Working down

TABLE 5

COMPARISONS OF THE RESULTS OF THE THREE GROUP LEADERSHIP MEASUREMENTS°

Group	Individual	A	E	C	Group	Individual	A	E	C
1	1	None	X	X	6	27	X	X	X
	2					33			
	3					40			
	4					28			
	5								
2	6		X	X		26	X	X	X
	7	X				34			
	8					25			
	9					28			
	44					17	—		
3	11	X	X	X	8	29	X	X	X
	12					35			
	13					30			
	14								
	15								
4	16	None	X		9	42	X	X	X
	10					41			
	36			X		21			
						31			
						32			
5	22	X	X	X	10	19			
	23					20	None	X	X
	24								
	43								
	18								

°Leadership measurements
  A = attraction
  E = expertness
  C = communications centrality.

TABLE 6

COMPARISONS OF FREQUENCY OF CHOICE OF BEST
LIKED BRANDS OF THE LEADER AND MEMBERS
OF EACH GROUP

Group Leader's Best Liked Brand	Percent Best Liked Brand Chosen by Leader (Ranked from Highest to Lowest in Percent of Time Chosen)	Entire Group's Best Liked Brand	Percent Best Liked Brand Chosen by Group (Leader Excluded)
M	100%	M	50%
M	100	M	48
P	83	P	50
H	68	H	56
P	43	M	34
H	43	H	31
M	43	P	28
H	43	H	25
L	40	H	29
M	37	P	28

the figures in the table, it is seen that the more frequently a leader chose one brand, the higher the probability that the rest of her group would like and take the same brand. Once the leader's preference for a certain brand dropped below 68 percent, the group's frequency and similarity of brand preference to that of the leader declined rapidly. In the four highest ranked groups, the leaders and members not only preferred the same best liked brand, but preferred them an exceptionally high percentage of the time compared to the rest of the groups. In only two of the six remaining groups did the leaders and other members prefer the same brand, and then only at percentage levels expected by chance.

To further substantiate the hypothesis that group leaders are a key element in understanding how groups influence the behavior of members, the data were analyzed in order to compare the leader's degree of brand loyalty[4] and the percentage of brand loyalty among the other members of the group. Table 7 summarizes the results of this analysis.

TABLE 7
COMPARISON OF THE DEGREE OF BRAND LOYALTY OF
THE GROUP LEADER WITH THE PERCENTAGE OF
BRAND LOYALTY IN THE GROUP

Group Leader's Degree of Brand Loyalty (Length of Longest Consecutive Run of One Brand)	Percent of Group (Excluding Leader) Becoming Brand Loyal (3 Consecutive Choices of One Brand)	Number in Group (n)
16	100%	2
15	100	5
12	75	5
9	100	3
6	100	3
5	100	5
3	50	5
3	25	5
2	45	5
2	55	4
		42

Once the leader's brand loyalty reached a certain degree of strength (5 consecutive times), then the probability was much greater that most of his group would also become brand loyal. Further increases, however, in the leader's degree of brand loyalty had no measurable effect, since 100 percent brand loyalty was the highest that could be obtained.

[4]While brand loyalty has been operationally defined as three consecutive choices of the same brand, it is logically assumed in this discussion that a person who selected the same brand 16 times in a row has a much higher degree of brand loyalty than an individual who selects the same brand three consecutive times.

SUMMARY AND CONCLUSIONS

The study led to the following tentative conclusions:

First, an analysis of variance test indicated that the informal groups had a definite influence on their members toward conformity behavior with respect to brands of bread preferred. At the same time, there was no significant preference shown for any one of the four brands used in the study. Interaction between the groups and brands was found not to be significant.

Second, it was hypothesized that the cohesiveness of a group would be an important determinant of the degree of brand loyalty exhibited by members. No statistical significance, however, was found between the level of cohesiveness and the degree of member brand loyalty. Only when cohesiveness and leadership were combined was any relationship with member brand loyalty uncovered. In more cohesive groups, the probability was much higher that the members would prefer the same brand as the group leader. Thus, cohesiveness appeared to have its most important function in providing an agreeable environment in which informal leaders could effectively operate.

Finally, leaders were found to influence fellow group members in two ways. First, the higher the degree of brand loyalty exhibited by a group leader, the more likely were the other members to prefer the same brand. Second, the greater the degree of leader brand loyalty, the higher was the percentage of his group also becoming brand loyal. In other words, the extent and degree of brand loyalty within a group was closely related to the behavior of the informal leader.

Like most exploratory studies of this nature, this experiment had certain inherent limitations—the groups obtained may not have been the ones most relevant to the purchase of bread, the number of groups studied was small, and only one product was used. Similarly, the product itself (bread) was a limiting factor. Susceptibility to group influence probably varies across products with the more conspicuous or socially important products being more susceptible. Also, the influence of the leaders on member brand preferences might be much less in the "real world" where differences do exist among products. If these statements are true, then the product used in this study may have been one which maximized the difficulty of locating and measuring the interpersonal influences of group members. Since in this experiment, the influence of groups (and leaders) was substantiated on such a common and minor purchase as bread, then there is good reason for presuming similar influence on a broad spectrum of consumer behavior. One of its primary values of this type of interdisciplinary study lies in the fact that the results usually lead to interesting and provocative implications, as well as providing new avenues and directions for research. By altering the selection process of the informal groups, and by testing products other than bread, a more thorough understanding of social influence on consumer behavior should be possible.

REFERENCES

1. W. C. Bonney and C. E. George, *Measurement of Affective Adaptation Residuals,* Technical Report 5 (Office of Naval Research, Agricultural and Mechanical College of Texas), 1961.
2. George Brown, "Brand Loyalty—Fact or Fiction?" *Advertising Age,* Vol. 23 (June 9, 1952), pp. 53–55.
3. Ross Cunningham, "Brand Loyalty—What, Where, How Much?" *Harvard Business Review,* Vol. 34 (January–February, 1956), pp. 116–28.
4. Ronald E. Frank, "Brand Choice as a Probability Process," *Journal of Business,* Vol. 35 (January, 1962), pp. 43–56.
5. Frank Harvey and Benjamin Lipstein, "The Dynamics of Brand Loyalty: A Markovian Process," *Operations Research,* Vol. 10 (January–February, 1962), pp. 19–40.
6. George Homans. *Social Behavior: Its Elementary Forms,* pp. 118–19. New York: Harcourt, Brace and World, Inc., 1961.
7. Elihu Katz and P. F. Lazarsfeld. *Personal Influence.* Glencoe, Ill.: The Free Press of Glencoe, 1955.
8. A. A. Kuehn, "Consumer Brand Choice—A Learning Process?" in *Quantitative Techniques in Marketing Analysis,* R. E. Frank, A. A. Kuehn, and W. F. Massy, eds., pp. 390–403. Homewood, Ill.: Richard D. Irwin, Inc., 1962.
9. S. J. Shaw, "Behavioral Science Offers Fresh Insights on New Product Acceptance," *Journal of Marketing,* Vol. 29 (January, 1965), p. 9.
10. W. T. Tucker, "The Development of Brand Loyalty," *Journal of Marketing Research,* Vol. 1 (August, 1964), pp. 32–35.

12. FASHION ADOPTION: A REBUTTAL TO THE "TRICKLE DOWN" THEORY*

Charles W. King

The oscillations and vagaries of fashions in women's apparel have been the topic of social critics for centuries. A sizable body of literature has developed in fashion based on over three hundred years of conceptual commentary and anecdotal evidence. Collectively, these contributions have become the core of modern day "fashion theory."

What is known as fashion theory, however, is more an amorphous network of concepts than an integrated paradigm predictive of modern fashion behavior. *The loose conceptual framework is organized around*

*From *Toward Scientific Marketing,* American Marketing Association, December, 1963, pp. 108–25.

a basic model of the fashion adoption process—the "trickle down" theory of fashion adoption. The theory unfortunately lacks contemporary validation in empirical research. Virtually none of the proponents of the "trickle down" process has tested the details of the model. Historically, specific anecdotal evidence supporting the traditional notion has been limited. Even in the era of the consumer survey, published studies of fashion behavior are scarce.

In this project, fashion adoption has been attacked as a specific type of innovative behavior within the broader contexts of social change and product innovation. Contemporary innovation research and methodology have been applied in the fashion adoption context. Specifically, the project has involved an exploratory consumer survey of the consumer change agents—the innovator (the early season buyer) and the influential (the opinion leader) in the fashion adoption process within the product category of women's millinery. The central theme of the research is that the traditional fashion adoption process model—the "trickle down" theory—does not reflect contemporary fashion behavior.

THE "TRICKLE DOWN" THEORY

What is the "trickle down" theory? The flavor of the theory can be most fully appreciated by quoting directly from its supporters. Though the theory has been implied by many early economists such as Rae,[1] Foley,[2] and Veblen,[3] one of the first detailed presentations was made by Simmel,[4] a sociologist:

"Social forms, apparel, aesthetic judgment, the whole style of human expression are constantly transformed by fashion, in such a way, however, that fashion—in all these things affects only the upper classes. Just as soon as the lower classes begin to copy their style, thereby crossing the line of demarcation the upper classes have drawn and destroying the uniformity of their coherence, the upper classes turn away from this style and adopt a new one, which in its turn differentiates them from the masses; and thus the game goes merrily on. Naturally, the lower classes look and strive toward the upper, and they encounter least resistance in those fields which are subject to the whims of fashion; for it is here that mere external imitation is most readily applied. The same process is at work as between the different sets within the upper classes, although it is not always as visible here . . ."

Barber in more recent research on social stratification has emphasized

[1]John Rae, *The Sociological Theory of Capital* (London: Macmillan & Co., 1834), chap. 13, and appendix i.
[2]Caroline R. Foley, "Fashion," *Economic Journal*, Vol. 3 (1893), p. 458.
[3]Thorstein Veblen, *The Theory of the Leisure Class* (New York: Macmillan Co., 1912).
[4]Georg Simmel, "Fashion," *American Journal of Sociology*, Vol. 62 (May, 1957), pp. 541–58. (Reprinted from the International Quarterly, Vol. X [October, 1904], pp. 130–55).

the "trickle down" process in women's clothes,[5] and Robinson argues essentially the same vertical flow notion, modifying it slightly to include horizontal movement within particular social strata:

". . . any given group (or cluster of groups forming a class) will tend to take its cues from those contiguous with it. Horizontally fashions will spread outward from central loci; and vertically—the more important consideration— any given group will tend to adopt as its mentor not the highest distinguishable group, but, rather, those immediately above it. In consequence of the vertical continuity of class groupings, new fashions tend to filter down by stages through the levels of affluence. The process of discarding any fashion will be a mere reflex of its proliferation. For an object of fashion to lose its meaning for the topmost class, it is only necessary for it to be taken up by the secondmost and so on down the line."[6]

In essence, then, *the vertical flow hypothesis simply states that the upper socio-economic classes adopt fashions first in the time dimension as symbols of distinction and exclusiveness.* In the course of inter-intra class competition, the lower classes, each and in turn, emulate and follow the upper class leaders. At a certain level of adoption by the lower levels the syndrome of styles becomes vulgarized and is discarded by the upper class in favor of a new set of fashion symbols. The "trickle" is again activated and the process repeats itself.

For the sophisticated marketer and social scientist, this discussion of the vertical flow hypothesis may have added little in terms of substantive knowledge. The purpose of the detailed quotations from these theorists has been to highlight the similarity of the fashion adoption process model among different writers over time (Simmel wrote in 1904, Robinson in 1961). Despite a changing social and business environment, the conceptualizations have remained essentially static in theme and detail for at least sixty years.

A REBUTTAL TO "TRICKLE DOWN"

The basic question is, *does the "trickle down" theory accurately describe the contemporary fashion adoption process?* The traditional notion is vulnerable. The historical evidence quoted by the early theorists strongly indicates the vertical flow process may have been functional in earlier periods in different types of class structures. The modern social environment, mass communications, and the fashion industry's manufacturing and merchandising strategies, however, almost impede any systematic vertical flow process.

---

[5]Bernard Barber, *Social Stratification* (New York: Harcourt, Brace & Co., 1957), p. 150.

[6]Dwight E. Robinson, "The Economics of Fashion Demand," *The Quarterly Journal of Economics,* Vol. 75, No. 3 (1961), p. 376.

CHANGING SOCIAL ENVIRONMENT

During the past 30 years in the United States, social and economic "leveling influences" have changed the entire profile of the consumer market. The once obviously structured class system has changed; class lines are clearly drawn only at extreme points on the social class continuum. As a result of the leveling influences, a much broader slice of the population can afford to be in fashion. The traditional value of material and craftsmanship in labeling social position still exists. But quality apparel is now within the reach of more people. The population's affluence reverberates through other facets of the theory also.

IMPACT OF MASS MEDIA

Mass communication media rapidly accelerate the spread of fashion awareness and influence mass market endorsement. The traditional upper class fashion leader directing the lower levels is largely short-circuited in the communication process. Within hours after the exclusive Paris and American designers' showings, the season's styles have been passed to the mass audiences via newspaper and television. The mass media "fashion seminars" also reflect the short-cutting of upper class influence in a direct sense. The woman's fashion page universally geared to "middle majority," the "woman's problems" columns, the fashion journals, and the broadcast media's fashion programs provide detailed "what to wear" and "how to wear it" instruction aimed directly at the mass market buyer. The traditional process of vertical personal transmission is again challenged.

FASHION INDUSTRY MANUFACTURING AND MERCHANDISING

Fashion industry manufacturing and merchandising methods actually impede any vertical flow process of fashion adoption.

Adoption and the fashion season. Fashion adoption is a process of social contagion by which a new style or product is adopted by the consumer after commercial introduction by the designer or manufacturer. Though gradual long term secular trends in apparel fashions have been documented,[7] the actual consumer adoption decision is made within the time dimension of a season. Though historically, the fashion seasons have roughly paralleled climatic seasons, in recent years fashion merchandisers have tended to accelerate the transitions from season to season. In women's apparel, the season is typically three to six months in length.

---

[7]For example, see A. L. Kroeber, "Order in Changes in Fashion" (1919), *The Nature of Culture* (Chicago: University of Chicago Press, 1952), pp. 332–37; Jane Richardson and A. L. Kroeber, "Three Centuries of Women's Dress Fashions: A Quantitative Analysis," *Anthropological Records,* October, 1940, pp. 111–53; Agnes Brooks Young, *Recurring Cycles of Fashion, 1760–1937* (New York: Harper and Bros., 1937).

As a merchandising strategy, designers and manufacturers strive to differentiate products between comparable seasons over time. Though classic styles and silhouettes may carry over, new styles are introduced and colors and fabrics changed. Therefore, the adoption of a new fashion entails a shift within the population from the styles appropriate at a given time the previous year to the new style offerings. Individuals make the adoption decisions at different speeds and at different times. The aggregate fashion cycle for a style is an expression of this continuum of adoption.

The effect of adoption within the season. The net impact of operating within the time dimension of a season is to compress the adoption process into a blur. The rapidity of adoption dictated by the fashion season directly challenges the operationality of the "trickle down" process.

The lag time for vertical flow of fashion adoption at the consumer level is almost non-existent. From creation to mass market introduction, there may be virtually no opportunity for vertical flow. Paris fashions pose a good example. Many of the Paris designers are concentrating almost exclusively on "originals" for the mass fashion industry. In 1957, an estimated 30 percent of Paris *haute couture* volume was accounted for by manufacturers and retail syndicate and store buyers.[8] In these cases, there is little upper class style endorsement supporting mass market adoption. In 1960, for further support, the August showings in Paris that were purchased or leased by American concerns were flown to the United States on the same plane on August 23. On September 5, New York fashion houses introduced the fall collection of copied Paris originals to the fashion press. Following five days of manufacturing and merchandise preparation, Macy's, Gimbels, and other leading New York department stores introduced the "popular priced" fall fashions to the consumers.[9] Again, where was the vertical flow process and upper class initiation and lower class emulation?

Product design and consumer choice. In the area of product design, the consumer moves from one extreme of virtually no choice in fashion selection to the other extreme of wide freedom of choice. The fashion industry defines basic colors, fabrics, and silhouettes for all price lines for a given season months before the season actually gets under way at the retail level. Once the basic dimensions of a season's fashions are set, a multiplicity of contemporary and classic styles are introduced. These decisions are certainly the result of a vast distillation of fashion design experience, success, and failure. These product decisions are rarely the result of empirical research beyond review of last season's trends.

---

[8]"Yield from High Fashion Is Low: Paris Haute," *Business Week*, February 16, 1957, pp. 68–70.

[9]"Bringing Paris Fashions Down to the Mass Market," *Business Week*, August 20, 1960, pp. 72–77.

Theoretically, the consumer can select from a wide range of current and classic designs and still be entirely "in fashion" regardless of the particular selection she makes. The consumer has comparative freedom across styles to satisfy personal tastes and physical features with little social penalty.

Product differentiation. Product differences between price lines are almost exclusively quality based rather than design based. The same basic silhouettes, materials and imitations, and colors are featured in each broad price range. The higher priced lines tend to be merely of higher quality in material and craftsmanship. Styling may be more versatile and creative in the higher priced lines because of the wider profit margins. The obvious differences, however, are difficult to recognize once the economy lines are excluded.

Fashion retailing—simultaneous introduction across price levels. The time factor in retail merchandising impedes much vertical flow except on a very rapid basis. In fact, modern retailing almost guarantees simultaneous adoption of the same basic styles across status levels. The volume fashion manufacturing and retailing industry operates essentially in the same way and on the same basic seasonal schedules in the higher priced and in the lower priced categories. The season's styles at each price level tend to be introduced at approximately the same time. In millinery, departments introduce new season items at essentially the same time in the seasons. Stores at all price levels tend to follow basically the same fashion calendar in fashion promotion.

WHY CONTINUED SUPPORT OF THE THEORY?

Given these contradictions of the vertical flow process, how does the notion marshal support from sophisticated fashion theorists?

Vertical flow within the fashion industry. The confusion is, in part, a product of using the fashion industry as a source of information.[10] Defining the broad fashion innovation process as the entire range of activities from conceptualization of a new style through detailed design to market introduction, a vertical flow definitely operates *within* the industry. The character of that process is entirely different from the consumer reaction outlined by Simmel and others.

The three elements of the innovation process—manufacturers, trade channel buyers, and consumers—represent a great filtering system. The three elements or sub-systems operate as interdependent yet independent evaluation and adoption centers. The manufacturers select a finite number of styles to feature from an almost infinite array of possibilities. The trade channel buyers then select a sampling of styles for ultimate sales from the universe of lines offered by all manufacturers. The con-

---

[10]Robinson, for example, relied heavily on fashion industry interviews. No formal consumer research was reported.

sumers then adopt a sampling of these selections and endorse them as accepted fashions.

Within the industry subsets, a vertical flow exists also. The exclusive and famous designers are watched closely and emulated by lesser designers. Major manufacturers are studied and copied by smaller and less expert competitors. Design piracy is a well established competitive strategy.

Little factual consumer information. In describing the consumer fashion adoption process, industry spokesmen are surprisingly uninformed.[11] An enigmatic "fashionable woman" guides many fashion managers. Others refer to the all pervasive importance of celebrity endorsement in influencing fashion trends. Some recognize the mass market influence but understand little of its complexity.

Some "trickle" may exist. In modest defense of the vertical flow supporters, it must be granted that some upper class influence undoubtedly exists. The question really is: *does it dictate market behavior as predicted by the theory?* In one segment of the market, a narrowly defined vertical flow can be recognized. The small, chic, and very wealthy upper class indirectly influences styles through the private designer. The social elite nurture the private designers through their patronage. More importantly, the private designers test new styles with this group and adapt successful trends for mass market showings. The garment manufacturers' and retail buyers' offerings, then, are partially distillations of upper class taste. Therefore, an indirect and hazy "vertical flow" process might be considered at work.

This type of function, however, falls short of the all pervasive social status emulation outlined by Simmel, Barber, Robinson, and others. To use this evidence in defense of the traditional vertical flow theory may be theoretically appropriate but pragmatically irrelevant.

If this limited interpretation of the "trickle down" process is to be applied then there is no current fashion adoption theory. The great adoption function occurs within the mass period. This limited interpretation gives no explanation of mass market adoption. What goes on there? This is the crucial question of fashion management and social scientists.

RESEARCH DESIGN

The research described here has involved an exploratory consumer survey of the key figures in fashion adoption, the innovator (the early buyer) and the influential (the opinion leader). The context has been confined to the product category of women's millinery and the geographical area of Metropolitan Boston. The field research was conducted

---

[11]Based on approximately 30 interviews with major millinery manufacturers, retail syndicate and retail buyers, and leading fashion journalists and researchers.

immediately following the close of the fall (1962) millinery season.

The millinery buying context has proven particularly suitable to fashion adoption research. Millinery is recognized as a highly fashion oriented item of women's apparel. Fashion change occurs semi-annually and is an accepted social phenomenon. Involvement in millinery adoption is high and almost all women can discuss the adoption process with some expertise.

The cornerstone of the project involved inclusion of the time of adoption as the critical variable in the research design. Respondents were qualified on a continuum of adoption based on their fall buying behavior. The objective was to segment the adoption continuum into independent parts as accurately as possible within the financial constraints. Time of adoption was defined as the month of first purchase of a hat during the fall season. The adoption decision was not defined as adoption of any specific style but merely purchase in time since the consumer can "adopt" from a wide range of styles *within the season's merchandise* and be "in style" regardless of the specific selection. The "early" and "late" buyers were operationally defined:

1. "early" buyers—late August or September purchasers representing the first 35% of the fall season's buyers.
2. "late" buyers—October through mid-January purchasers representing the latter 65% of the season's buyers.

The field research involved two phases: a brief telephone interview, and a one hour personal interview with selected respondents.

Based on the Metropolitan Boston Telephone Directory, a random cluster sampling procedure was used to select 1,934 adult women, who were classified into the adopter categories. Of these, 303 respondents in the early and late buyer categories were selected and personally interviewed to probe their general fashion and hat adoption processes in detail, including coverage of an extensive array of demographic, psychological, social, and mass communication, and personal influence variables.

REJECTIONS OF THE "TRICKLE DOWN" THEORY

The empirical data support rejection of the "trickle down" theory of fashion adoption in this product context. Two broad questions central to the theory have been analyzed:

1. Are the early buyers, in fact, the high status "elite esotery" depicted by the vertical flow notion?
2. Are early buyers more influential than late buyers in dictating fashion adoption?

The traditional theory implies a form of personal influence in which the high status, early buyers directly influence the lower status, later adopters in the personal network of information transmission.

SOCIOECONOMIC STATUS OF THE ADOPTER CATEGORIES

The socioeconomic status of the respondents was measured on three levels: total annual family income, husband's occupational status, and self designated or perceived social class position. The three measures are obviously highly intercorrelated but each taps a somewhat different dimension of social status. The three measures produced essentially identical results.

The basic conclusion to be drawn from the analysis of social status was that early buyers were consistently higher status than late buyers *but* the early buyers were not "upper class." Specifically:

In terms of annual family income, 59% of the early buyers had income under $9,000 per year; 19% had income of less than $6,000.

In terms of husband's occupational status, 62% of the early buyers were "middle class" or lower; 33% were "lower middle class" or lower.

In terms of respondent's perceived class position, despite the expected clustering of reports in the "middle class," 16% of the early buyers located themselves in "lower middle" or "lower class" social positions.

Is this group of early buyers the "elite esotery" the traditional theorists have labeled as the fashion innovators initiating the "trickle down" process?

PERSONAL INFLUENCE AND THE ADOPTER CATEGORIES

Even if the early buyers were assumed to meet the status requirements for the "elite esotery," the second question of personal influence in fashion adoption must be answered. Admittedly, the early buyer does levy some visual influence through displaying the season's fashions early in the season. In turn, because of the reliance of retailers on early season sales as a guide to later season inventory purchases, the early buyer exercises influence over retail inventories. The issue here, however, centers on the early buyer's role as a personal influential in the interpersonal network of information transmission.

As a first step in the analysis, "influentials" were identified in two contexts: general fashion and hat buying. In the general fashion context an influential was anyone who had "been asked her advice" or "offered any suggestions" on fashions recently or felt she was "more likely" to be asked than any of her friends. The hat influentials were those respondents who felt they were "more likely" to be asked their advice about hats than their friends. This approach to identifying influential opinion leaders has frequently been used in other contexts.[12]

Reliance on personal interactions in information receiving and trans-

---

[12]See Elihu Katz and Paul F. Lazarsfeld, *Personal Influence* (Glencoe, Ill., The Free Press, 1955); and Everett M. Rogers and David G. Cartano, "Methods of Measuring Opinion Leadership," *Public Opinion Quarterly*, Vol. 26, No. 3 (Fall, 1962), p. 435.

mitting is high, particularly in the general fashion context. Approximately 73% and 25% of the respondents relied on personal interactions in the general fashion and hat buying contexts respectively. The lower incidence of interaction in hat buying is largely a result of narrowing the reporting context from broad fashion to the specific product category of women's millinery.

Given the role of personal influence and the identification of influentials, three dimensions were explored in measuring the dynamics of influence exercised by early versus late buyers:

1. The frequency of interaction by the influentials within adopter groups.
2. The number of influentials within the adopter group.
3. The status compatibility between the receiver and the influential in the reported interactions.

Frequency of interactions. There were no significant patterned differences in the frequency of reported interactions by influentials in the early versus late adopter groups as indicated in Table 1. It should be noted that only the interactions from the general fashion context are reported in Tables 1 and 4. Too few interactions were fully reported in the hat context to justify detailed presentation. The general pattern reflected by the data in the two contexts, however, were essentially identical.

TABLE 1
COMPARISON OF EARLY VS. LATE BUYERS BY
INFLUENCE INTERACTION FREQUENCY
GENERAL FASHION CONTEXT

	Early Buyer	Late Buyer
Number of interactions per influential	1.06*	1.10
Base number of influentials	66	86

*I.e., Early buyer influentials reported 1.06 interactions per influential.

The influentials within the adopter groups. Recognizing the importance of the level of influence, the analysis has concentrated on the influentials within the adopter groups. Though the early buyers have been found to be well distributed across the class structure rather than "upper class," supporters of the "trickle down" theory could argue that the influence in the early buyer group was concentrated in the upper income sector. If this were the case, greater credence might be given the "trickle down" concept.

To attack this hypothesis, the adopter groups were divided into high, medium, and low income subsets. To eliminate the impact of the slightly larger number of higher income respondents in the early group, the percentage of respondents qualifying as influentials *within each income subset* was calculated. As presented in Table 2, in both the general fashion and hat buying contexts, influence was not concentrated in the early buyer, high income subset.

TABLE 2

COMPARISON OF EARLY VS. LATE BUYERS BY
INCIDENCE OF INFLUENCE WITHIN INCOME SUBSETS
GENERAL FASHION AND HAT BUYING CONTEXTS

Family Income	General Fashion Context		Hat Buying Context	
	Early Buyer	*Late Buyer*	*Early Buyer*	*Late Buyer*
Under $6,000	50%*	41%	4%	13%†
$6,000 to $8,999	50%	51%	17%	10%
$9,000 or more	51%	62%	10%	21%

Note: Percentages do not add to 100%.
 *I.e., 50% of the early buyers reporting "under $6,000" income qualified as influentials in the general fashion context.
 †I.e., 13% of the late buyers reporting "under $6,000" income qualified as influentials in the hat buying contest.

In the general fashion context, the early buyers within each income subset had essentially identical probabilities of being influentials. In the hat buying context the early buyer, middle income respondents had a somewhat higher probability of qualifying as influentials. Nor were the early buyer, high income respondents more influential than their late buyer, high income counterparts. In fact the late buyer, high income subset had more per capita influence in both contexts than any other subset—further refutation of the "trickle down" theory.

A logical question would be: *are early buyers in total more influential than late buyers?* The basic data presented in Table 3 indicate that in both the general fashion and hat buying contexts, the percentage of respondents qualifying as influentials *within* the early buyer and late buyer groups was essentially identical. Though the general incidence of influence was lower in the hat context, the relationship of the adopter categories remained the same. Clearly in contradiction to the traditional theory, the early buyers were no more likely to be influentials than late buyers.

A critical blow to the traditional "trickle down" notion is provided when the early and late buyer groups are weighted according to their relative importance in the fall hat buying market. By definition, the early buyer group (August and September buyers) represented 35% of the total buyers, and the late buyers represented 65% of the market. Therefore, since the two adopter groups had essentially identical levels of influence *within* the categories, weighting for market importance indi-

TABLE 3
COMPARISON OF EARLY VS. LATE BUYERS BY
INCIDENCE OF INFLUENCE
GENERAL FASHION AND HAT BUYING CONTEXTS

Respondents Qualified as:	General Fashion Context		Hat Buying Context	
	Early Buyer	Late Buyer	Early Buyer	Late Buyer
Receiver	23%	23%	14%	16%
Influential	49*	51	11†	14
Uninvolved	28	26	75	70
Total	100%	100%	100%	100%
Base	135	168	135	168

*I.e., 49% of the early buyer group qualified as influentials in the general fashion context.

†I.e., 11% of the early buyer group qualified as influentials in the hat buying context.

cated there were *86 percent more late buyer influentials compared with early buyer influentials* in the total fall season hat buying population. *In direct contradiction to the "trickle down" theory, the total impact of influence by late buyers was markedly greater than that of early buyers.*

Status compatibility in reported interactions. The third question to be answered centers around the interpersonal interaction itself. Who talks to whom? The traditional notion would predict that influentials influence those lower in social status and receivers receive from those higher in social status than themselves. In the personal interview, each time an interaction was reported, a series of questions was asked concerning the referent with whom the respondent had talked. The referent's husband's occupation was defined and compared with the respondent's husband's occupation as the basis for the status compatibility measure.

Analysis of non-family interactions is presented in Table 4. Though some "trickle" might be read into the data, the basic conclusion is that the vast majority of receiving and influencing interactions by both early and late buyer were *between individuals of the same social status.* Personal transmission of fashion information moves primarily horizontally rather than vertically in the class hierarchy.

A NEW APPROACH TO FASHION ADOPTION

The critique and rejection of the "trickle down" theory have set the scene for a counter theory—*a "mass market" or "trickle across" scheme of fashion adoption.* The purpose of this discussion is not to present a highly structured or detailed paradigm in the tradition of the deductive method. Rather, the objective is to draw the data presented earlier into a broad conceptual scheme descriptive of modern adoption behavior.

TABLE 4
COMPARISON OF EARLY AND LATE BUYERS'
NON-FAMILY INTERACTIONS BY
SOCIAL STATUS COMPATIBILITY
GENERAL FASHION CONTEXT

Referent Compared to Respondent	Receiving Interactions*		Influencing Interactions*	
	Early Buyer	Late Buyer	Early Buyer	Late Buyer
Referent of higher social status	16%†	11%	13%‡	—
Referent of same social status	80	82	74	86%
Referent of lower social status	4	7	13	14
Total	100%	100%	100%	100%
Base number of interactions	25	27	23	35

*"Receiving" interactions were those where the respondent primarily received information; in "influencing" interactions the respondent *gave* advice.
†I.e., in 16% of the "receiving" interactions, the referent had a higher social status than the respondent in the early buyer group.
‡I.e., in 13% of the "influencing" interactions, the referent had a higher social status than the respondent in the early buyer group.

The scheme represents only a loose framework of notions but is a first step toward a more definitive model of the adoption process.

In essence, the "mass market" or "trickle across" theory of fashion adoption centers around four broad arguments:

1. Within the fashion season, the social culture and the fashion industry's manufacturing and merchandising strategies almost guarantee adoption by consumers across socioeconomic groups simultaneously in the time dimension.
2. Consumers theoretically have the freedom to select from a wide range of contemporary and classic styles in the season's inventory to satisfy the dictates of their physical features and personal tastes.
3. The innovators and influentials play key roles in directing fashion adoption and represent discrete market segments within social strata.
4. The transmission of information and personal influence "trickles across" or flows primarily horizontally within social strata rather than vertically across strata.

The basic contribution of this scheme is to refocus on the horizontal versus the vertical flow and on the major consumer change agents—the innovator and the influential—in the adoption process. Though some vertical flow undoubtedly exists, it does not represent the dominant movement in adoption. Given simultaneous adoption across socioeconomic strata and freedom of choice among consumers, the innovators and the influentials tend to direct fashion adoption within social strata.

In general, the functions of the innovator and the influential appear to differ. The innovator is the earliest visual communicator of the season's styles for the mass of fashion consumers. The influential appears to define and endorse appropriate standards. Both the innovator and the influential are performing advisory functions but the nature of the advice and the respective power are different. For example, in a particular social network, the influential may define the dress appropriate for the bridge party, cocktail party, etc. The innovator, in turn, may present the current offerings consistent with these broad standards. The separate roles of the innovator and the influential are graphically supported by the concentration of the influentials in the late buyer sector of the total fall millinery market.

Within this framework, the horizontal flow concept is fundamental. When the new fashions are introduced, the innovators and influentials play out their roles within social strata. Given initial introduction across social strata, adoption processes are operative simultaneously within different strata. An abundance of anecdotal evidence exists illustrating products and fashions that have received wide acceptance within some social strata, but have not been successful at other levels.

The new conceptual approach has important implications for fashion management. Though the fashion industry typically segments the market on price dimensions, merchandisers deal in aggregate terms within specific price ranges. To be sure, fashion merchandisers often "sense" style and color trends with uncanny accuracy and intuitively segment markets in this manner. More precise segmentation, however, is rare.

The "mass market" model suggests a form of "functional" segmentation. The innovators and the influentials are identified as discrete market segments within social strata. These groups represent prime sales targets themselves. More importantly, however, they represent the key links to the volume fashion market. Obviously, the fashion manufacturer and merchandiser should cultivate these market segments and utilize them in expediting the fashion flow.

SUMMARY

The central theme of this research has been that the traditional fashion adoption process model—the "trickle down" theory—does not reflect contemporary fashion behavior. Based on a consumer survey of adoption in women's millinery, the empirical data indicated that the innovators or early buyers in the fashion season were not an "elite esotery" of upper class consumers. Nor were the early buyers the dominant personal influentials in the adoption process. In contrast, the fashion influentials were concentrated in the late buyer group. Based on the anecdotal and empirical evidence, the "mass market" or "trickle across" scheme has been presented. The major contribution of this approach is the emphasis on the horizontal flow of adoption within strata and the roles of the innovators and the influentials in the process.

While the scheme is based on research in the product category of millinery, the conclusions have relevance for the entire area of fashion adoption. The specific identity and profile of the innovators and the influentials may vary with fashion products. The *adoption process* outlined in this paper, however, seems applicable across fashion products. Utilization of the scheme by fashion merchandisers is contingent upon identification of the innovator and influential market segments within specific contexts. The scheme does represent a general analytical approach to the mysteries of fashion adoption more descriptive of modern adoption behavior than the traditional "trickle down" theory.

Suggested additional AMA readings

Carman, James M. "The Fate of Fashion Cycles in Our Modern Society," in *Science, Technology, and Marketing* (ed. Raymond M. Haas), pp. 722–37. Chicago: American Marketing Association, 1966.

Cunningham, Scott M. "Perceived Risk as a Factor in the Diffusion of New Product Information," in *Science, Technology, and Marketing* (ed. Raymond M. Haas), pp. 698–721. Chicago: American Marketing Association, 1966.

Engel, James F.; Knapp, David A.; and Knapp, Deanne E. "Sources of Influence in the Acceptance of New Products for Self-Medication: Preliminary Findings," in *Science, Technology, and Marketing* (ed. Raymond M. Haas), pp. 776–84. Chicago: American Marketing Association, 1966.

Feldman, Sidney P. "Some Dyadic Relationships Associated with Consumer Choice," in *Science, Technology, and Marketing* (ed. Raymond M. Haas), pp. 758–75. Chicago: American Marketing Association, 1966.

Haines, George H., Jr. "A Study of Why People Purchase New Products," in *Science, Technology, and Marketing* (ed. Raymond M. Haas), pp. 685–97. Chicago: American Marketing Association, 1966.

Kelly, Robert F. "The Diffusion Model as a Predictor of Ultimate Patronage Levels in New Retail Outlets," in *Science, Technology, and Marketing* (ed. Raymond M. Haas), pp. 738–49. Chicago: American Marketing Association, 1966.

King, Charles W. "Adoption and Diffusion Research in Marketing: An Overview," in *Science, Technology, and Marketing* (ed. Raymond M. Haas), pp. 665–84. Chicago: American Marketing Association, 1966.

Levy, Sidney J. "Symbolism and Life Style," *Proceedings of the Winter Conference of the American Marketing Association* (ed. Stephen A. Greyser), pp. 140–50. Chicago: American Marketing Association, 1963.

Martineau, Pierre. "Social Classes and Spending Behavior," *Journal of Marketing*, Vol. 23 (1958), pp. 121–31.

Myers, John G. "Patterns of Interpersonal Influence in the Adoption of New Products," in *Science, Technology, and Marketing* (ed. Raymond M. Haas), pp. 750–57. Chicago: American Marketing Association, 1966.

FIGURE B
THE DECISION-MAKING PROCESS

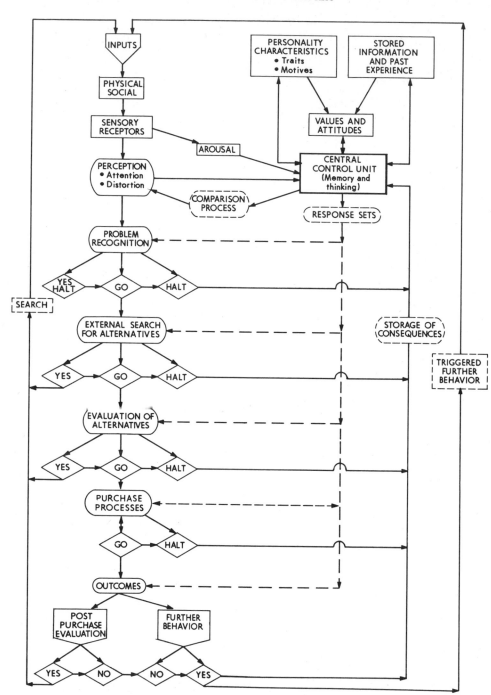

Part IV

CONSUMER DECISION MAKING

The readings in Part IV focus primarily on the last part of the model as is shown in Figure B on the facing page. The emphasis is on true problem-solving behavior—its stages, the search for information, purchasing behavior, and the consequences of decisions. At this point, however, there is a key gap in the literature because it is not possible to present a large quantity of knowledge on habitual decisions. Much on the subject has been published, but, unfortunately, the best contributions appear outside the literature published by the AMA. Nevertheless, the readings presented here push back the frontiers considerably, and serve as a good introduction to the subject.

A. Fundamental concepts and processes

Three important articles appear in this section. The first, by Bauer, has become a classic in the marketing literature. While he reports little in the way of rigorous research, Bauer suggests that perceived risk can underlie much of what the consumer says and does. Risk is defined primarily to include doubts about an intended action, and he has identified some strong consequences when perceived risk is high. High-risk consumers not only perceive differently from their counterparts, but it also appears that perceived risk functions as an important response set and thereby affects all stages of buying action. The reader will notice that risk is mentioned in many later readings as well, but Bauer deserves the credit for opening a meaningful area of inquiry.

Granbois represents a thorough review of the entire subject of household decision making, with special reference to the information that is required and used. He identifies the various stages and pulls together much of the related literature. Of special interest is his use of the concept of perceived risk as the stimulus for search behavior.

Cox builds on the background presented by Granbois and assesses analytically the sources of information used in search behavior. This also is a rigorous review of available literature, and Cox has synthesized the relevant findings in the area of personal influence (informal channels) and advertising and selling (market-dominated channels). The marketing implications emerge with exceptional clarity.

13. CONSUMER BEHAVIOR AS RISK TAKING*

Raymond A. Bauer

One of the fads in discussions of marketing research is to say that the field of marketing research has been marked by fads. Thus, we have become accustomed to the statement: "Last year it was Motivation Research; this year it's Operations Research; I wonder what it will be next year." Seldom is any such new emphasis a radical departure from the past. At least there is always a handful of protesting orthodox practitioners to exclaim: "—but we've been doing it all along." Operations Research, properly speaking, probably should be considered as concerned with simulation as much as with experimentation. But most of the operations research work I have seen in market research uses experimentation rather than simulation, and in this is continuous with traditional, albeit rare, well-executed experiments in marketing research. These new approaches are characterized by a distinctive concentration of attention on particular variables, concepts or techniques. After their potential has been pretty well explored and developed they get absorbed into the general body of research knowledge and technique, usually after having generated a few healthy antibodies.

I make these general remarks about fads in marketing research because I am about to make a modest effort to start a new one. However, if I am to be as modest as my effort I should also state that I have neither confidence nor anxiety that my proposal will cause any major stir. At most, it is to be hoped that it will attract the attention of a few researchers and practitioners and at least survive through infancy. The proposal is that we look at consumer behavior as an instance of risk taking.

We are accustomed to use the term "consumer decision making." Yet, there has been little concentration of research on the element of risk taking that is as characteristic of consumer behavior as it is of all decision making. A conspicuous exception is the work of Katona and Mueller on prepurchase deliberation. They found, when buying durable goods, that middle-income people deliberated more than either lower- or upper-

*From *Dynamic Marketing for a Changing World,* American Marketing Association, June, 1960, pp. 389–98.

income people. When buying sport shirts, lower-income people deliberated most.

Consumer behavior involves risk in the sense that any action of a consumer will produce consequences which he cannot anticipate with anything approximating certainty, and some of which at least are likely to
be unpleasant. At the very least, any one purchase competes for the
consumer's financial resources with a vast array of alternate uses of that
money. The man who buys a pint of whiskey today does not know to
what degree he prejudices his son's college education 20 years hence.
But, he risks more than alternate purchases. Unfortunate consumer decisions have cost men frustration and blisters, their self-esteem and the
esteem of others, their wives, their jobs, and even their lives. Nor is the
problem of calculation of consequences a trivial one. It is inconceivable
that the consumer can consider more than a few of the possible consequences of his actions, and it is seldom that he can anticipate even these
few consequences with a high degree of certainty. When it comes to the
purchase of large ticket items the perception of risk can become trau-
matic. Paul Lazarsfeld tells me that certain unpublished data show that
the prospective automobile buyer often goes into a state of virtual panic
as he reaches the point of decision, and rushes into his purchase as an
escape from the enormity of the problem.

If I may now anticipate what is on your minds, I suspect that about
·at this point you are saying to yourselves that I have painted an un-
realistic picture of the consumer. He simply does not in most instances
stand about trying to calculate probabilities and consequences nor is he
overtaken by anxiety. True, these things happen on occasion, and particularly on big ticket items, but only in rare instances does the consumer
appear to tackle these problems as "risk taking."

If these objections are on your mind, I agree with them. The consumer
who consistently tried to act like the classical "rational man" would
quickly sink into inaction. This, in fact, is precisely what I would like
to stress. Consumer characteristically develop decision strategies and
ways of reducing risk that enable them to act with relative confidence
and ease in situations where their information is inadequate and the
consequences of their actions are in some meaningful sense incalculable.
(When I say "in some meaningful sense incalculable," I mean that not
only can the outcomes not be anticipated reliably, but the consequences
may be drastic.)

Up to now, what I have to say has been abstract and general. Therefore, for the next few minutes I would like to move back to familiar
ground and argue that many of the phenomena with which we habitually
deal have a strong bearing on the problem of "risk taking." I am not
going to contend that risk taking is the only thing involved in these
phenomena, but rather that it is a common thread which runs through
them and is worth pulling out for inspection.

One of our traditional problems is that of brand loyalty. Brand loyalty may involve a number of considerations. In recent years we have heard stressed the compatibility of the brand image with one's self-image, or with the norms of one's reference group. Brand loyalty is also seen as a means of economizing of decision effort by substituting habit for repeated, deliberate, decisions. Without for a moment minimizing such considerations, I would like to reintroduce the old-fashioned concept of "reliability." Much brand loyalty is a device for reducing the risks of consumer decisions. I am told that sugar is one product for which it has traditionally been difficult to develop brand loyalty. But my friend Edward Bursk tells me that when he was a salesman in Lancaster, Pennsylvania, there was a strong loyalty to a particular brand of sugar. The Pennsylvania Dutch housewives of that area are avid and proud bakers and there is more risk involved in making a cake than in sweetening a cup of coffee or a bowl of cereal. Suppose we were to limit ourselves to small ticket items, and to interview a sample of housewives as to the risks—that is a combination of uncertainty plus seriousness of outcome involved—associated with each category of product. I would predict a strong correlation between degree of risk and brand loyalty.

The recently popular phrase that advertising gives "added value" to a product also bears on the question of risk taking. The "added value" of advertising has usually been discussed in terms of the satisfaction of consumer motives that extend beyond the primary function of the product. It is perhaps worth recalling that one of the customer's motives is to have a feeling of confidence in the product he buys. Some, but not all, consumers are willing to pay added money for added confidence. Others prefer to read "Consumers Reports" in the hope that some obscure, unadvertised, low-priced brand will be rated a best buy. And, it is worth recalling, there are still other consumers in whom advertising does not generate confidence but rather the suspicion that it is added, worthless cost.

Now, relating the questions of brand loyalty and the "added value" of advertising to risk taking, or its reciprocal "confidence," is scarcely a radical departure from tradition. This must be the working assumption of every competent marketing practitioner. It is instructive, however, to note how little this relationship has been exploited as a research problem. We know that some people are inclined to favor advertised brands in some categories, and that other people will consistently buy the cheapest product in these same categories. This is about the level on which our knowledge rests. It is my suspicion that our recent concern with the prestige element of advertising and well known brands has deflected our attention from the problem of risk taking even when it was right under our nose.

Another recently popular area of concern where the problem of risk taking has been obscured is the phenomenon known as "personal influence." There are exceptions to what I am about to say, but *in general* discussions of personal influence on consumer behavior have been couched in terms that suggest only that opinion leaders are followed because they are style setters and that the follower wants to accrue to himself the prestige of behaving like the pace setters. Seldom is the fact made explicit that one of the very important functions of opinion leaders is to reduce the perceived risk of the behavior in question.

The work of Katz, Menzel, and Coleman on physicians' adoption of a new drug is very pertinent. They found that the doctors they studied tended to follow the lead of respected colleagues *early* in the life history of the drug when adequate information was lacking. Once the drug became sufficiently well established, personal influence no longer played a role. The period of risk was passed.

I have seen data on related products that reenforce the notion that the Katz, Menzel, Coleman findings are related to risk taking. We studied two types of products in the same general product category. We were interested in whether the probability of trial of a product and subsequent preference for that product was influenced by preference for one or another of the companies, or by preference for the salesmen of the various companies. For these particular types of products we confirmed the findings of the drug studies. Both company and salesmen preference were more strongly correlated with product trial and preference in the newer products in the general line. That is to say, apparently both company *and* salesmen preference had more influence when product was new and relatively unknown.

However, if I may be permitted some freedom of assumptions and inference, and a certain amount of liberty in filtering out the noise in the data, there were some findings that bore in a more interesting fashion on the problem of personal influence and risk taking. Let me start with some assumptions about the difference between company preference and salesman preference. Relative to each other, company preference is more associated with risk reduction, and salesman preference more with personal influence in the sense of "compliance," of one person "going along" with someone whom he likes. The company is a relatively impersonal entity, and the main function of its reputation is in this instance to guarantee the quality of the product. The salesman, to some extent, also guarantees quality. However, he also exploits his strictly personal relationships to the buyer. Thus we have personal influence operating in two ways, to produce compliance, and to reduce risk. Compliance is relatively more associated with salesman preference, and risk reduction with company preference.

If you accept the above assumptions as reasonable, then certain findings are quite interesting. You will remember that I said we studied two product types. These product types differed as to the degree of risk associated with them. Product type A was by common consent risky.

Product type B was safe. In the case of product type A, the risky type of product, the relationship of company preference to product preference was twice as strong as the "effect" (in quotes) of salesman preference. In the case of product type B, the "effect" of company and salesman preference was just about equal. My interpretation of these findings is that when risk was high, the risk relevant factor of company image was the dominant source of influence, and that when risk was low, "personal influence" in the sense of compliance played a relatively more prominent role.

In addition to "personal influence" we have recently been concerned with the effect of "group influence" on consumer behavior. We have heard a great deal in the past few years about the fact that consumers judge their behavior by the standards of groups with whom they identify themselves, or—although this is seldom dealt with—from whom they dissociate themselves. This has been treated predominantly like the classical "keeping up with the Joneses." The consumer looks to his reference groups for cues as to the type of consumption that is valued by people whose esteem he in turn values. "But, dahling, everybody, but everybody, knows Wente Brothers' chablis is the best California chablis!"

In his recent work, "Sociological Reflection on Business," Paul Lazarsfeld suggests that group influence will be stronger in those instances in which the wisdom of one's decision is difficult to assess. Interpreted in one way, this suggestion could lead us to the popular notion that when the primary functions of a product are hard to assess, or when all products in a category work equally well, then "secondary attributes" such as group approval come to the fore. Under this interpretation the influence of the group is to get the consumer to pay attention to different attributes of the product. It is equally plausible that in many instances the function of group influence is to reduce perceived risk by confirming the wisdom of the choice. That is to say, the individual may already share the values of his group and agree on the desirability of a given type of purchase but look to the group for guidance as to what is a wise purchase. By a "wise" purchase, I mean one that is likely to satisfy the values for which it is made. In other words, we not only look to our reference groups for standards of values, but on occasion we also use the judgment of the people around us as an informal "Consumer Report." This is what the psychological student of cognition would call "consensual validation." Lacking any sound basis of judgment, we accept the judgment of others.

A final traditional problem worth considering in terms of risk taking is impulse buying, or perhaps we might prefer the label of "prepurchase deliberation." A simple economic approach to impulse buying would suggest that it should increase as a function of the discretionary funds available to the consumer. This would be consistent with Katona and Mueller's finding that the amount of deliberation involved in buying sports shirts was inverse to the consumer's income. Yet, a number of studies show that in many instances the middle-class consumer is more given to deliberation than is the lower-class consumer. When we compare the middle- and lower-class consumers something more than economics simply considered seems to be involved. We speak of the tendency of the middle-class person to plan over a longer period and of various other aspects of middle-class and lower-class culture. Not for a moment would I want to underplay the importance of such cultural factors. However, it is worth while to think of the fact that the middle-class person has both a greater possibility of planning and a greater reason to plan. He has more of an investment in career, reputation, and accumulated property to risk if he gets into serious financial difficulty. The lower-class person has less to risk in terms of such long-run investments. Perhaps more pertinently it is more difficult for him to calculate the consequences of his actions because among other things he is likely to have less information. He is also less likely to have time for deliberation, because, as Katona and Mueller found with respect to durable goods, people of lower income are more likely to make a purchase in a situation where the product to be replaced has already broken down.

So that I may not seem to be arguing against a cultural interpretation, let me say simply that the lower-class consumer seems more prone to a decision strategy based on the assumption that the consequences of one's behavior are essentially incalculable in any event, so one may as well take a plunge and do what seems immediately desirable.

My argument to this point has been that the issue of risk taking is readily seen as an integral part of many familiar phenomena of consumer behavior. This is by no mean surprising, and is probably novel only in the degree that I have stressed the fact of risk taking. What will be of more interest will be to understand with more elaboration the devices through which consumers handle the problem of risk. In effect I have suggested mainly one device, namely reliance on some outside source for guidance, whether that outside source be the reputation of the manufacturer of product, an opinion leader or a reference group. This can scarcely exhaust the means that consumers employ to reduce perceived risk, nor does it tell us how the consumer decides where to place his confidence. The discussion of lower- v. middle-class deliberation in purchases of durable goods suggests an additional mechanism of reducing perceived risk, namely, to suppress the possible consequences from consciousness and rush through the process with rapidity. This is no more than a caricature of what we all do at times.

It should be noted that I have carefully said "perceived risk" whenever I referred to risk reduction. This is because the individual can respond to and deal with risk only as he perceives it subjectively. If risk exists in the "real world" and the individual does not perceive it, he cannot be influenced by it. On the other hand, he may reduce "perceived risk" by means which have no effect of affairs in the real world. Thus, if he reads advertisements favoring an automobile he has just bought, he may console himself on the wisdom of his action, but he does not reduce the objective probability of the muffler falling off.

Close study will probably reveal a wide range of decision rules which consumers invoke with regularity to reduce the perceived uncertainty involved in the outcome of their decisions. We are not totally oblivious to the existence of such rules. For example, there is a dying race of Americans who abide by the decision rule of not buying anything for which they cannot pay cash. A recent study shows that this is still a dominant decision rule for eating in restaurants. A majority of respondents thought it was improper to use credit cards for eating out, because "you should not eat out when you cannot afford it."[1] Other persons will buy products with plain and sensible design, fearing that surface aesthetics are designed to cover up bad workmanship and material. Some others will buy the most expensive product, and still others the cheapest product when both have equal amounts of money at their disposal. Such persons, for reasons about which we can only speculate, vary in the extent to which they are willing to pay money to minimize the risk of being disappointed in a product. There may be others who expect a certain rate of product failure as assurance that they are not wasting money on overly engineered and constructed products. It is doubtful that they will be joyful over the failure of any individual product, but they may persist in patronizing an outlet that features low prices and poor service. The shabbiness of the store and the rudeness of sales personnel may give further reassurance that one is not paying too much for what he buys.

A long list of such decision rules could probably be produced by the reader. However, I suspect that as ingenious as we all are, it is still worth turning to actual consumers to find out from them what their operating decision rules are. We may be in for some surprises. It is of course difficult for a consumer to articulate a notion such as a "decision rule." In an effort to get at such difficult-to-articulate notions, Donald Cox, one of our doctoral students, interviewed two consumers at very great length—an hour or two a week for several months—on their shopping habits. Many of the decision rules reported by these respondents were ones familiar to us. The following two, I suspect, are not entirely familiar. One of the respondents favored shopping in small shops because she saw the proprietor or buyer as having reduced her range of decision by having reduced the number of brands among which he had to choose, and also as having weeded out the least preferable lines. The same consumer would look about to see if a store carried advertised brands. She used this as a means of legitimizing *the store*. Once having satisfied herself on this score she was willing to buy off-brands from this same store. The

[1]Study by Benson and Benson reported in *Wall Street Journal*, May 12, 1960.

novelty of individual decision rules is not so important as the fact that the decision rules of each of these subjects appeared to form coherent but contrasting strategies for stabilizing the uncertain world of shopping. Both of these young women could be characterized as highly conscious of the risk involved in shopping. But one regularly relied on external sources of reassurance, while the other was extremely energetic in seeking out information and attempting to achieve the guise of rationality. We plan to continue such exploratory work with consumers. But in the meantime the problem of decision making has been tackled in other quarters.

There has been a good deal of research on decision making under conditions of uncertainty, but not much of this work can at this point be translated into terms useful for students of consumer behavior. The students of statistical decision theory have concentrated on how decisions *ought* to be made. That is to say that the decision theorists have been concerned with the calculation of an optimum decision within the framework of an explicitly defined limited set of conditions, rather than with how many people habitually *do* make decisions in the real world. Experimental psychological research on decision making, on the other hand, has studied how people *do* make restricted types of decisions in a laboratory situation. Such research shows minimally that problems of risk and uncertainty are handled variously by different people and under different conditions. Even though it is doubtful that any of these findings are directly applicable in the field of marketing, they have an important general implication for us by demonstrating that people do in fact evolve preferred decision rules even in situations much less complicated than that faced by the consumer on a day-to-day basis.

One body of work deserves our attention. Most of it is reported in Leon Festinger's book called *A Theory of Cognitive Dissonance*. Festinger and his associates have concentrated on the ways in which people reduce perceived risk *after* decisions are made. People will seek out information that confirms the wisdom of their decisions. Thus, people who have just bought an automobile tend preferentially to read ads in favor of the automobile they have bought. People will also perceive information in a way to reenforce their decision; smokers are less likely than nonsmokers to believe that cigarettes cause lung cancer, and this relationship holds even after these people who stopped smoking, because they believed in this relationship, were eliminated from the sample. People, finally, change their own attitudes to bolster their perception of the desirability of their actions. They have more favorable attitudes toward products after they have selected them than before they made the decision. Festinger has amassed considerable data to demonstrate that people do employ devices to reduce the perceived risk associated with consumer-type behavior.

Certain psychological research on problems of cognition also promises to be helpful. The book of Bruner, Goodnow, and Austin, *A Study of Thinking*, for example, deals with the way in which people develop decision strategies in handling situations of incomplete information.

The major reason for my remarks on the importance of the risk taking in consumer decision making is my conviction, frankly still in a somewhat less clear state than I would wish, that this is a fruitful area of research. It is my hope that others will suggest leads of which I am ignorant.

14. THE ROLE OF COMMUNICATION IN THE FAMILY DECISION-MAKING PROCESS*

Donald H. Granbois

The review on which this paper is based attempted to summarize and evaluate published research on family decision-making processes. Its broad aim was to assess the role of "outside" communications in family consumption decisions. The focus on consumer decision processes—how consumers first learn of alternatives, the sources and amounts of information they use in evaluating alternatives, etc.—was found particularly appropriate for appraising the impact of firms' promotional efforts and other sources of influence in consumer decision making.

Although there have been relatively few empirical studies of consumer decision-making performance, the evidence summarized in the review suggests strongly that *great variations exist in the types and sources of information used, the extent of information seeking, and the roles or functions of information in consumption decisions.* Three classes of independent variables, which have been found to be related to empirically observed variations in decision-making performance, were explored: the type of product, the aspects of the situation affecting the degree of uncertainty perceived by the decision makers, and the characteristics of the decision makers. This paper first summarizes the review of empirical studies documenting variations in decision-making process variables and then explores the possible effects of each of these three classes of independent variables.

PHASES OF THE DECISION-MAKING PROCESS

Studies that have explored specific aspects of the decision-making process can be classified according to a scheme based on stages of the process, such as the following:

1. Identification of the problem.

*From *Toward Scientific Marketing*, American Marketing Association, December, 1963, pp. 44–57.

2. Obtaining information.
3. Recognition of alternative solutions.
4. Evaluation of solutions.
5. Selection of a strategy.
6. Actual performance of an action or actions and subsequent learning and revision.

PROBLEM IDENTIFICATION

Research dealing with the way in which families first become aware of consumption problems has followed several somewhat different approaches. Some studies have focused on the diffusion of innovations through consumer populations, emphasizing the differing characteristics of new users at each level of market penetration and the differing sources of information and influence that affect adoption at each stage. Other researchers have emphasized how the interplay of changing family circumstances and changing environmental conditions leads to changes in the assortment of items purchased.[1] Studies of family decision-making role structure have been concerned with the family member who first "brings up" the problem (or the member who "typically" brings up the problem). Each of these approaches reveals the variety and complexity of the circumstances leading to changes in consumption patterns, indicating a high potential value for further study of this complex phase.

INFORMATION HANDLING

Although all phases of the decision-making process can be treated as aspects of information-handling behavior, a number of studies have dealt with this behavior alone, frequently without reference to the particular decision stages in which information was pertinent. These studies have typically been concerned with over-all measures of the number and types of information sources consulted and the relative importance of different types of sources in specific purchase situations. Results defy simple generalizations; variations among families have been found in each study in the extent of information seeking, the mix of sources consulted, and the relative importance of each type of source.

Studies that have attempted to relate information-seeking behavior to the other stages of the decision-making process have sought to discover the roles of various types of information sources (such as impersonal media, other people, etc.) at each stage. Research dealing explicitly with family decision processes has explored the roles of family members in receiving, transmitting to other family members, and evaluating information from sources outside the family.

---

[1]Especially valuable studies include Eva Mueller, "The Desire for Innovations in Household Goods," in Lincoln H. Clark (ed.), *Research on Consumer Reactions: Consumer Behavior, Volume III* (New York: Harper & Bros., 1958), pp. 13–37, and Peter Rossi, *Why Families Move* (Glencoe, Ill.: The Free Press, 1955).

Scant attention has been paid to the questions of how and to what extent information feedback from past experience influences family decisions. Studies of family processes have not dealt explicitly with the questions of who evaluates the family's experience, how the evaluation influences information "stored" for future use, and who draws on this information storage when the need arises.

EVALUATION AND SELECTION OF SOLUTIONS

The next three phases—the production of solutions, their evaluation, and the final selection—have usually been treated together in the literature, and clear distinctions among them have usually not been made. Cultural, social class, and family life cycle determinants and constraints on perceived consumption solutions have been emphasized as likely determinants of variations in the number and mix of alternatives considered by particular segments of large, diverse consumer populations. The special problems of conceptualizing the process by which family members contribute alternatives and reach consensus (or compromise) in their evaluation of perceived solutions have recently been undertaken,[2] although it is by no means clear that all families even attempt to agree on each decision. Research directed specifically at the decision-making role structure exhibited by families (to be cited in a later section) indicates that the responsibility for purchase decisions may be divided among family members to reduce the chances of conflict. Some promising investigation of consumers' strategies of search for alternatives includes means of assessing retail outlets and media in terms of the likelihood of their producing acceptable alternatives.

A limited number of experimental studies relating to the evaluation and selection phases—and the precise way in which consumers use information in these phases—show them to be more susceptible to study in a laboratory or experimental setting than the other phases of the decision-making process. Techniques used include the shopping game developed by Alderson and Sessions[3] and the use of interaction process analysis categories in studying how husbands and wives resolve hypothetical consumption problems.[4]

Future study may well borrow techniques developed in other areas of decision research, where attempts have been made to measure both desirability and probability dimensions of the "outcomes" associated

[2]Several examples are included in Nelson N. Foote (ed.), *Household Decision-Making: Consumer Behavior, Volume IV* (New York: New York University Press, 1961).

[3]Alderson and Sessions, "Basic Research Report on Consumer Behavior: Report on a Study of Shopping Behavior and Methods for Its Investigation," in Ronald E. Frank, Alfred A. Kuehn, and William F. Massy, *Quantitative Techniques in Marketing Analysis* (Homewood, Ill.: Richard D. Irwin, Inc., 1962), pp. 129–45.

[4]William F. Kenkel, "Family Interaction in Decision-Making on Spending," in Nelson N. Foote (ed.), *Household Decision-Making: Consumer Behavior, Volume IV* (New York: New York University Press, 1961), pp. 140–64.

with each perceived alternative solution through "paper and pencil" tests of decision making.[5]

STUDIES OF SEVERAL PHASES

A few researchers have developed measures spanning several phases of the decision-making process and have used these as measures of pre-purchase "deliberation." In a study of household durable goods purchases, Katona and Mueller measured five dimensions of deliberation: extent of circumspectness (length of planning period, family discussions, and consideration of alternative purchases), extent of information-seeking activity, influence of price, consideration of alternative brands, and consideration of features other than price and brand. Families were classified according to an index that combined these dimensions of deliberation, and family characteristics and situational variables were examined as explanatory variables associated with variations in the dimensions of deliberation.[6]

Hill has reported preliminary findings from a unique three-generation consumer study of major expenditure decisions. Three dimensions of "family consumership" were studied: planning (extensity, length of planning horizon, and specificity of commitment to act); efficiency of decision process (information seeking for costs and for alternatives, consideration of long-range as well as immediate consequences, conferring within the family, and reference to or creation of a policy to cover the action); and planfulness of actions taken (quantity of actions taken, proportion of actions preceded by plans, and proportion of plans carried out on schedule). Of these three dimensions, efficiency of decision making was found to be the most highly associated with consumer satisfaction.[7]

SUMMARY OF FINDINGS

(1) All of the studies reviewed have treated one or more aspects of the performance of the decision-making process as dependent variables, and have typically found a great deal of variation among families in this performance. These variations are apparently accounted for by complex combinations of independent variables including type of product, situation, and decision makers' characteristics. Later sections will summarize studies concerning the effects of each of these classifications of independent variables. A major conclusion of the review is that the validity of studies in which one or more of these groups of variables are not

---

[5]Orville G. Brim, David C. Glass, David E. Lavin, and Norman Goodman, *Personality and Decision Processes* (Stanford, Calif.: Stanford University Press, 1962).

[6]George Katona and Eva Mueller, "A Study of Purchase Decisions," in Lincoln H. Clark (ed.), *The Dynamics of Consumer Reaction: Consumer Behavior, Volume 1* (New York: New York University Press, 1954), pp. 30–87.

[7]Reuben Hill, "Judgment and Consumership in the Management of Family Resources," *Sociology and Social Research*, Vol. 47 (July, 1963), pp. 446–60.

accounted for—either through specific attempts to assess their impact or devices to control for their effects—may be open to serious question.

(2) Most of the studies have investigated only one stage of the decision-making process or have been concerned with relatively few dimensions of the process. A better understanding of relationships among types of performance of each phase can best be obtained in studies encompassing all stages of the process.

(3) With a few exceptions, these studies have been confined to decision processes that resulted in actual purchases. A more complete understanding might be gained through the study of families whose considerations of possible acquisitions did not end in a purchase. The marketing decision maker may find the study of abortive decision processes particularly useful in suggesting ways in which promotional efforts may be planned to counteract factors that cause consumers to postpone or abandon purchase plans.

(4) Many studies have used (at least implicitly) a decision model appropriate for an individual, and some have structured field research as if the entire process were performed by a single family member. Studies that recognized the family as the relevant decision-making unit have often dealt with family "preferences," ignoring the process by which consensus or compromise was reached. (Even explicit studies of family decision-making role structure—to be reviewed in a later section—have tended to use only *summary* descriptions rather than studying structure throughout the process.)

(5) Precise comparisons of the findings of these studies are hampered by the tendency of researchers to develop their own indexes for measuring general dimensions of the decision process, such as extent of information seeking and length of decision-making period. This problem of comparability is accentuated by the failure of a few published studies to report methodological details.

(6) The few studies concerned with all phases of the decision-making process have been based on recent purchasers' responses to questions asking them to "reconstruct" the act of decision and have perhaps overemphasized the sequential nature of phases of the process. Attention has thus been diverted from the role of past experience from previous purchases of the same or similar products and the role of information "stored" for future use after casual exposure to advertising or the experience of friends. Riesman and Roseborough[8] have emphasized the importance of anticipatory socialization in the learning of purchase motives and brand preferences, even among pre-teen children. Future research might well explore consumers' abilities to produce alternative "solutions"

[8]David Riesman and Howard Roseborough, "Careers and Consumer Behavior," in Lincoln H. Clark (ed.), *The Life Cycle and Consumer Behavior: Consumer Behavior, Volume II* (New York: New York University Press, 1955), pp. 1–18.

to purchase problems and their evaluations of these alternatives at different stages of "nearness" to actual purchase.

TYPE OF PROJECT

Several published studies have illustrated differences in such dimensions of the consumption decision-making process as the length of decision period, extent of information seeking, and number of alternatives considered, depending upon the generic type of product purchased.

A number of studies centering on the purchase of small, frequently purchased items illustrate diverse conceptual approaches and methodologies, but all of them document the role of learning and that of reliance on past experience and habit in routine, repetitive purchasing behavior. Changes in products and brands are nevertheless quite common, and the factors influencing these changes are apparently diverse. In the studies of major purchases cited, far more deliberation was typically found than was associated with small, frequent purchases, with the amount of deliberation increasing roughly in proportion to the size of the purchase and the length of time elapsing between purchases.

Important differences in behavior among purchasers of the same generic product have typically emerged from all of these studies. The failure of generic product type to account for all the observed differences in purchase behavior indicates a need to use product categories based on other factors in addition to unit value and frequency of replacement.

CATEGORIES OF PURCHASING DECISIONS

Several efforts have been made to establish categories for the classification of product purchasing decisions according to the type of purchasing behavior evoked. Probably the earliest attempt was the distinction between convenience, shopping, and specialty goods. Although several different definitions of these terms have been advanced, Bucklin's distinction among them—based on whether or not the shopper has a predetermined preference may and, in the former category, whether only one or several alternatives are acceptable—clearly suggests additional factors which may affect purchasing behavior.[9] Bucklin shows that such factors as frequencies of change in price, style, and product technology may be partial determinants of the presence or absence of a predetermined preference map.

The categories developed by Norris[10] and Alderson[11] also appear suitable for classifying consumption decisions according to the type of

[9] Louis P. Bucklin, "Retail Strategy and the Classification of Consumer Goods," *Journal of Marketing*, Vol. 27 (January, 1963), pp. 50–55.

[10] Ruby Norris, *The Theory of Consumers' Demand* (rev. ed.; New Haven: Yale University Press, 1952), chap. 6.

[11] Wroe Alderson, *Marketing Behavior and Executive Action* (Homewood, Ill.: Richard D. Irwin, Inc., 1957), pp. 267–69.

decision-making process they are likely to evoke. Both classification systems explicitly assume the decision-making unit to be the household or family, and both include predictions of the type of decision making that will be associated with each category of their schemes.

Norris builds her approach on the disposition of income during the income period. In the short run, little true decision making or deliberation precedes two categories of outlays: *commitments* (including such outlays as house rent, taxes, fuel and light, life insurance, and auto purchase and expense) and *petty goods* (which are habitually purchased and are not thought to be worth an "expenditure" of deliberation). The unallocated income that remains after outlays have been made for commitments and petty goods is spent experimentally in ways that often start commitments for future income periods. Experimental outlays are not planned in advance; they are by definition the result of a decision process triggered by sales efforts and persuasion to which the shopper is exposed during the income period. In fact, income left over is defined as unplanned, residual saving and may be considered an index of resistance to sales appeals received during the income period. In the long run, commitments are evaluated, new commitments are added to the pattern, and existing commitments are sometimes terminated. Thus, commitments evoke considerable deliberation at times.

Alderson's system is framed in terms of the relationship between the category of purchase and the total assortment or inventory of goods held by the family. Purchases may be replacements of items used over and over (for which the purchaser has to follow a schedule that will minimize "outs"); substitutes of new products or brands for items that have been previously used; or additions to the inventory. Building on this simple framework, he identifies eight purchase situations, ranging from the replacement of a depleted item with an identical item (for which little deliberation is required) to the purchase of a technical innovation (requiring much deliberation). Unfortunately, neither the Norris nor the Alderson categories have been tested empirically.

CONCLUSION

The conclusion to be drawn from this brief discussion is that attempts to relate variations in decision-making performance to generic product types have been only partly successful, and the usefulness of schemes categorizing purchase decisions has never been empirically tested. The conceptualization of these categories, however, seems to draw on characteristics of the specific situation in which products are purchased, and is therefore closely related to the second major group of independent variables summarized in this review.

SITUATIONAL FACTORS

The emphasis on situational factors affecting purchasing decision making grows out of an emerging tendency for writers and researchers to consider decision making as an information-handling process. Actions are determined mostly by habits, attitudes, and the accumulated stock of knowledge, but stored information must often be supplemented, revised, or replaced by current or "outside" information. In general, the functions of outside information can be expressed in terms of its ability to reduce uncertainty (the absence of information), and the extent of information-seeking and handling behavior can therefore be expected to vary with the degree of uncertainty perceived in the specific situation.

"Outside" information in consumption decision making becomes important when several basic conditions are met. First, the decision maker must face uncertainty of an order high enough to evoke behavior intended to reduce that uncertainty. Second, the perceived consequences of making an error must be important enough to justify an expenditure of effort to reduce the chance of error. (This condition—really a decision in itself—can be compared with an organization's somewhat more formal calculations of the value of researching a problem.) Third, information stored in the memory must be considered inadequate, either because there is little or no relevant past experience or because data from past experience are thought to be out of date. Finally, the uncertainty-reducing strategies in the decision maker's repertoire must be judged inadequate for the situation. Bauer has suggested that consumers may use these strategies as alternatives to information seeking in situations they perceive as risky; sample strategies include "buy the most expensive product," "buy the cheapest product," "patronize the lowest priced outlet," etc.[12]

DETERMINANTS OF PERCEIVED UNCERTAINTY

Specific ways in which information may reduce uncertainty are suggested by a consideration of the factors influencing both the degree of perceived uncertainty and its importance. A tentative list of some illustrative factors suggested by the review follows.

(1) The consumer has little or no relevant past experience because he has never purchased the product. Uncertainty may exist as to what future needs will be—as in the case of the couple expecting their first child or the inexperienced traveler planning a trip abroad—or concerning the availability and characteristics of products suitable for the need.

(2) The consumer has had no past experience because the product is "new."

(3) Past experience with a product has been unsatisfactory.

(4) The purchase is considered discretionary rather than necessary.

[12]Raymond A. Bauer, "Consumer Behavior as Risk Taking," in Robert S. Hancock (ed.), *Proceedings of the 43rd National Conference of the American Marketing Association* (Chicago: The American Marketing Association, 1960), pp. 389–98.

(5) The "correct" selection is especially important to the consumer, as when the purchase is for a gift.

(6) The purchase is socially "visible."

(7) All available alternatives may have both desirable and undesirable consequences, and positive arguments may be needed.

(8) Disagreement among members of the family unit as to requirements and/or the evaluation of alternatives results in the need for further information to persuade dissenters or to discover a satisfactory compromise. A family member may refer repeatedly to certain sources as a means of legitimizing his position.

(9) The consumer recognizes that his behavior deviates from that of an important reference group.

(10) The consumer perceives important changes in the economic or political environment.

Previously cited product characteristics may also be interpreted in terms of uncertainty. The replacement of an infrequently purchased product may generate a high degree of perceived uncertainty, since the consumer's past experience yields out-of-date information and since the long service life of the product makes forecasts of future needs and/or future product performance more difficult. High unit price may evoke uncertainty because purchase of the item would displace many alternative expenditures. Perceived uncertainty may also vary—independently of product type or situation—with personality characteristics of decision makers. A review of the literature on personality was not within the scope of this review, however.

Clearly, the functions of information in consumer decision making may be quite complex and may vary greatly from one situation to another, depending upon the factor or factors affecting the need for information. An attempt to determine functions in empirical studies of decision making, therefore, promises to be helpful in interpreting findings of at least two sorts.

First, the functional approach suggests an important set of determinants of variations in the *amount* of outside information sought by decision makers. Several of the factors listed above, for example, were suggested by empirical studies in which variations in the amount of information seeking were at least partially explained by situational factors affecting perceived uncertainty.

Second, there is some evidence that information sources may vary in terms of the functions for which they are thought appropriate. The function of information from different sources has been found to vary in several studies. Generally, the mass media have been found to perform an informing function (particularly in introducing an innovation), whereas personal sources have typically assumed a legitimizing or evaluating function.

The formulation of a functional approach based on determinants of perceived uncertainty focuses attention on the varying kinds and amounts of information "needed" in the decision. This emphasis contrasts with the notion sometimes incorrectly inferred from economic theory that consumer "rationality" can somehow be measured in terms of the amount of information seeking that precedes a purchase. Brim *et al.*[13] have pointed out how complicated the concept of rational decision making is and have shown the pitfalls of using single indexes of rationality based either on characteristics of decision outcomes or on those of decision processes. Hopefully, this kind of error in interpreting studies of consumer behavior will be less common in the future.

DECISION MAKERS' CHARACTERISTICS

Attempts to relate observed variations in decision-making performance to decision makers' characteristics have followed two different approaches. Studies assuming the orientation of an individual decision maker have found economic and demographic attributes (such as income and education) and personality variables related to variations in decision-making performance. Katona and Mueller, for example, found deliberation (incidence of planning, family discussions, information-seeking, consideration of several product attributes) highest among buyers with a college education, with incomes between $5,000 and $7,500, who were under 35 years of age, and who were white collar workers.[14] Brim has recently reported an excellent study exploring the impact of certain personality variables on variations in decision-making performance.[15]

Other research that has explicitly recognized the family as the relevant decision-making unit has suggested that the role structure exhibited by family members in influencing and performing the purchase decision-making process may affect the performance of the process. Bott's study, for example, suggested the hypothesis that segregation in family role structure (where each partner specialized in certain decision areas) varies directly with the importance of personal influence exerted by the social networks outside the family to which each partner belongs.[16] Thus, family role structure may be related to the types of sources of information influencing the decision process. A field study of major durable purchases supported this hypothesis and suggested, additionally, that the degree of information seeking may be lower among families in which the decision-making function is performed by one partner than among families in which both partners participate.[17]

---

[13]Brim, *loc. cit.*

[14]Katona and Mueller, *loc. cit.*

[15]Brim, *loc. cit.*

[16]Elizabeth Bott, *Family and Social Network* (London, Tavistock Publications Limited), 1957.

[17]Donald H. Granbois, *A Study of the Family Decision-Making Process in the*

These latter studies suggest that family decision-making role structure variables may be treated as "mediating" variables affecting decision-making performance and that the effects on decision making of economic, demographic, and personality characteristics of family members may best be understood by exploring these characteristics as possible determinants of family role structure.

A review of the many studies that have dealt with family role structure revealed a diversity of methodological and conceptual approaches. Despite certain limitations on many of these studies several possible theoretical explanations of observed differences in family role structure have emerged.

THEORETICAL EXPLANATIONS OF FAMILY ROLE STRUCTURE

Many studies have been structured around modifications of a conceptual framework devised by Herbst, which generated four basic patterns of decision making: automatic (where an equal number of separate decisions is made by each partner); husband dominance; wife dominance; and syncratic (in which most decisions are made jointly).[18] Although most studies have documented fairly large amounts of joint decision making, significant variations among families (and *within* families in studies that have dealt with a variety of decision areas) have been the rule. Cross-classification analyses have typically explored such variables as product type, family characteristics (for example, social class and husband's education), and comparative characteristics of husbands and wives. Drawing on this evidence, various writers have suggested the following bases of family structure.

(1) *Life cycle.* Scattered evidence (and common sense) supports the idea that joint decision making declines over the life cycle. The tendency is usually explained in terms of an increased efficiency or competence that people presumably develop over time in making decisions that will be acceptable to their partners, eliminating the need for extensive interaction.

(2) *Product type.* Komarovsky has suggested that joint decision making is more likely to occur in connection with purchases that represent significant outlays, whereas smaller purchases are more likely to be delegated to one partner.[19] When specialization does occur, certain products may tend to be handled by men and others by women. This

---

Purchase of Major Durable Household Goods (Unpublished doctoral dissertation, Graduate School of Business, Indiana University, 1962).

[18]P. G. Herbst, "Conceptual Framework for Studying the Family," in O. A. Oeser, and S. B. Hammond (eds.), *Social Structure and Personality in a City* (London: Routledge and Kegan Paul Ltd., 1954), chap. 10.

[19]Mirra Komarovsky, "Class Differences in Family Decision-Making on Expenditures, in Nelson N. Foote (ed.), *Household Decision-Making: Consumer Behavior, Volume IV* (New York, New York University Press, 1961), p. 257.

tendency has been discussed in terms of the relative involvement of husband and wife. The existence of specialized skills and knowledge of men and women in different areas seems an equally plausible explanation.

(3) *Social class.* Komarovsky has advanced a "curvilinear hypothesis" and has cited several studies in apparent support of the theory.[20] Specifically, she postulates that joint decision making is less common at both extremes of the socioeconomic hierarchy than at the middle, with women playing the most important role in lower class families and men dominating upper class families.

(4) *Relative contributions.* Blood and Wolfe interpreted the results of their study in terms of the relative contribution of "resources" (education and income, for example) made by each partner.[21] The dominant spouses they identified tended to contribute more resources to the marriage than did their partners. The relative contributions hypothesis presumably accounts for the comparatively greater power exercised by higher class husbands, since the indexes used to determine social class can also be interpreted as measures of a husband's success and, therefore, of his contribution to the marriage.

15. THE AUDIENCE AS COMMUNICATORS*

Donald F. Cox

The marketing research director of a large and sophisticated consumer goods manufacturing company recently told me, "We've known about 'word of mouth advertising' at our company since the year One." And in the next breath, he said, "But we don't really know what to do about it."

His statement is full of meaning. Because if we stop to think about it, it is not difficult to conclude that what we call "word of mouth advertising" probably *has* been going on since the year One. Word of mouth advertising is nothing more than a particular type of conversation—conversation about products. And both conversation and products have existed throughout the ages of man. It is not unreasonable to conclude that products were one of the earliest of man's topics of conversation. In the absence of mass media, man had to obtain product information somewhere, and aside from information derived from direct observation, what more likely source than his fellow man?

It is rather interesting that although all this conversation about products has been going on for so many years, Paul Lazarsfeld and his co-

[20]*Ibid.*

[21]Robert O. Blood, Jr. and Donald M. Wolfe, *Husbands and Wives: The Dynamics of Married Living* (Glencoe, Ill., The Free Press, 1960).

*From *Toward Scientific Marketing,* American Marketing Association, December, 1963, pp. 58–72.

workers are often credited with its discovery just over 20 years ago.[1] Lazarsfeld did not "discover" word of mouth advertising, nor would he claim such a discovery. What he did do, in a now classic book written with Elihu Katz,[2] was to demonstrate a *relationship* between the formal channels of communication—the mass media—and the informal channels of communication—the conversational media.

The *relationship* between the formal and informal channels of communication is the crux of the problem I want to consider. I think this relationship is an important problem for two reasons. First, I don't believe that we really understand the nature of the relationship, despite, or perhaps even because of, the work of Lazarsfeld and his disciples. Second, as marketers, until we gain some *understanding* of this relationship we will remain in the position of the marketing research director I referred to earlier. We will recognize the existence of informal communications, but we won't really know what to do about it.

Part of the reason for the lack of understanding is a lack of research. Marketers have shown rather little interest in researching the relationship between the two types of communications. And I am afraid that a lack of interest is our only excuse. To be sure, research in this area is difficult and expensive, but researchers in fields other than marketing have been working on similar problems for many years. For example, rural sociologists have been studying the relationship between formal and informal communication as it applies to the diffusion and adoption of new farming practices and products since 1938. By now, approximately 300 studies of the diffusion of agricultural innovations have been published.[3] Marketers can't begin to match this achievement, at least in published research.

But lack of research is not the only reason for our lack of understanding. Our research, in general, is a reflection of our way of conceptualizing a problem. And concepts or points of view have both advantages and limitations. We think of concepts as being helpful because they focus our attention on certain aspects of reality, but we are inclined to forget that concepts can be blinding as well as illuminating. Our attention may be so steadily focused on one aspect of reality that we neglect other aspects which may be equally important.

I think that research on the relationship of formal and informal communications in marketing may have been blinded by one commonly held

[1]The notion of the "two-step flow of communication" was first developed as the result of a study of the 1940 presidential election; Paul F. Lazarsfeld, Bernard Berelson, and Hazel Gaudet, *The People's Choice* (New York: Columbia University Press, 1948), p. 151.

[2]The two-step flow of communication concept was subjected to its first serious empirical test in a study conducted in Decatur, Illinois in 1945. This study was published in Elihu Katz and Paul F. Lazarsfeld, *Personal Influence* (Glencoe, Ill.: Free Press, 1955).

[3]Many of these studies are reviewed in Everett M. Rogers, *Diffusion of Innovations* (New York: The Free Press of Glencoe, 1962).

concept, namely that of *the passive audience*. When we think of an audience, we think of an assembly of listeners or readers or viewers. We think of this assembly as being primarily passive receivers of information. They listen, or read, or view, but they do not, in general, actively seek information. Armed with a concept like this, research on the link between formal and informal communications can only proceed in one direction: the direction of the "two-step flow of communication."

THE TWO-STEP FLOW CONCEPT

The concept of the two-step flow of communication is the classic model of the link between the mass media and interpersonal communication. Although the two-step model has been revised, updated,[4] modified, and elaborated on over the past 20 years (e.g., it is sometimes referred to as a multistep flow), its essential features remain unchanged from its earliest formal statement which was that influences and ideas "flow *from* [the mass media] *to* opinion leaders and *from them* to the less active sections of the population."[5] Thus the two-step flow model assumes that the bulk of the audience is composed of passive receivers of information. The link between the passive masses and the mass media is the opinion leader.

The two-step flow of communication concept added an intermediary or relay point—the opinion leader—to the communications process. But the basic concept of the mass audience remained unchanged. The mass audience is thought of as being composed largely of information receivers. The two-step flow suggested that many people receive their information from interpersonal sources instead of, or in addition to, mass media sources. But the *initiative* in the transmission of information was assumed to lie with the *communicator*—either the mass media or the opinion leader—and not with the audience.

This point of view has had some rather interesting effects on the type of research conducted on the relationship between formal and informal communications.

For one thing, attention has been directed to the issue of which source formal or interpersonal—has more influence on consumer behavior. One assumption was that since the audience is passive, and is largely content to receive rather than to seek information, the two types of information channels are often competitive rather than complementary; given a passive audience, the question then is who gets to them firstest with the mostest.

Katz and Lazarsfeld presented data which suggest that personal influ-

---

[4]For example, see Elihu Katz, "The Two-Step Flow of Communications: An Up-to-Date Report on an Hypothesis," *Public Opinion Quarterly*, Vol. 21 (Spring, 1957), pp. 61–78.

[5]Lazarsfeld, Berelson, and Gaudet, *loc. cit.*

ence was seven times more effective than magazine or newspaper advertising in persuading women to switch brands of household products.[6] Beal and Rogers found interpersonal sources to be the most influential in convincing housewives to purchase new fabrics such as Dacron and nylon.[7] Atkin presented data which indicate that while 48 percent of housewives reporting heavy exposure to advertising which advocated switching to another supermarket actually switched, 80 percent of women who reported strong interpersonal pressure switched.[8]

Research of this type may reaffirm the importance of informal communications. But it left the marketer a little confused. If formal and informal channels are competitive, and if the informal channels are the more effective of the two, what can the marketer do? How can he act more effectively in light of this knowledge?

At this point the marketer was left with only one hope: that in some way he could reach the opinion leader and persuade her to endorse his product or brand. But how? *How does one even identify opinion leaders,* particularly since they tend to specialize in particular opinion areas? Katz and Lazarsfeld identified four areas of specialization among opinion leaders: household products, fashions, movies, and public affairs; and that was merely a first cut. The degree of specialization could be almost infinite. It is not inconceivable that a housewife might consult with one friend about cake mixes, and another about laundry detergents.

As a practical matter it is virtually impossible to identify all of the specific opinion leaders for most consumer products. At best, one might be able to describe some of their general characteristics. As a consequence, direct communication between the marketer and the opinion leader is not possible. The marketer, if he wished to communicate at all with opinion leaders, would be forced to use the mass media.

Katz and Lazarsfeld provided a partial answer to the marketer's dilemma with their finding that opinion leaders are more likely to be exposed to the mass media, and in some cases may be more influenced by the mass media than are nonleaders.[9] However, research subsequent to the publication of *Personal Influence* has not, to my knowledge, addressed itself to the question of what types of messages in media may be most likely to stimulate the opinion leader to relay certain kinds of information about a product.

I will return to the problem of stimulating opinion leaders. But before I do, I would like to place the two-step flow concept in proper perspective. The two-step flow concept is a fairly adequate model—as far as it

---

[6]Katz and Lazarsfeld, *op. cit.*, p. 176.

[7]George M. Beal and Everett M. Rogers, "Informational Sources in the Adoption Process of New Fabrics," *Journal of Home Economics,* Vol. 49 (1957), pp. 630–44.

[8]Kenward L. Atkin, "Advertising and Store Patronage," *Journal of Advertising Research,* Vol. 2 (December, 1962), pp. 18–23. The 48% and 80% figures are derived from an analysis of data contained in Table 2, p. 20.

[9]Katz and Lazarsfeld, *op. cit.*, chap. 14.

goes. My objection is that the model is much more incomplete than it appears. One gets the impression that the two-step concept is seen as describing *the* basic relationship between formal and informal communication channels. Actually it presents only a partial picture of the way in which the audience obtains information, and thus describes only a part of the relationship.

My intention today is to try to describe another part of the relationship. Perhaps the best way to begin doing this is to examine the information needs of consumers and to look at the ways in which these information needs may be satisfied.

CONSUMER INFORMATION NEEDS AND SOURCES

Before making a buying decision, the consumer needs, in the most general sense, three types of information. First, since she must be aware of a product before she can buy it, she needs information about the existence or availability of a product or brand, i.e., *awareness*. Second, on the assumption that interest is a necessary precondition of consideration, the consumer needs information which will give her a reason to become *interested* in a product—at least if she is to be motivated to give further consideration to the product. Third, the consumer needs information which will help her *evaluate* the product, in terms of its ability to satisfy her buying goals.

This latter type of information will include information about the product itself—its cost, characteristics, functions, variations, performance, and so on. It may include comparative product information, i.e., information which will allow a comparison of the several products or brands which may be involved in the choice to be made, and may also include information which will help the consumer to evaluate the psychological and social consequences of purchasing the product.

The consumer has three basic types of information sources to which she can turn in order to satisfy her information needs. First there are the *marketer dominated* channels of communication, that is, those means of communicating with the consumer which are under the direct control of the marketer: the product itself, packaging, advertising, promotion, distribution channels, display, personal selling, and so forth. Second are the *consumer dominated* or consumer-oriented channels of communication; i.e., all interpersonal sources of information which are not under the direct control of the marketer. Third are the generally neutral information sources not directly influenced by either the marketer or the consumer, such as *Consumer Reports* and magazine and newspaper articles about products.

The question is which source or sources of information will the audience use in order to satisfy its information needs? A substantial part of the answer to this question will depend on how much initiative we accord to the audience. If we view the audience as being largely passive, the question may be which source gets to the audience firstest with the mostest. On the other hand, if we place much of the initiative in the choice of information sources with the audience, the question is which source is most likely to satisfy the audience's *various* information needs? We might assume that the audience will try to choose those sources which appear to achieve an optimum combination in terms of information cost vs. information value.

If we examine the characteristics of the three major channels of information, it becomes apparent that each has rather distinctive characteristics and, from the point of view of the audience, each has rather distinctive advantages and limitations.

Marketer dominated channels, for instance, may be valued by the audience for their ability to present quickly, and frequently in a sophisticated manner, a broad range of technically accurate, if often superficial, information. These channels may also be perceived as a low-cost source of information. That is, the consumer usually has ready access, with relatively little effort on her part, to information provided by marketer dominated channels.

However, while they may be perceived as being *competent* sources of information, there is some question as to consumer's perception of the *trustworthiness* of marketer dominated channels. After all, the marketer is trying to sell something, and knowing this intention consumers may raise questions both about the information the marketer provides ("Is it trustworthy?") and about the information he withholds ("Are there some disadvantages to the product which we aren't told about?").

Even so, for many of the decisions faced by a consumer, the information provided by marketer dominated channels may be perfectly adequate. This is most likely when the consumer's perceived risk and uncertainty is sufficiently low that the time and effort required to obtain information from alternate sources is not justified. For example, Maloney has shown that for some products advertising can stimulate curiosity and thus develop willingness to buy, even though the advertising claims may not be believed.[10] (Presumably this would happen with only low-risk products.)

Consumer dominated channels may be valued by the audience for their flexibility, trustworthiness, and for the amount of information they may convey about any one product. Consumer channels are flexible in that interpersonally communicated information can often be tailored to meet an individual's particular information needs. Furthermore, a consumer may be able to develop a great deal more information about a product through consumer channels—particularly information concerning product performance and information about the social or psychological conse-

---

[10]John C. Maloney, "Curiosity vs. Disbelief in Advertising," *Journal of Advertising Research,* Vol. 2 (June, 1962), pp. 2–8.

quences of a purchase decision. Finally, consumer channels may be perceived as being more trustworthy sources of information.

However, consumer channels may at times be perceived as less competent sources of information than marketer dominated channels. You may assume that your neighbor will speak the truth as he sees it, but there is no guarantee that he always knows what he is talking about. With marketer dominated channels the problem is reversed. Consumers may assume that the marketer knows what he is talking about, but may perceive no guarantee that he is speaking the truth.

There are other distinctive advantages and disadvantages of consumer channels which depend on the way in which they are used. The two-step flow concept implies that consumers obtain information from consumer channels in one way—by passively receiving information from an opinion leader. But this overlooks another important possibility—that the consumer may take the initiative and actively *seek* information from consumer channels. There are some rather sharp differences between information receiving and information seeking.

Information receiving seems like an almost ideal way of obtaining information. The consumer sits back, and without any effort on her part, except for listening, receives the advantages of both the marketer and consumer channels. Since the opinion leader is an intermediary she screens and filters marketer originated information and passes it along, perhaps together with her own personal evaluation.

However, from the consumer's point of view there are some serious disadvantages to this procedure. The opinion leader, no matter how vocal, can't compete with the mass media of today in terms of coverage. Yet, the opinion leader is interested in providing her audience with information which she feels has not already reached them via the mass media. An opinion leader who habitually passed on information which had already become common knowledge would lose her reputation as an opinion leader and quickly gain a reputation as a bore. Consequently, the opinion leader is likely to be selective, to deal with information which has not been communicated to the audience via the mass media. The consumer, therefore, is less likely to *depend* on the opinion leader for this type of information. As the effectiveness of the mass media increases, we might expect that the role of the opinion leader as a relayer of information (as described by the two-step flow concept) will be diminished. However, the opinion leader may still play an initiating role by either adding to or filtering mass media information in order to provide "new" information to her audience.

Information seeking is a much more costly way of obtaining information. The process of seeking out friends and neighbors or neutral sources who possess a particular type of product knowledge can be very time-consuming. Considering its cost, information seeking is most likely to occur when three conditions are present: when the consumer has become aware of a need for information; when she has become sufficiently interested or motivated to want to acquire more information; and when she perceives sufficient risk and uncertainty to justify the time and effort required to secure information from consumer channels or from neutral sources. These three conditions are most likely to be present when the marketer dominated channels or an opinion leader have created awareness and stimulated the consumer's interest, but have not provided her with all the information she needs in order to evaluate the product.

COMPLEMENTARY INFORMATION SOURCES

If the assumptions I have made are correct, then it may well be that *the audience uses the types of channels as complementary rather than competing sources of information.* The consumer may develop a set of expectations or decision rules which cause her to tune in one type of channel for certain kinds of information and another channel for other kinds of information. The primary role of the marketer dominated channels may be to create awareness, to stimulate interest in a product, and in some cases to provide consumers with information which can be used to evaluate a product. Where the marketer dominated channels fail to get through to the mass audience, the opinion leader, acting as an information relayer, may enter the picture. And where either marketer channels or opinion leaders have stimulated the consumer's interest, but have failed to satisfy her information needs, she may begin to seek information from consumer channels or from neutral sources. Since the most likely area of weakness of the marketer dominated channels (providing information which can be used to evaluate products) happens to be the area of greatest strength of consumer channels, the major role of consumer dominated channels may be to provide information which can be used to evaluate products.

To summarize, I have presented a model of the relationship between marketer dominated and consumer dominated channels of communication which suggest that:

1. These channels are viewed by consumers as being primarily complementary rather than competitive.
2. Information seeking is an important aspect in the way in which consumer dominated channels are used.

Since both of these assumptions are in conflict with the two-step flow of information concept, and since both have rather important implications for marketing action, let me support them with some hard data. Let me emphasize, however, that on the issue of information seeking versus information receiving, I am not trying to disprove the two-step flow concept. I am not saying that information receiving, as described by the two-step concept, does not occur. I am saying that this is not the only way in which consumers use informal channels of communications, and furthermore, in terms of implications for marketing action, *it is extremely important to recognize the existence of information seeking.*

Two side comments are necessary at this point. First, to conserve time I have not discussed the role of the so-called neutral information sources such as *Consumer Reports.* With full awareness that there are exceptions to the statement, let me say that in general, these neutral sources play a role similar to that played by the consumer channels. As a second aside, I will use the terms formal channels and marketer dominated channels synonymously and will equate consumer channels with informal channels. I prefer the terms marketer and consumer dominated channels because they spotlight the importance of the issue of the *intent* of the communicator. However, I will be referring to data outside of the area of marketing, and these terms would not be appropriate.

The basic distinction between the two-step flow concept and the information seeking model is the *degree of initiative accorded to the audience.* The alternate model rests on the assumption that the audience takes a good deal of the initiative in the communications process. The two-step flow model views the audience as being largely passive.

The two-step flow concept, which seems to be the most widely accepted model of the relationship between formal and informal communications in marketing, has been exposed to marketers for only the past eight years. But the two-step concept was developed over 20 years ago, at a time when the notion of a passive audience was widely accepted in communications research.[11] Considering this fact, the two-step flow concept was consistent with most of the knowledge and assumptions available at the time of its development.

But that was over 20 years ago. In the intervening period, available knowledge from communications research has changed greatly. With regard to formal channels of communication, research now shows quite clearly that the audience takes a good deal of initiative in deciding to what information it will be exposed, in deciding what information it will retain, and so forth.

And some evidence is available which suggests that the audience takes a good deal of initiative in utilizing informal channels of communication as well. For instance, in an unpublished commercial study which I have seen, 47 percent of the product conversations were initiated by the so-called influence. In another unpublished commercial study, 45 percent of the users of a particular brand indicated they had started using that brand as the result of asking someone else for information about suitable brands in the product class in question. Some of the research of rural sociologists also indicates that the audience may play an active

---

[11] Raymond A. Bauer, "The Initiative of the Audience," *Journal of Advertising Research,* Vol. 3 (June, 1963), pp. 2–7.

information seeking role in utilizing informal communications channels.[12]

And, as a matter of fact, even though they did not focus on this point, data from the Katz and Lazarsfeld study suggest that probably at least half of the two-person conversations about products were initiated, not by the opinion leader, but by the so-called influencee.[13] (For various reasons, including problems in the research methodology, it is not possible to pin this figure down precisely.)

In sum, evidence is available which indicates that when consumer channels are used, information seeking takes place roughly at least as often as does information receiving. The notion of a largely passive audience no longer seems valid.

The second basic difference between the two-step flow concept and the alternate approach revolves around the issue of whether formal and informal channels play largely *competitive*, or primarily complementary roles in the communications process. While recognizing that different information sources could play *complementary* roles in other areas, Katz and Lazarsfeld argued that consumer buying decisions for household products are made within such a short span of time that the notion of complementarity was not relevant.[14] Actually, in the case of both of the unpublished commercial studies which I referred to earlier, the products were household products similar in nature to those investigated in the Decatur study. And in both cases there was evidence that the marketer dominated channels stimulated at least a portion of the information seeking activity. Outside of the area of household products, the work of Bauer in studying differences between Negro and white women's fashion buying behavior has developed data which are consistent with the notion that marketer dominated, consumer dominated, and neutral information channels play complementary roles in the buying decision process.[15] And outside of the area of consumer goods marketing, Rogers has reviewed a number of studies of the diffusion of farming innovations which support the notion that "impersonal information sources are most important at the awareness stage, and personal sources are most important as the evaluation stage in the adoption process."[16]

Although the model of the relationship between formal and informal channels which I have presented is highly consistent with Rogers' notion, there is one important difference. I have argued that consumers tend to use informal channels primarily in those situations in which perceived risk and uncertainty have not been sufficiently reduced by

[12]Herbert F. Lionberger, "Information Seeking Habits and Characteristics of Farm Operators" (Columbia, Missouri Agricultural Experiment Station Bulletin 581, 1955).

[13]Katz and Lazarsfeld, *op. cit.*, p. 156.

[14]*Ibid.*, p. 195.

[15]Raymond A. Bauer, Harvard University, work in progress.

[16]Rogers, *op. cit.*, p. 99.

formal information sources; and where risk, and uncertainty, and involvement are high enough to justify seeking information through informal channels. Thus, for many "low risk" products, informal channels may play a relatively minor role. Since agricultural innovations tend to involve substantial amounts of perceived risk, informal sources of information may be more generally important to farmers than to housewives.

A third major distinction between the two-step model and the alternate model which was presented relates to the issue of *why* informal channels are effective sources of influence. Some writers (e.g., Whyte)[17] have implied that the opinion leaders' influence is derived from her ability to punish deviant behavior and reward conforming behavior. In my opinion, this may be part of the reason, but only part. Consumers don't choose just anyone to provide product information. Generally, they look to friends or neighbors who have a particular expertise with regard to the product in question. The reason for this is that they want accurate information because they want to make satisfactory buying decisions. Katz and Lazarsfeld argue that "control" or compliance which results from interpersonal relationships is "probably the most important reason [why they] found the impact of personal contact to be greater than the impact of formal media."[18] Raymond Bauer and I have recently completed a study which lends support to an opposite conclusion, namely that the desire to achieve a satisfactory solution to a problem such as a buying decision may, in many situations, outweigh conformity motives.[19] Thus, it is possible that much of the effectiveness of informal channels results from consumers' desires to make good buying decisions, coupled with a feeling on their part that consumer channels may provide more trustworthy information than do marketer dominated channels.

MARKETING IMPLICATIONS

At this point it is time to ask "So what?" Even if the model helps achieve a better understanding of the relationship between marketer dominated and consumer dominated communications channels, is there any way in which the marketer can act more effectively in light of this knowledge? While the final answer to this question will be up to the marketer, I believe there are some bases for hope.

For one thing, the model suggests that to the extent that marketers can resolve consumer uncertainty through formal communications, they may not have to be too concerned with informal channels.

---

[17]William H. Whyte, Jr., "The Web of Word of Mouth," *Fortune*, Vol. 50 (November, 1954), pp. 140 ff.

[18]Katz and Lazarsfeld, *op. cit.*, p. 185.

[19]Donald F. Cox and Raymond A. Bauer, "Self-Confidence and Persuasibility in Women," unpublished manuscript.

However, where it seems desirable to do so, it may be possible to stimulate opinion leaders to relay certain types of information to the audience. Research on the transmissibility of information is in short supply, but it is probable that some types of information are more likely to be transmitted than others. Further thinking and research are needed to identify the dimensions of information transmissibility; although perceived novelty and perceived relevance to the opinion leader's audience are certain to be found important. For example, a soon to be published study found that advertising of a certain type for a household product was able, over a period of several months, steadily to increase word of mouth activity, particularly among people who might be regarded as prospective users of the product. In an unpublished commercial study of a very novel consumer service, of those responding to a mail questionnaire, 73 percent of consumers who had tried the service as the result of direct mail advertising indicated that they had recommended the service to friends and relatives. Furthermore, 48 percent of these respondents claimed that they had told at least 10 people about the new service.

The information seeking model suggests that by creating awareness and interest in the product among the mass audience, the marketer may be able to stimulate information seeking activity. When this can be accomplished, and when the right kind of information is flowing through the informal channels, the marketer may be able to make substantial savings in resources which might otherwise have to be committed to formal communications campaigns. For example, one company in a highly competitive consumer products field regularly spends only one-third as much on advertising as its two major competitors, yet retains a market share roughly equal to that of the two leading competitors. It would be overstating the case to say that this was a planned strategy, but investigation revealed that the apparent reason for their ability to succeed with relatively little advertising was the fact that their brand received vastly more word of mouth activity than did the two other brands which had about the same market shares. The other brands were moved by muscle. The word of mouth brand had developed an advertising program which apparently aroused curiosity, which in turn stimulated some of the information seeking. In addition, the company had a good product which was well regarded by certain opinion leaders, and this resulted in favorable word of mouth activity.

The moral of this story is not that you can influence opinion leaders to act as unpaid salesmen for a brand. This may or may not be the case. The important thing is that it may pay the marketer to monitor continuously the amount and nature of the information about his product which is flowing through informal channels. If a brand is receiving favorable mentions in consumer channels, and if a large number of people are talking about it, it might be wise to conserve some of the marketing resources allocated to the brand on the grounds that since the informal channels are doing a good job of providing information, less emphasis need be placed on formal channels. On the other hand, a company which found a favorable, but limited flow of information might be wise to act through formal channels to create more awareness and interest in order to stimulate information seeking activity and thus take advantage of the favorable word of mouth activity.

To summarize, the marketer has several types of opportunities to work with, rather than in ignorance of, consumer communications channels. Primarily, there is the possibility of influencing the opinion leader. But even where this can't be achieved, the marketer may be able to stimulate information seeking activity in order to take advantage of a limited but favorable flow of information through consumer channels. And even in situations where there is nothing the marketer can do to influence either opinion leaders or information seekers, he can still coordinate his formal communications program with the information the consumer is already receiving through informal channels. This requires that consumer channels be kept under steady surveillance.

Today the marketer is primarily concerned with achieving a balanced communications program by adjusting the timing and relative emphasis given to the various elements of his formal channels of communication. In the future, informal channels may, in a sense, be considered a part of the marketing mix. Marketers may attempt to achieve communications programs in which not only are the elements of the formal channels internally balanced, but also in which the amount and type of information provided by formal channels is coordinated with information the consumer is already receiving through informal channels.

The marketer's communications objective in the future may be to provide the consumer with relevant information about his product which she is *not* receiving through informal channels.

B. Behavior in the retail store

One of the most relevant yet least investigated questions pertains to what happens once the buyer enters the retail store. The two articles presented here shed significant new light on this subject.

Willett and Pennington report the results of a study that considered the interaction between buyer and salesman. The purpose was to learn what roles were assumed by each and what were the outcomes of the interaction process. The Bales process analysis procedure was utilized in an imaginative way, and the results are worthy of careful analysis.

Kollat asks the related question: How does impulse buying, or instore decision making, take place? He reports findings that challenge much that has traditionally been assumed by practitioners in the field, and he suggests new insights that have potential importance in the planning of instore communications.

16. CUSTOMER AND SALESMAN: THE ANATOMY OF CHOICE AND INFLUENCE IN A RETAIL SETTING*

Ronald P. Willett and Allan L. Pennington

There is a paradox of heroic proportions in the low esteem accorded personal selling as an area of inquiry by the academic researcher in marketing. Few visible marketing phenomena would appear to offer as rich a setting for the study of choice and influence processes as the interaction of a buyer and seller in the pursuit of a completed transaction. To add to the paradox there has been extensive investigation of selling by researchers of a different bent, for as Miner suggests, the salesman has been one of the most extensively studied men in the business world.[1] But the great strength of this stream of research—its singleness of purpose in seeking predictors of occupational performance—also limits its applicability in explaining transactional behavior and differentiating the successful from unsuccessful transaction. An endorsement of this latter focus is implied in an articulate critique of research in personal selling by Hauk.[2] Viewing personal selling as a central part of certain types of marketing transactions, the question becomes the causation for a successful transaction.

A PROCESS APPROACH

The central thesis of this paper is that personal selling of consumer durables—specifically household appliances—can be viewed usefully as a problem-solving process, requiring the joint participation and interaction of customer and salesman for a successful outcome. Components of this conceptualization of personal selling include: (1) The actors (customer shopping party and salesman) and a stage (retail appliance selling floors) for the action that is to be played out; (2) An organizing scheme that determines the roles of the participants; (3) The mechanisms for maintenance and mediation of the process implicit in buyer-seller

*From *Science, Technology, and Marketing,* American Marketing Association, September, 1966, pp. 598–616.
[1]J. B. Miner, "Personality and Ability Factors in Sales Performance," *Journal of Applied Psychology,* Vol. XLVI, No. 1 (February, 1962), p. 6.
[2]James G. Hauk, "Research in Personal Selling," in George Schwartz (ed.), *Science in Marketing* (New York: John Wiley & Sons, Inc., 1965), p. 217.

interaction; and (4) Assumed starting positions for the players. The first and last components are in a sense not functional, and their existence and configuration must be specified. Normally, these givens will not change appreciably during the transaction itself.

THE SETTING FOR THE TRANSACTION

Assumptions about the starting positions of the two parties to the transaction are most meaningful presented in terms of latent predispositions for action. For example, on the salesman's side in a retail appliance setting there is little basis for predicting from one potential transaction to the next exactly what customer intent or action will prevail. The retail floor salesman is confronted by a continuous stream of customers, with little consistency in the order of their appearance or the characteristics of those who do appear. Floor salesmen normally will have little opportunity—unless a particular customer has been a prior patron of that salesman—to form any extensive set of expectations about specific customers prior to contact. On the other hand, on the customer's side, a significant selection process has been exercised. The customer's choice of retail store, and perhaps even his selection of a salesman, may be quite deliberate.

Another assumption relating to the customer concerns his predisposition to purchase at the time of customer-salesman contact. It is contended, and was documented in the present study, that the decision to purchase as a generic choice in most appliance transactions is no longer an issue at the time that customer-salesman contact is made. If this is true one might infer that the substance of a potential transaction is more likely to revolve around the specific offer alternatives from which choice can be made, and the conditions under which execution of the purchase decision might be possible.

BUYER AND SELLER AS A GROUP

At the very heart of the interaction approach to personal selling is the view that, since buyer and seller share participation in the marketing transaction, they might meaningfully be considered as a group, specifically, a dyad. Admittedly this is an attractive point of view. Viewing buyer and seller as a dyad allows one to bring a great number of variables and a great deal of insight from social psychology into the explanations for transactional behavior. If this is an attractive strategy, it is also a risky strategy, for although certain kinds of buyer-seller relationships—especially those in the industrial area—may last over time, the occasional contact that accompanies the great majority of retail transactions raises serious doubts as to the true presence of a dyad. Becker and Useem define a dyad in terms of the length of time of relations of members of the pair, pointing out that the relationship must have persisted over a length of time sufficient for the establishment of a discernible pattern of interacting personalities.[3] It is assumed that the dyad will continue to exist and will form the basis for future relationships. This does not appear to be the case in the large portion of typical retail transactions.

Goffman offers a very persuasive alternative to automatic classification of a two person relationship as a group. He suggests that the designation "encounter" or "focused gathering" may be much more appropriate, allowing one to explore what is uniquely characteristic of the less formal relationship. He points out that some of the properties important to encounters are much less important to groups as such. For example, embarrassment, maintenance of poise, capacity for verbal communication, exchange of speaker role, and in particular, maintenance of continuous focus on the official activity of the encounter are not properties of social groups in general.[4]

Use of the encounter as a potential frame of reference for the analysis of buyer-seller behavior has both strengths and limitations. Highly situational properties of the transaction assume additional significance, and this orientation seems to match more closely the reality of the retail marketing transaction. Additionally, enough is known about durable goods purchasing to infer that it would be difficult to maintain a true dyad given the spacing of durable goods purchases and their dispersion across sellers. With its principal focus on the immediate interaction between participants an "encounters" approach offers a better chance of supplying inductive explanation. Conversely, it would be more difficult to draw inferences from this concentration on social interaction without the benefit of the additional conceptual insight that accompanies viewing buyer and seller as a true group. Sources of explanatory variables are drastically reduced. Despite these limitations it was concluded that this approach offered the greatest possibility of generating defensible and useful findings.

THE PROCESS MECHANISMS

To define the exchange between buyer and seller in the transaction as interaction is, in and of itself, of only limited usefulness. Interaction takes place by definition when the parties to the transaction emit behavior in each other's presence.[5] But if behavior can take on various forms it can be argued that highly subtle forms of behavior might not be perceptible to even a careful observer. Interaction nevertheless serves, in communications parlance, as the carrier for the modulating effects of both parties' purposeful behaviors.

[3]Howard Becker and Ruth Hill Useem, "Sociological Analysis of the Dyad," *American Sociological Review,* Vol. 7 (January, 1942), p. 13.

[4]Erving Goffman, *Encounters* (Indianapolis: The Bobbs-Merrill Co., Inc., 1961), pp. 9–14.

[5]John W. Thibaut and Harold H. Kelly, *The Social Psychology of Groups* (New York: John Wiley & Sons, Inc., 1959), p. 10.

Of all the possible process orientations that could be adopted to guide investigation of buyer-seller interaction, the problem-solving or decision process perspective seemed the most cogent. There has been a virtual explosion of work dealing with problem-solving behavior, and meaningful inductive evidence has begun to stack up in support of this kind of explanatory model.[6] The problem-solving approach adopted implies that a continuous problem-solving role be exercised by the buyer. Extending this logic, customer and salesman might be expected to specialize in the performance of the phases of the problem-solving process. Further, the exclusion of one or more phases of the problem-solving process would seem to reduce the likelihood of a successful outcome to the transaction. Finally, the problem-solving approach supplies in its internal structure the guidelines for detecting its presence, given longitudinal measurements of customer–salesman interaction.

To implement a process approach required that some method be devised that would permit a systematic analysis of the content of customer–salesman interaction. Although the possibilities here are legion the more conservative strategy—using an extant classification system— was employed. Bales has developed and recorded substantial experience with a method for interaction analysis which he refers to as Interaction Process Analysis. As defined by Bales, the heart of the method is a way of classifying behavior in face-to-face groups on an act by act basis, permitting one to obtain indices that provide description of group process.[7] A simplified statement of categories employed by Bales appears in Figure 1.

It should be noted that the indicated categories are not only pragmatic definitional units. As Bales points out, the terms are related to a conception of an over-arching problem-solving sequence of interaction between two or more persons. He postulates six interlocking functional problems applicable to any concrete type of interaction system. These conform in part to the previously noted stages of decision-making. Bales describes the early stages of interaction in terms of emphasis on problems of orientation, that is, describing or deciding what the situation is like. Problems of evaluation, involving decisions about what attitude should be taken toward the situation, occur next. As interaction continues, and behavior ideally moves closer and closer to some ultimate agreement or solution, problems of control become paramount. This phase of interaction takes the form of decisions about the solutions to the problem. During this entire process it is possible that members of the group can contribute positively or negatively toward the maintenance of group rapport.[8] Each of the Interaction Process categories, then, permits the

---

[6]See, for example, Barry E. Collins and Harold Guetzkow, *A Social Psychology of Group Processes for Decision-Making* (New York: John Wiley & Sons, Inc., 1964).

[7]Robert F. Bales, "A Set of Categories for the Analysis of Small Group Interaction," *American Sociological Review*, Vol. 15 (April, 1950), p. 258.

[8]*Ibid.*, pp. 259–61.

FIGURE 1

DEFINITION OF SOCIAL INTERACTION CATEGORIES

Social-emotional area: Positive reactions	1.	*Shows solidarity,* raises other's status, gives help, reward¶
	2.	*Shows tension release,* jokes, laughs, shows satisfaction‖
	3.	*Agrees,* shows passive acceptance, understands, concurs, complies§
Task area: Attempted answers	4.	*Gives suggestion,* direction, implying autonomy for other‡
	5.	*Gives opinion,* evaluation, analysis, expresses feeling, wish†
	6.	*Gives orientation,* information, repeats, clarifies, confirms*
Task area: Questions	7.	*Asks for orientation,* information, repeats, clarifies, confirms*
	8.	*Asks for opinion,* evaluation, analysis, expression of feeling†
	9.	*Asks for suggestion,* direction, possible ways of action‡
Social-emotional area: Negative reactions	10.	*Disagrees,* shows passive rejection, formality, withholds help§
	11.	*Shows tension,* asks for help, withdraws out of field‖
	12.	*Shows antagonism,* deflates other's status, defends or asserts self¶

*Problems of orientation.
†Problems of evaluation.
‡Problems of control.
§Problems of decision.
‖Problems of tension-management.
¶Problems of integration.
    Source: Robert F. Bales, "A Set of Categories for the Analysis of Small Group Interaction," *American Sociological Review,* April, 1950, p. 258.

classification of individual acts, but also maintains these acts in a system of coding that retains the underlying problem-solving context for the interaction. This analytical scheme was adopted and forms the basis for subsequent findings.

THE STUDY

A multidimensional research approach—involving both direct observation of retail appliance customers and salesmen, and consumer survey—was required to carry out the study objectives. Because the methodology employed is complex, a brief review of the techniques used may be helpful in understanding and interpreting specific findings.

STUDY'S DESIGN AND SETTING

Research operations in the study started on the retail sales floor and ended with consumer survey work. First, selected appliance shoppers were identified as they entered retail appliance stores. Second, provision was made to observe and record the exchange between customer and salesman while the customer was on the floor. Prior to the time that the customer exited the store, he was given the opportunity to win a door prize. The customer's name, address and phone number were secured in this fashion.

The second phase of the data gathering involved two waves of follow-up interviews with the appliance customers identified in the stores. Within three days after the customer had been observed shopping, he was contacted to determine: (a) whether or not he had purchased a major appliance; (b) His intentions to purchase an appliance; and (c) The extent of deliberation and shopping associated with the purchase or potential purchase. All customers who had not purchased by the time of the first interview were reinterviewed in approximately two weeks. In this terminal interview, it was determined whether the customer had purchased since the first interview, and whether he had conducted additional shopping during that period.

Customers included in the study came from eleven appliance stores, located in seven midwestern metropolitan areas. Three types of appliance floors were included in the study. They were: (a) Department store major appliance departments; (b) The multi-line appliance store, that is, the appliance store that handled more than one major full line brand; and (c) The brand specialist, or retailer that handled the full line of only one major appliance manufacturer. A total of fourteen salesmen were included in the study, and study observations are based on a sample of each of these salesman's customers over a period of time.

RESPONDENT SELECTION

Fifteen of each salesman's customers, or a total of 210 appliance shoppers, were included in the study. Participating customers were selected systematically at store entry. As the customer was not aware of his participation in the study at this time, observations were obtained for every customer selected. To further avoid systematic bias, salesmen were given no latitude to select customers to be included. Consequently, every selected shopper, no matter how poor a prospect he appeared to be, was covered in the analysis. Specific exclusions in the selection process were made for service calls—where there was no potential for a sale—and for customers shopping appliances tagged at less than $100. Both brown goods (electronics) and white goods (kitchen appliances) were included in the study in approximately equal proportions.

MEASUREMENT OF INTERACTION

The most critical part of the study involved the record of customer–salesman interaction. This was accomplished by equipping the salesman with a wireless microphone, a combination of microphone and miniature FM transmitter. This device was carried by the salesman in a convenient pocket. The transaction was picked up on a remote FM receiver and tape recorded for later analysis. This aural record of the transaction was supplemented by visual observations made by one member of the research team. From a distance this observer systematically timed and noted physical actions or gestures, facial expression, and other events that would not be identifiable from the taped record. These observations were later synchronized with the taped record, and this evidence of interaction was analyzed using Interaction Process Analysis.

CUSTOMER–SALESMAN INTERACTION

Appliance shoppers, no matter how disinterested they appeared to be in immediate purchase, by an overwhelming majority had definite intentions to purchase. Over 53 percent of the 210 customer subjects indicated definite plans to purchase an appliance and could articulate that they intended to carry out that decision soon. An additional 35 percent of all respondents indicated definite plans to purchase accompanied by some uncertainty as to the time of purchase. Further, the majority of these high intentions shoppers quickly implemented their intentions to purchase. A total of 132 or 63 percent of all appliance shoppers completed their major appliance purchase either at the time they were observed on the retail floor or within two weeks of that time. These findings help validate the earlier assumption that the decision to purchase is generally concluded by the time serious shopping starts, and pinpoints a customer group, homogeneous in intentions, that can serve as a basis for accumulating interaction data. Accordingly, subsequent data on interaction are confined to the transactions associated with the 132 respondents who completed purchase.

SOME PARAMETERS OF APPLIANCE TRANSACTIONS

The average retail appliance transaction observed lasted approximately 23 minutes from the point of customer–salesman contact to the point where the interaction was either terminated or a sale had been consummated. As one might expect, the length of time of transactions differed markedly in individual cases, and ranged from approximately one minute to nearly two hours. A distribution of lengths of time for transactions appears in Table 1. Noteworthy is the 75 percent of all transactions that lasted less than 30 minutes. Potential for true dyad

TABLE 1
TEMPORAL LENGTH OF RETAIL APPLIANCE
CUSTOMER–SALESMAN TRANSACTIONS

Length of Time from Customer–Salesman Contact to Close or Termination of Transaction	Percent of Transactions
0–7.5 minutes	17.4
7.6–15.0 minutes	31.1
15.1–30.0 minutes	26.5
Over 30.0 minutes	25.0
All Transactions°	100.0

°N = 132.

information can, of course, not be based merely on time alone; however, the findings would seem to support the proposition that true group formation in this kind of personal selling situation is highly tenuous, if not unlikely.

The 132 instances of customer–salesman interaction produced a total of over 26,000 interaction acts, with a mean number of acts per transaction of 198. Again, as in the case of the lengths of transactions, there was high dispersion, and in individual cases the total number of acts per transaction was as low as seven and as high as 920. While these data indicate enormous variability, a more stable pattern develops when the effect of length of transaction is netted out, and gross interaction is converted into interaction per minute. The distribution of interaction rates appears in Table 2. It is apparent that transactions show a much

TABLE 2
RATE OF CUSTOMER–SALESMAN INTERACTION
DURING RETAIL APPLIANCE TRANSACTIONS

Interaction Acts per Minute	Percent of Interactions
0–6.0/ minute	12.1
6.1–11.0/ minute	50.8
11.1–16.0/ minute	30.3
Over 16.0/ minute	6.8
All Transactions°	100.0

°N = 132.

higher degree of consistency than would be suggested by either time spent in the transaction or the gross transaction alone. Over 50 percent of all transactions generated rates of between six and eleven acts per minute, and the mean interaction rate for all transactions was approximately ten acts per minute. Bales has ordinarily recorded interaction rates of from 15 to 20 acts per minute in problem-solving groups, although he is dealing with substantially different groups.[9]

CONTENT OF CUSTOMER–SALESMAN INTERACTION

Table 3 presents the pattern of customer–salesman interaction, showing the mean number of acts per transaction and percent distribution of acts across each of the interaction categories. Category 6, gives

TABLE 3
COMPOSITION OF RETAIL APPLIANCE CUSTOMER–
SALESMAN SOCIAL INTERACTION

Interaction Process Categories		Mean Number of Acts per Transaction	Percent Distri- bution
Social-emotional area: Positive reactions	1. Shows solidarity	.08	.04
	2. Shows tension release	5.64	2.84
	3. Agrees	7.60	3.83
Task area: Attempted answers	4. Gives suggestion	4.07	2.05
	5. Gives opinion	74.56	37.61
	6. Gives orientation	76.74	38.71
Task area: Questions	7. Asks for orientation	22.84	11.52
	8. Asks for opinion	6.15	3.10
	9. Asks for suggestion	.24	.12
Social-emotional Area: Negative reactions	10. Disagrees	.31	.16
	11. Shows tension	.01	.01
	12. Shows antagonism	.02	.01
All Transactions°		198.26	100.00

°The distributions encompass 26,170 "acts" in 132 customer-salesman encounters.

orientation, was the most frequent type of exchange recorded, representing on the average over 38 percent of total interaction acts. Following closely in terms of volume of acts is Category 5, gives opinion, and together these two categories of acts account for, on the average, over 75 percent of the total interaction between customer and salesman. These categories of interaction denote attempted answers, specifically, attempts to define problems or issues and to evaluate problems or issues. Thus, three quarters of total customer–salesman interaction was concentrated on efforts to simply lay the groundwork for effective communication.

Low volumes of acts in the functional problem areas of control and decision should not be construed as indicating a lack of importance, for despite low frequency of occurrence, these acts become instrumental in predicting the outcome of the transaction.

Some preliminary evaluation of the problem-solving hypothesis is

[9]Robert F. Bales, "Task Roles and Social Roles in Problem-Solving Groups," in Eleanor E. Maccoby, Theodore M. Newcomb, and Eugene L. Hartley (eds.), *Readings in Social Psychology* (New York: Holt, Rinehart & Winston, Inc., 1958), p. 438.

possible at this point by comparing the pattern of customer–salesman interaction with the pattern of interaction that Bales has recorded for groups facing a standard task.[10] Despite the differences in setting, amount of control over the situation, and kind of task facing the participants, it might be argued that if the sales situation does represent problem-solving, the common thread of a decision process running through even such diverse situations would generate at least roughly comparable kinds of behavior. In fact, the parallel between findings recorded by Bales and the present study is encouraging. There are, of course, differences in the percentage concentrations in specific categories, but the structural patterns of interaction are congruent. Customer–salesman interaction was characterized by lower proportions of categories 3 and 10 (involving problems of decision), lower proportions of categories 4 and 9 (involving problems of control), and a higher proportion of requests for information than has generally been recorded by Bales.

CUSTOMER AND SALESMAN INTERACTION ROLES

The overall pattern of interaction, while useful, fails to provide any insight about the roles played by customer and salesman. Consequently, a further stage of analysis was initiated to trace the origin of interaction, and the source of control of interaction. The origin of interaction is a measurable property of customer–salesman behavior, and was evaluated by separately analyzing the customer and salesman interaction acts. Questions of control, however, constitute a separate problem, in that here an attempt is being made to infer the source of power over the course of interaction. This latter question was tested through the use of analysis of variance. Essentially, the total variation of each interaction category across the customers of each salesman was compared with the variation among salesmen's customer groups. If a particular variable was consistent for all transactions of a given salesman, but varied greatly among salesmen, the inference would be that this variable was subject to control by the salesman. On the other hand, if a given variable fluctuated widely for each salesman's customers, but there were few differences in the behavior of that variable averaged and compared across salesmen, the variable would appear to be controlled by the customer. Note that this analysis does not imply that either party consciously exercises his power in controlling the course of interaction.

CUSTOMER–SALESMAN INTERACTION SEGMENTATION

Comparisons of the interaction contributions of customer and salesman appear in Table 4. Data reflect the ratios of customer to salesman acts in each transaction averaged across all transactions. In general, the customer performed half as many interaction acts as the salesman.

[10] *Loc. cit.*

TABLE 4
RELATIVE CONTRIBUTIONS OF CUSTOMER AND
SALESMAN TO INTERACTION IN THE TRANSACTION

Interaction Process Categories	Mean of Ratios of Customer to Salesman Acts (Number of Ratios Equals 132 for Each Category Set)
Total Interaction Acts	.56
Task area:	
Attempted answers . . . . (Categories 4 to 6)	.36
Questions . . . . (Categories 7 to 9)	3.86
Social-emotional area:	
Positive reactions . . . . (Categories 1 to 3)	1.41
Negative reactions . . . . (Categories 10 to 12)	.12

However, there is wide variation in the customer to salesman ratios across the interaction categories. As the table indicates, attempted answers were primarily the prerogative of the salesman, while in the question categories customer acts outnumbered salesman acts nearly four to one. One jarring finding concerned customers' and salesmen's contributions to the social-emotional area. Customers were more frequently responsible for positive reactions (embracing categories 1 to 3), while salesmen were almost uniquely responsible for disagreement, tension, and antagonism in the transaction.

SOURCES OF CONTROL OF INTERACTION

A second test, to determine the inferred source of control over interaction, was applied to two dimensions of total interaction—the relative contributions of each interaction category and the ratio of customer to salesman participation by interaction category. The analysis of relative contributions of each interaction category to total interaction appears in Table 5. Without exception, salesmen acting in concert with their selling environment appear to control customer–salesman interaction. Whether he is aware of it or not, by virtue of his patterning of interaction and his response to customer interaction, the salesman does exercise the power to shape the content of interaction.

If it would appear that the influence of salesmen is almost complete, the analysis appearing in Table 6 will help to build a more balanced perspective. This table contains the products of a comparable analysis applied to the relative contributions of customer and salesman to the transaction by interaction process category. The salesman is truly in control of total interaction, as evidenced by the significant F Ratio in the

TABLE 5
ANALYSIS OF VARIANCE OF CUSTOMER–SALESMAN
INTERACTION ACROSS SALESMEN

Variable: Percent Contribution of Interaction Process Category to Total Interaction	F Ratio	Inferred Source of Control of Relative Occurrence of Interaction Category
Categories 1 to 3: Shows solidarity; shows tension release; and agrees	3.62°	Salesman
Category 4: Gives suggestion	3.43°	Salesman
Category 5: Gives opinion	7.38°	Salesman
Category 6: Gives orientation	3.26°	Salesman
Category 7: Asks for orientation	4.29°	Salesman
Category 8: Asks for opinion	3.67°	Salesman
Category 9: Asks for suggestion	3.29°	Salesman
Categories 10 to 12: Disagrees; shows tension; and shows antagonism	3.05†	Salesman

°Significant at .01.
†Significant at .05.

TABLE 6
ANALYSIS OF VARIANCE OF RELATIVE CUSTOMER TO
SALESMAN INTERACTION CONTRIBUTIONS ACROSS SALESMEN

Variable: Ratio of Customer to Salesman Contributions of Interaction Process Categories	F Ratio	Inferred Source of Control of Ratio of Customer to Salesman Interaction
Total Interaction Acts	3.81°	Salesman
Task area:		
Attempted answers (Categories 4 to 6)	1.56	Customer
Questions (Categories 7 to 9)	2.29†	Salesman
Social-emotional area:		
Positive reactions (Categories 1 to 3)	1.70	Customer
Negative reactions (Categories 10 to 12)	1.01	Customer

°Significant at .01.
†Just significant at .05.

case of customer to salesman total interaction. However, when interaction is examined by category it is revealed that the customer is influential in determining the parties' relative contributions in the case of attempted answers, positive social-emotional reactions, and negative social-emotional reactions. Conversely, the salesman appears to hold the key to the relative contributions made by both parties to the question categories.

Additional insight is provided if one compares the findings in Tables 4 and 6. It will be recalled that Table 4 shows the relative contributions of interaction by customer and salesman, while Table 6 supplies inferences as to the source of influence. The salesman is the major contributor to interaction and also the source of influence in affecting total interaction. In contrast, attempted answers, representing possible problem-solving attempts, are contributed most heavily by the salesman, but as evidenced by Table 6, can be inferred to be controlled by the customer. Conversely, the question categories are contributed heavily by the customer, yet appear to be influenced predominantly by the salesman. While this evidence is hardly conclusive it is exciting. In this pattern of reciprocal question and answer control there is a suggestion of a true problem-solving process in operation.

INTERACTION DETERMINANTS OF
SUCCESSFUL TRANSACTIONS

Thus far, the data presented have served to clarify the structure of customer–salesman interaction in the appliance transaction and portray the roles played by customer and salesman in contributing and influencing interaction. Some indication of the hypothesized problem-solving orientation has appeared, but this evidence is, of course, merely suggestive. Additionally, there is no indication from the foregoing data that the interaction is in any definitive way related to some success criterion. Consequently, a more discrete test was conducted, relating interaction to transactional outcomes. The basis for such a test exists in the potential discrepancies between interaction in transactions where purchase occurred at the time customer and salesman were observed, as opposed to transactions where purchase occurred at a later time and not necessarily in the same store. Out of the 132 customers who had purchased within two weeks of the time observed, 58 of these transactions were closed at the time the shopper was observed on the floor.

INTERACTION COMPONENT PREDICTORS

Mean interaction acts per transaction for transactions producing spontaneous purchase and transactions not closed were virtually identical. However, significant differences appeared in the structure of interaction. Table 7 presents the ratios of the mean percents of acts by category for transactions closed at the time observed to the mean percents of acts for transactions that were not closed. Significant differences occurred in two categories, category 4 (attempted answers in the form of suggestions) and category 8 (requests for opinions). More importantly, the

TABLE 7
DIFFERENCES IN THE COMPOSITION OF CUSTOMER–SALESMAN
INTERACTION ASSOCIATED WITH CUSTOMERS PURCHASING AT TIME
OBSERVED VERSUS CUSTOMERS PURCHASING LATER

Interaction Process Category	*Ratio, Mean Percent of Acts for Transactions Closed at Time Observed to Mean Percent of Acts for Transactions Not Closed*
Categories 1 to 3: Shows solidarity; shows tension release; and agrees	.96
Category 4: Gives suggestion	1.97°
Category 5: Gives opinion	.98
Category 6: Gives orientation	.99
Category 7: Asks for orientation	.96
Category 8: Asks for opinion	1.28†
Category 9: Asks for suggestion	1.33
Categories 10 to 12: Disagrees; shows tension; and shows antagonism	.80

°Difference significant at .02.
†Difference significant at .09.

categories that registered significant differences are the evaluation and control categories.

Another significant indicator of the successful transaction, not contained explicitly in Table 7, was the relationship between customer and salesman contributions of task-question acts; successful transactions were likely to involve a significantly higher proportion of instances where the ratios of customer to salesman task-question acts were low. Interpreting this, the lower the ratio the greater the contribution of the salesman to the task-question categories. Task-question categories are customer contributed; consequently, a smaller ratio means that the salesman has participated more heavily in asking for information, asking for opinions, and asking for suggestions. Overall, then, interaction in that group of transactions associated with spontaneous purchase was marked by significantly higher rates of offerings of attempted solutions, accompanied by significantly greater amounts of search for evaluation (attempts to determine what attitude should be taken toward the situations represented in the transaction).

THE TIME PATH TO PURCHASE

Significant differences in interaction between the spontaneous purchase group and the group representing transactions that were not closed, while consistent and seemingly meaningful, were not great in number. There is, of course, a chance—given that problem-solving does constitute a meaningful explanation for transactional behavior—that differences between the two groups could have been cancelled out over the time path of the transaction. A final stage of analysis—involving an examination of the longitudinal change in components of interaction during the transaction—served a dual purpose, supplying clarification of the differences between the two purchase groups and also providing a more definitive test of the problem-solving hypothesis. Analysis of change during the transaction were conducted in the following fashion. Interaction associated with each transaction was first divided into thirds on the basis of total number of interaction acts. The composition of interaction by category was then reconstructed.

LONGITUDINAL CHANGE IN INTERACTION COMPONENTS

Table 8 presents the pattern of longitudinal change in the components of customer–salesman interaction during the transaction. Using the proportion of interaction acts in each category during the first third of the transaction as a base, the index values for the second third and last third of the transaction were calculated. Viewing Table 8 and the index values for transactions that were closed at the time they were observed, a pattern of movement toward purchase appears to emerge. Problems of

TABLE 8
PATTERN OF LONGITUDINAL CHANGE IN THE COMPONENTS OF
CUSTOMER–SALESMAN INTERACTION DURING THE TRANSACTION

Interaction Process Category	Index of Change First Third Acts = 100		
	First Third	Second Third	Last Third
Transactions closed at time observed:			
Categories 1 to 3: Shows solidarity; shows tension; agrees	100	127	165
Category 4: Gives suggestion	100	156	346
Category 5: Gives opinion	100	107	118
Category 6: Gives orientation	100	89	74
Category 7: Asks for orientation	100	100	85
Category 8: Asks for opinion	100	107	124
Category 9: Asks for suggestion	100	137	262
Categories 10 to 12: Disagrees; shows tension; shows antagonism	100	72	45
Transactions not closed:			
Categories 1 to 3: Shows solidarity; shows tension; agrees	100	116	165
Category 4: Gives suggestion	100	142	262
Category 5: Gives opinion	100	117	113
Category 6: Gives orientation	100	85	91
Category 7: Asks for orientation	100	99	68
Category 8: Asks for opinion	100	119	68
Category 9: Asks for suggestion	100	137	62
Categories 10 to 12: Disagrees; shows tension; shows antagonism	100	225	575

orientation (problem definition) decline as the transaction moves toward a conclusion. The evaluative and control areas experienced rather sharp increases in acts. Finally, there was a noticeable increase in positive social-emotional content as the transaction moved toward a conclusion, accompanied by a parallel decline in the amounts of negative social-emotional interaction.

In contrast, in transactions that were not closed somewhat different patterns of change emerged. Categories 8 and 9, representing search for solutions, decline sharply in the last third of the transaction, despite the fact that attempted solutions increase through the last third of the transaction, although not as much as in transactions that resulted in spontaneous purchase. Transactions that were not closed also experienced substantial increases in the amount of disagreement, tension and antagonism, although interestingly, this is accompanied by a seemingly paradoxical increase in positive social-emotional acts. This latter finding may be explained in part by customers' efforts to detach themselves from the transaction, in effect, to "cool-out" the salesman but to do so amicably. Another interesting feature of transactions that were not closed was an indication of regression in problem-solving attempts beginning in the second third of the transaction. Attempts to supply evaluation as manifested by category 5 decline from the second third to the last third of the transaction, while attempts to supply orientation, as evidenced by category 6, actually show a modest increase.

CONCLUSIONS

Taken together, results from this study seem uniformly consonant with a problem-solving conceptualization of selling behavior in major appliance transactions. Longitudinal changes in interaction during successful transactions show discernible parallels with descriptions by Bales of interaction in groups created specifically for purposes of generating problem-solving behavior. Indeed, one abstract by Bales of the act sequencing observed in his groups could have been applied almost without modification to the pattern of change in interaction in successful customer–salesman transactions.[11]

On a more cautious note, it is highly unlikely that problem-solving as a process constitutes a sufficient explanation for successful outcomes in these transactions. Full study findings demonstrated to be significant indicators of purchase included, in addition to interaction, specific customer shopping behaviors and elements of a formal bargaining process. It would also be presumptuous to rule out the possibility that more durable psychological traits of customer and salesman are affective, operating through the mediating processes of social interaction and communication.

[11]Robert F. Bales, "How People Interact in Conferences," *Scientific American*, Vol. CXCII (March, 1955), pp. 31–35.

17. A DECISION-PROCESS APPROACH TO IMPULSE PURCHASING*

David T. Kollat

Although "impulse" or "unplanned" purchasing actually has a variety of meanings, the term is probably most commonly used to refer to purchases that were not anticipated or planned before the shopper entered a retailing establishment.[1] While unplanned purchasing is not confined to any product or retail setting, it is probably most often used in the context of food purchasing decisions.[2] The importance of unplanned purchasing in this setting is "documented" by the latest du Pont study which indicates that 50 percent of the purchases in food supermarkets are transacted on an unplanned basis.[3]

Several studies have investigated unplanned purchasing in food supermarkets. The studies sponsored by du Pont have measured the overall rate of unplanned purchasing and have shown how different types of products are affected by this type of behavior.[4] Other studies have investigated how product location,[5] shelf space,[6] display location,[7] and other store

*From *Science, Technology, and Marketing,* American Marketing Association, September, 1966, pp. 626–39.

The author wishes to express his deep appreciation to Dr. Ronald P. Willett, Associate Professor of Marketing, Indiana University, for the invaluable role that he played in all phases of this study.

[1]*Consumer Buying Habits Studies,* E. I. du Pont de Nemours and Company, 1945, 1949, 1954, 1959, 1965, pp. 1–6. For other definitions of unplanned purchasing, see James D. Schaffer, "The Influence of Impulse Buying or In-the-Store Decisions on Consumers' Food Purchases," Journal Paper No. 2591 from the Michigan Agricultural Experimental Station, pp. 317–24; Vernon T. Clover, "Relative Importance of Impulse Buying in Retail Stores," *Journal of Marketing,* Vol. XV (July, 1950), pp. 66–70; Hawkins Stern, "The Significance of Impulse Buying Today," *Journal of Marketing,* Vol. XXVI (April, 1962), pp. 59–62; Saul Nesbitt, "Today's Housewives Plan Menus as They Shop," Nesbitt Associates Release, 1959, pp. 2–3.

[2]For studies of unplanned purchasing in other retail settings, see: *Drugstore Brand Switching and Impulse Buying* (New York: Point-of-Purchase Advertising Institute, 1963); *Package Store Brand Switching and Impulse Buying* (New York: Point-of-Purchase Advertising Institute, 1963); C. John West, "Results of Two Years of Study into Impulse Buying," *Journal of Marketing,* Vol. XV (January, 1951), pp. 362–63.

[3]*Consumer Buying Habits Studies, op. cit.,* pp. 3–4.

[4]*Ibid.*

[5]Lawrence W. Patterson, *In-Store Traffic Flow* (New York: Point-of-Purchase Advertising Institute, 1963).

[6]Keith Cox, "The Responsiveness of Food Sales to Shelf-Space Changes in Supermarkets," *Journal of Marketing Research* (May, 1964), pp. 63–67.

[7]Robert F. Kelly, "An Evaluation of Selected Variables of End Display Effectiveness" (Unpublished doctoral dissertation, Harvard University, Boston, 1965); *A First Study of the Totality of Impact of Point-of-Purchase Materials on Plus Sales in Supermarkets* (New York: Point-of-Purchase Advertising Institute, 1959).

layout characteristics[8] affect unplanned purchasing. Other investigations purport to have identified and measured various "reasons" for unplanned purchasing[9] while another has hypothesized circumstances which appear to be associated with the occurrence of the behavior.[10]

These studies are similar in that they have all been primarily concerned with the influence of various in-store strategies—product location, shelf location, end-aisle displays—on the rate of unplanned purchasing. Despite the fact that these strategies influence unplanned purchasing through their effects on shoppers, past studies have not explicitly investigated customer differences in unplanned purchasing behavior.[11]

The present study takes a customer-oriented approach to unplanned purchasing. The basic objectives were: (1) to identify the decision-processes involved in unplanned purchasing and determine the ways in which these processes differ from those associated with other types and degrees of planning; and (2) to determine whether customers differ in their susceptibility to unplanned purchasing, and, if so, to ascertain what customer characteristics are associated with differential susceptibility to this type of behavior.

METHODOLOGY

Unplanned Purchasing Defined

An unplanned purchase is defined here as one of the planning categories that results from a comparison of purchase intentions and actual behavior. A purchase was classified as *unplanned* if the shopper did not indicate that she planned to purchase the product before she did her shopping. The other planning categories used include: (1) *Specifically Planned* (a specific product and brand are purchased as planned); (2) *Generally Planned* (a need is recognized before shopping but the choice of a specific product and brand are made in the store); and (3) *Brand Substitution* (the brand purchased differs from the one that was planned).[12]

Research Design

This investigation was a field study rather than a survey. That is, the present study was more concerned with a comprehensive account of the processes under investigation than it was with their typicality in a larger

[8]C. John West, *loc. cit.*, p. 363; and Vernon T. Clover, *loc. cit.*, p. 67.

[9]*One on the Aisle* (New York: Life Marketing Laboratory, undated and unnumbered manuscript).

[10]Hawkins Stern, *loc. cit.*, p. 61.

[11]For the exceptions to this statement, see *How People Shop for Food* (New York: Market Research Corporation of America, undated and unnumbered manuscript); *Impulse Buying* (Philadelphia: the Curtis Publishing Company Research Department, February, 1952); *One on the Aisle, loc. cit.*, and James D. Schaffer, *loc. cit.*, pp. 320–21.

[12]This definition of planning categories is essentially the same as those used in the du Pont studies. See *Consumer Buying Habits Studies, op. cit.*, p. 2.

universe.[13] The research plan consisted of two phases: (1) Store interviewing; and (2) Home interviewing.

Store interviewing. The objective of this phase was to identify the rate of customer unplanned purchasing. Using a 4 x 4 latin square design, eight stores of a national supermarket chain were paired into four groups and randomly assigned to treatments A through D. Within each cell, the stores were randomly assigned for either morning or afternoon-evening interviewing. Interviews were conducted over a four-week period on Fridays, Saturdays, Sundays, and either Tuesdays or Wednesdays with the occurrence of the latter two days being randomly determined.

Employing a *Pretest-Posttest Control Group Design,* sampling fractions were used both to identify eligible shopping parties and to assign them to experimental and control groups.[14] Shoppers in the experimental group were asked what they intended to buy and were not told that their actual purchases would be checked. Those shoppers comprising the control group were not queried about their purchase plans. Customers in both groups then did their shopping and their actual purchases were recorded. Sample size was 596 for the experimental group and 196 for the control group. A comparison of purchase plans with actual purchases permits the identification of the appropriate planning category.

Home interviewing. This phase of the study was necessary in order to reconstruct the decision-processes associated with unplanned purchasing. Followup interviews were conducted within two days with 196 of the original 596 shopping parties.

Writers have suggested several formal properties of decisions that are likely to influence the configuration of decision-making.[15] These characteristics were used to select products that seemed most likely to involve differential decision-making processes. The product categories chosen were: (1) Soft drinks; (2) Selected grocery products including jams, jellies, spreads, sauces, and dressings; (3) Paper products including napkins, towels, and tissues; and (4) Laundry and dishwashing products.

---

[13]For a discussion of the differences between a field study and a survey, see Leon Festinger and Daniel Katz (eds.), *Research Methods in the Behavioral Sciences* (New York: Holt, Rinehart & Winston, 1953), chap. 2.

[14]Seymour Banks, *Experimentation in Marketing* (New York: McGraw-Hill Book Co., Inc., 1965), p. 31. A comparison of experimental and control group respondents revealed that the process of asking respondents what they planned to purchase did not affect the amount of money spent in the store or the number of different products purchased and had little or no effect on the mixture of products that the customer purchased. (Independent at the .05 level of significance—chi-square and correlation coefficients.)

[15]See Donald H. Granbois, "The Role of Communication in the Family Decision-Making Process," in Stephen A. Greyser (ed.), *Toward Scientific Marketing* (Chicago: American Marketing Association, 1963), p. 50; Orville Brim, *et al., Personality and Decision-Processes* (Stanford: Stanford University Press, 1963), pp. 14–17; Louis P. Bucklin, "Retail Strategy and the Classification of Consumer Goods," *Journal of Marketing,* Vol. XXVII (January, 1963), pp. 50–55; and Hawkins Stern, *op. cit.,* p. 61.

Decision-process questions were administered to those respondents that purchased a product in these categories.

FINDINGS—DECISION-PROCESSES INVOLVED IN UNPLANNED PURCHASING

Decision-making has typically been studied by dividing the process into various phases or steps.[16] The phase formulation used here consists of four steps linked in a sequence: (1) Problem identification; (2) Information seeking; (3) Alternative evaluation; and (4) Decision. This phase formulation is used to describe the anatomy of an unplanned purchase.

The discussion of decision-processes is divided into two parts. The first part will describe the general nature of decision-making involved in grocery purchasing. The question of how unplanned purchase decision-making differs from the decision processes associated with other types and degrees of planning will be explored in the second part.

THE GENERAL NATURE OF GROCERY PURCHASING DECISION-MAKING

Problem identification.   Past studies of consumption decision-making have typically been couched in the context of durable goods purchasing. These studies have rather consistently documented the roles of changing family circumstances, changing environmental conditions, and dissatisfaction with previously used problem solutions as problem identification cues.[17]

The types of products at issue here, however, have a drastically different pattern of consumption. The short life of these products, coupled with the continuity of the underlying needs, results in a high frequency of purchase. Shoppers typically alternate their purchases between two or three brands of the products. They have usually known about all of these brands for several years and have been purchasing them for usually a year or more.

One result of this pattern of consumption is that problem identification usually results from the depletion of a product that has only recently been purchased. In-store problem identification becomes a combination of personal searching for the product and/or seeing the product—usually

---

[16]See, for example, Robert M. Gagne, "Problem Solving and Thinking," in R. Farsworth and Q. McNeman (eds.), *Annual Review of Psychology* (Palo Alto: Annual Reviews, 1959), pp. 147–73; James G. March and Herbert A. Simon, *Organizations* (New York: John Wiley & Sons, 1963).

[17]See, for example, George Katona and Eva Mueller, "A Study of Purchase Decisions," in Lincoln Clark (ed.), *The Dynamics of Consumer Reactions* (New York: New York University Press, 1955); pp. 30–88; Ruby T. Norris, "Processes and Objectives of House Purchasing in the New London Area," in *The Dynamics of Consumer Reactions, op cit.*, pp. 25–50; William T. Kelly, "How Buyers Shop for a New Home," *The Appraisal Journal*, Vol. XXV (1957), pp. 209–14; and Donald H. Granbois, *op. cit.*, p. 45.

in its regular location—and being reminded of the need to remedy the state of depletion and/or to store-up for future needs.

Information seeking. Shoppers typically engage in a minimal amount of information seeking. Only 40 percent of the respondents could recall seeing any recent advertisements featuring either the brand that they purchased or other brands of the product. Further, only 20 percent of the shoppers had recently discussed the brand that they purchased with other persons.

The amount of exposure to in-store sources of information is even less. Only 4 percent of the respondents recalled obtaining any information from product displays, and less than 7 percent of the shoppers interviewed said that they read or examined the package or container of either the brand that they purchased or other brands of the product. Finally, less than 1 percent of the respondents talked to anyone in the store about the brand that they purchased.

Some observers have suggested that many supermarket purchases are triggered by the recall of previously obtained information.[18] In the present study, 87 percent of the respondents said that while they were shopping they did not remember any information that they had recently seen or heard about either the brand that they purchased or other brands of the product. Thus, although some recall of previously obtained information occurs, the frequency of occurrence is perhaps not as great as some have suggested.

Finally, a fairly large percentage of those respondents who were exposed to various information sources indicated that the experience produced "no useful information." Overall, then, there is typically only a minimal amount of exposure to both out-of-store and in-store information sources.

Alternative evaluation. Approximately 82 percent of the respondents said that they considered only one brand before they made a decision. This low level of brand evaluation is particularly intriguing in view of the fact that most shoppers have regularly purchased several brands of the product. Shoppers appear to display a need for variety, purchasing one brand for a period of time, switching to another brand for a period of time, and then perhaps switching back to the first brand. Thus, there is a pronounced tendency for shoppers to be loyal to a single brand in the short run and loyal to several brands in the long run.

UNPLANNED PURCHASING DECISION-MAKING

The configuration of decision-making described above was termed "general" because it represents only a brief summary of the dimensions of decision-making that were actually investigated. Figure 1 contains an itemization of all of the facets of decision-making that were included in

---

[18]See, for example, Hawkins Stern, *loc. cit.*, pp. 59–62.

FIGURE 1

DIMENSIONS OF DECISION-MAKING THAT DO NOT DIFFERENTIATE AN
UNPLANNED PURCHASE FROM PURCHASES INVOLVING OTHER TYPES
AND DEGREES OF PLANNING

1. Whether the product has been purchased before.
2. Whether the brand has been purchased before.
3. Length of time the brand has been purchased.
4. The frequency with which the product has been purchased.
5. Number of brands that have regularly been purchased.
6. Family members who use the product.
7. Whether any family member insists that a particular brand be purchased.
8. Family members who insist the brand be purchased.
9. What happened in the store that caused the brand to be first noticed.
10. Family member that first noticed the brand.
11. Whether advertisements featuring the brand or other brands had recently been seen.
12. What useful information, if any, was obtained from these advertisements.
13. Whether the product or brand had been recently mentioned during conversation with other people. Who are these people?
14. What useful information, if any, was obtained from these conversations.
15. Whether the shopper saw any displays for the brand purchased and/or other brands.
16. Whether product packages or containers were read or examined.
17. What useful information, if any, was obtained from product packages or containers.
18. Whether shopper talked with anyone in the store about the brand purchased or other brands of the product.
19. Whether while in the store the shopper remembered any information she had recently seen or heard about the brand purchased and/or other brands.
20. What happened that caused the shopper to remember this information.
21. Number of brands considered before the purchase decision.
22. Length of time that the purchase could have been postponed.

Sample size: 196. These dimensions of decision-making fail to differentiate an unplanned purchase from other categories of planning at the .05 level of significance (chi-square).

the study. In order to investigate the degree to which unplanned purchasing decision-making differs from that associated with other types and degrees of planning, the decision-making dimensions listed in Figure 1 were cross-classified by planning category.

The analysis reveals that unplanned purchasing decision-making does not differ significantly from the decision-making behavior associated with other types of purchases. That is, none of the dimensions of decision-making differentiates an unplanned purchase from purchases involving other types and degrees of planning. Thus, in terms of decision-processes, there does not appear to be anything unique about unplanned purchasing.

These findings are perhaps not so surprising if one considers the types of purchase situations represented by unplanned purchases. Using an abbreviated version of Alderson's classification of purchase situations,[19] respondents were asked to indicate the appropriate purchase situation category for the products that they purchased on an unplanned basis.

---

[19]Wroe Alderson, *Marketing Behavior and Executive Action* (Homewood, Ill.: Richard D. Irwin, Inc., 1957).

As Table 1 indicates, 97 percent of the unplanned purchases involved products that had been purchased before. Of those unplanned purchases represented by products that had been purchased before, nearly 64 percent were "out-of-stock-same-brand" purchases and 23 percent were "inventory-addition-same-brand" purchases. Apparently, most unplanned purchases represent routine re-stocking of the same brand or adding to an existing inventory of the brand in anticipation of future needs.

TABLE 1
UNPLANNED PURCHASES CROSS CLASSIFIED BY
TYPE OF PURCHASE SITUATION

Type of Purchase Situations	Unplanned Purchases	
	Number of Purchases	Percent of Purchases
Purchased Before:		
Out-of-stock; same brand	813	63.6
Out-of-stock; different brand	78	6.1
Inventory-addition; same brand	297	23.2
Inventory-addition; different brand	52	4.1
Not Purchased Before	39	3.0
Total	1,279	100.0

FINDINGS—CORRELATES OF CUSTOMER UNPLANNED PURCHASING BEHAVIOR

Thus far the analysis has been concerned with a grocery purchase decision in general and an unplanned purchase decision in particular. The analysis now shifts to focus on the shopper's overall rate of unplanned purchasing. The dependent variable becomes the percentage of purchases that were unplanned.[20]

The average shopper in this study purchased 50.5 percent of her products on an unplanned basis. Thus, the incidence of unplanned purchasing is greater than all of the other planning categories combined. The mean percentage of "specifically planned" purchases is only 25.9 percent while the highest mean for any of the remaining planning categories is a mere 8.2 percent.

Shoppers differ considerably in their susceptibility to unplanned purchasing. The percentage of customer unplanned purchases has the maximum range of 100 percent and a standard deviation of 28.1.

A large number of variables were employed in an attempt to account for this variation in unplanned purchasing behavior. The analysis yielded three categories of variables: (1) Variables that are not related to unplanned purchasing and do not affect it; (2) Variables that are related

[20]Number of unplanned purchases divided by the total number of products purchased by the shopper.

to but do not affect unplanned purchasing; and (3) Variables that are related to and affect unplanned purchasing.

VARIABLES THAT ARE NOT ASSOCIATED WITH

CUSTOMER DIFFERENCES IN UNPLANNED PURCHASING

Figure 2 itemizes those variables that do not affect the rate of unplanned purchasing. Several economic and demographic variables, all personality variables,[21] and many food shopping characteristics, including the existence of a food budget, food coupons, and trading stamps, do not affect the percentage of purchases that shoppers transact on an unplanned basis.

FIGURE 2

VARIABLES THAT ARE NOT ASSOCIATED WITH
CUSTOMER DIFFERENCES IN UNPLANNED PURCHASING

A. *Economic and Demographic Variables**

1. Income of the household
2. Number of full-time wage earners in the household
3. Occupation of the household head
4. Formal education of the household head

B. *Personality Variables†*

1. Impulsivity
2. Dominance
3. Optimism
4. Self-confidence
5. Self-sufficiency
6. Belief in fate
7. Future time orientation
8. Desire for certainty
9. Belief in the predictability of life
10. Belief in multiple causation of events

C. *General Food Shopping Behavior Variables‡*

1. Size of shopping party
2. Existence of a food budget
3. Frequency of food budget revision
4. Role of wife in determining food budget
5. Use of food coupons
6. Use of trading stamps
7. Amount of recalled exposure to newspaper advertisements for grocery products
8. Frequency with which grocery products are discussed with others

*Sample size: 596. These variables are independent of the percentage of customer unplanned purchases at the .05 level of probability (chi-square).

†Sample size: 196. These variables are independent of the percentage of customer unplanned purchases at the .01 level of probability (both chi-square and correlation coefficients).

‡Sample size: 196. These variables are independent of the percentage of customer unplanned purchases at the .05 level of probability (chi-square).

VARIABLES THAT ARE ASSOCIATED WITH CUSTOMER DIFFERENCES

IN UNPLANNED PURCHASING BUT DO NOT AFFECT THE BEHAVIOR

Several variables are related to customer differences in unplanned purchasing only because of their relationship to another variable—the

---

[21] These personality variables have been used by Brim and were derived from French's factor analytic review of personality tests. See Orville Brim, *op. cit.*, pp. 257–59; and John W. French, *The Description of Personality Measurements in Terms of Rotated Factors* (Princeton, N.J.: Educational Testing Service, Princeton University Press, 1953).

number of different products purchased. That is, although these variables are related to customer differences in unplanned purchasing, they do not, in and of themselves, affect the behavior. Figure 3 itemizes the variables in this category. Of particular interest is the fact that the day of the week does not influence the rate of unplanned purchasing despite the fact that in-store promotional activities are more intensive on Thursday, Friday, and Saturday.

FIGURE 3

VARIABLES THAT ARE ASSOCIATED WITH
CUSTOMER DIFFERENCES IN UNPLANNED
PURCHASING BUT DO NOT AFFECT
THE BEHAVIOR

A.   *Demographic Variables*
   1. Number of people living in the household
   2. Sex of the shopper

B.   *General Food Shopping Behavior Variables*
   1. Number of shopping trips made per week
   2. Distance traveled to the store
   3. Day of week
   4. Time of day
   5. Size of store

VARIABLES THAT AFFECT UNPLANNED PURCHASING

As Figure 4 indicates, this study found only six variables that affect customer rates of unplanned purchasing. The variables and the nature of the relationships are:

1. *Grocery bill.* The percentage of unplanned purchases increases as the shopper's grocery bill increases.
2. *Number of products purchased.* The percentage of unplanned purchases increases as the number of products that the shopper purchases increases. Moreover, as the number of products purchased increases, the probability that additional purchases will be unplanned approaches certainty.
3. *Type of shopping trip.* The percentage of unplanned purchases is higher during major shopping trips than during fill-in shopping trips.
4. *Product purchase frequencies.* The more frequently the product is purchased, the lower the probability that the product will be purchased on an unplanned basis.
5. *Shopping list.* The presence of a shopping list affects the percentage of unplanned purchases when a large number of products (15 or more) are purchased—shoppers with a list purchase a smaller percentage of products on an unplanned basis. When a small number of products are purchased (less than 15), the presence of a shopping list does not affect the percentage of unplanned purchases.
6. *Number of years married.* The percentage of unplanned purchases increases as the number of years that the shopping party has been married increases.

FIGURE 4

VARIABLES THAT AFFECT THE PERCENTAGE OF
PURCHASES THAT SHOPPERS TRANSACT ON
AN UNPLANNED BASIS

A.   *Transaction Size Variables*
1. Grocery bill*
2. Number of products purchased†

B.   *Transaction Structure Variables*
1. Type of shopping trip (major or fill-in)*
2. Product purchase frequencies‡

C.   *Characteristics of the Shopping Party*
1. Presence of shopping list*
2. Number of years married*

*Sample size: 596. These variables are significantly related to the percentage of customer unplanned purchases at the .05 level of probability (chi-square).

†Sample size: 596. This variable has a linear correlation coefficient of .44 which is significantly different from zero at the .01 level of probability.

‡Sample size: 63. The linear correlation coefficient between product unplanned purchase rates and product purchase frequencies is −.60 which is significantly different from zero at the .01 level of probability.

WHAT REALLY CAUSES UNPLANNED PURCHASING?

There are at least two competing explanations for the findings of this study. The two hypotheses are, in many ways, the antithesis of one another and, as will become apparent below, they lead to conspicuously different conclusions about the nature and significance of unplanned purchasing. The two competing hypotheses are: (1) the exposure to in-store stimuli hypothesis; and (2) the customer-commitment hypothesis.

THE EXPOSURE TO IN-STORE STIMULI HYPOTHESIS

The exposure hypothesis is the traditional explanation for unplanned purchasing and it can account for the findings of this study. This hypothesis maintains that differences between purchase intentions and actual purchases are due to the effects of in-store stimuli. According to this hypothesis, customer exposure to in-store stimuli produces unplanned purchases because: (1) the shopper uses in-store stimuli to remind her of her shopping needs; that is, the shopper makes purchase decisions in the store rather than relying on a shopping list; and/or (2) in-store promotional techniques create previously unrecognized needs.

THE CUSTOMER-COMMITMENT HYPOTHESIS

Figure 5 explains how the customer-commitment hypothesis was deduced from the findings of the study. While the exposure hypothesis maintains that unplanned purchases are attributable to in-store stimuli, the customer-commitment hypothesis asserts that these purchases are attributable to incomplete measures of purchase intentions. In other words, the customer-commitment hypothesis argues that the customer is *unwilling* and/or *unable* to commit the time and cognitive resources necessary to make "measured purchase intentions" equal to "actual purchase intentions."

FIGURE 5

HOW THE CUSTOMER-COMMITMENT HYPOTHESIS ACCOUNTS FOR
CUSTOMER DIFFERENCES IN UNPLANNED PURCHASING BEHAVIOR

1. Transaction size. As the number of products to be purchased increases, it becomes more difficult and time-consuming for the shopper to give a complete roster of purchase intentions. Therefore, as transaction size increases, the divergence between actual and measured purchase intentions also increases, resulting in an increase in the percentage of unplanned purchases.
2. Type of shopping trip. Products purchased during fill-in trips usually have higher purchase frequencies and longer purchase histories than products purchased during major trips. Fill-in trips involve a smaller cognitive and time commitment so that measured purchase intentions deviate less from actual purchase intentions, thereby producing a lower rate of unplanned purchasing.
3. Frequency of purchase. Frequently purchased products have lower unplanned purchase rates because it is easier for the shopper to remember that she plans to purchase them.
4. Shopping list. A shopping list affects unplanned purchasing only when a large number of products are purchased because only then does it significantly reduce the amount of time and effort necessary to itemize purchase plans.
5. Length of marriage. Shoppers married for shorter periods may be better able to itemize purchase intentions because: (1) relatively lower incomes may force them to plan purchases to a greater extent; (2) a relatively greater degree of husband-wife interaction over grocery purchases may mean that purchase plans are more complete before the shopping trip; and (3) they may purchase a smaller number and variety of products so that it is easier to give a complete itemization of purchase plans.

The shopper may be *unwilling* to itemize her purchase intentions because she does not want to invest the amount of time and thought necessary to give the interviewer a complete roster of her purchase plans. Instead, she articulates only an incomplete itemization of what she plans to purchase, thereby satisfying the requirements of the interview without spending too much time or having to think too much.

The shopper may be *unable* to itemize her purchase plans for a variety of reasons. First, the shopper may know what she will purchase but may be unable to articulate these purchase intentions because of the characteristics of the interview. The methodology used in most studies of unplanned purchasing forces the shopper, in the absence of a shopping list, to rely on memory for purchase intentions. In other words, unaided and nearly spontaneous recall is usually used to measure purchase plans. This methodology alone makes it highly probable that measured purchase plans will deviate to some degree from actual purchase plans.

Second, the shopper may know what she plans to purchase but may be unable, in the absence of a shopping list, to relate these intentions regardless of the amount of assistance given by the interviewer. That is to say, without exposure to in-store stimuli, the customer may be unable to cognitively construct and relate to the interviewer what she will purchase.

UNPLANNED PURCHASING: FACT AND ARTIFACT?

The findings of this study can be explained by both the exposure to in-store stimuli and customer-commitment hypotheses. Although the findings of this and past studies do not permit a conclusion as to the relative roles of these two explanations, it is the writer's opinion that both hypotheses actually cause unplanned purchasing. Some unplanned purchases are probably really triggered by customer exposure to product assortments and/or in-store promotional devices. However, some purchases that are presently termed unplanned are not unplanned at all but rather are an artifact of the way in which the behavior is usually measured. These purchases are classified as unplanned because "measured purchase intentions" deviate from "actual purchase intentions" due to the customer's inability and/or unwillingness to commit the amount of time and thought necessary to tell the interviewer what she will purchase.

IMPLICATIONS

To the extent that the customer-commitment hypothesis is valid, "true" unplanned purchasing rates are lower than those that are currently accepted. Or, stated conversely, pre-shopping decisions about products and brands to be purchased are far more common than past studies have indicated. As a consequence, presently accepted rates of unplanned purchasing probably exaggerate the potential for influencing food purchasing decisions.

Moreover, there do not appear to be any grounds for assuming that the customer-commitment hypothesis affects all product unplanned purchasing rates equally. Rather, some product unplanned purchasing rates are probably more overstated than are others. If this is true, then product unplanned purchase rates are likely to be a misleading criterion for selecting products for special promotional emphasis.

The plausibility of the customer-commitment hypothesis, coupled with the severity of its implications for marketing strategy, vividly documents the need for additional research. Future research efforts need to be designed in such a manner as to be able to determine the degree to which the customer-commitment hypothesis accounts for customer unplanned purchasing behavior.

C. The consequences of a decision

As was stated earlier, there are many possible consequences of a buying decision, and Cardozo discusses one that has intriguing possibilities. He found that it is important to assess the impact of the outcomes of the decision in terms of the buyer's expectancies about this outcome. If they do not match, the result can be to the misfortune of the seller.

In this context, Engel in an earlier article (Part IIB) reports findings from studies on advertising readership after purchase to reduce post-decision doubts. While the findings are only suggestive, they are worthy of review at this point.

18. CUSTOMER SATISFACTION: LABORATORY STUDY AND MARKETING ACTION*

Richard N. Cardozo

Customer satisfaction with a product presumably leads to repeat purchases, acceptance of other products in the same line, and favorable word-of-mouth publicity. If this presumption is correct, then understanding and control of factors influencing customers' satisfaction should be useful for marketing management.

A recent experiment indicates that customers' satisfaction with a product is influenced by (1) the effort customers expend to acquire the product and (2) expectations customers have concerning the product. Specifically, the experiment suggests that satisfaction with the product may be higher when customers expend considerable effort to obtain the product than when they put forth only modest effort. This finding is opposed to our usual notions of marketing efficiency and customer convenience. The research also suggests that customer satisfaction is lower when the product does not come up to the customer's expectations than when the product meets those expectations.

These findings are based upon a controlled laboratory experiment in which undergraduate students shopped for ballpoint pens. Effort and expectation were manipulated in a catalog shopping situation; the measure of satisfaction was the evaluation which student customers gave the product they received.

THE EXPERIMENT

Each of the independent variables, effort and expectation, appeared at two levels. The design of the experiment was a "two-by-two," as shown in the following table.

Expectation was manipulated by the use of two 31-item catalogs in the study. Both contained descriptions and prices of ballpoint pens of the type usually purchased by the subjects. The "high expectation"

*From *Reflections on Progress in Marketing*, American Marketing Association, December, 1964, pp. 283–89.

TABLE 1
DESIGN OF THE EXPERIMENT

	Expectation	
Effort	Low	High
Low	A	B
High	C	D

catalog contained products whose median price was about $1.95; only six of the 31 products were priced under 50¢. The products shown in the "low expectation" catalog were priced between 29¢ and 59¢; the average price was about 39¢. All subjects received the same 39¢ pen, ostensibly chosen by lot from the samples provided by the manufacturers whose products were shown in the catalog. Thus the "rational expectation" of a student who saw the "high expectation" catalog was a $1.95 writing instrument; of a student who used the "low expectation" catalog, a 39¢ pen.

Effort was manipulated by a simulated shopping task. The task required "low effort" subjects to look through one of the catalogs as if shopping, and to write down one feature which impressed them for half of the items shown. This minimum effort procedure took about 15 minutes. "High effort" subjects worked about an hour in uncomfortable surroundings. They were asked to comb one catalog carefully, and to record five different features about each of the 31 items. The purpose of their task was to force them to invest considerable "shopping" effort.

The dependent measure was a questionnaire on which the product and shopping situation was rated, each on several scales. Subjects evaluated both the pen they received and the simulated shopping experience immediately after receiving the product.

RESULTS AND IMPLICATIONS

The principal results of this experiment were (1) that subjects who expended "high effort" evaluated the product more favorably than did those who put forth only "low effort," and (2) that subjects for whom the product came up to expectations rated the product more favorably than did those for whom the product did *not* come up to expectations.

Since customers' effort and expectations do affect evaluation of, or satisfaction with a product, the marketer who wishes to understand and influence customers' satisfaction with his offering may be able to do so by understanding and influencing customers' effort and expectations. Although one must use caution in extending laboratory findings to the marketplace, these observations on customers' behavior at least suggest some avenues for marketing management to explore. As illustrations of this argument, let us examine the following three propositions.

PROPOSITION ONE

Since "effort" includes processing information to choose among products and since increased effort leads to a more favorable evaluation of a product, marketers who provide customers with more (positive and accurate) information about their products should find their products evaluated more favorably than products of marketers who provide less information. However, the amount of information customers will accept sets an upper limit on the amount which should be provided.

The results of this study appear to imply that one method of obtaining a favorable evaluation of a product is to increase customer's effort. But such an approach does not recognize that a customer is free to expend as much or as little effort as he or she wishes. What this study does imply is this: up to that point where customers cease to expend effort, expenditure of greater effort brings about a more favorable evaluation of a product. A product should be evaluated most favorably, then, when customers have to put forth the maximum shopping effort which they will expend upon it. If this is so, marketers who wish their products to be evaluated as favorably as possible should influence customers to put forth that maximum amount of shopping effort.

Since a major component of customers' "shopping effort" is their processing information to make a purchase decision, marketers may be able to maximize customers' evaluations of their products by communicating the proper amount of (positive and accurate) information to their customers. No doubt there is an upper limit on the amount of information customers will use to differentiate among products in making a purchase decision. Indeed, they may reject a complex message if it appears to increase the difficulty of their decision.

In fact, students exposed to considerable, detailed information ("high effort") found the products in the catalogs *harder* to differentiate than did students exposed to little information ("low effort") about the products. Many students reported that they had simply skimmed the more informative advertisements. Too much information may "cloud the issue," and make choosing among competing products very difficult. To avoid this confusion, customers may reject, or skim, messages which contain more information than they wish to use to make a purchase decision. On the other hand, customers may not attend to a very simple message, if it appears to offer them no help in making a purchase decision. Even if they do accept the communication, they may not evaluate the product as favorably as they would a very similar one about which they had processed more information.

There appears to be some optimum amount of positive and accurate information customers prefer to use in making purchase decisions. To secure favorable evaluations of their products, it may be necessary (but not sufficient) for marketers to communicate to their customers an amount of information toward the upper end of this "optimum range." In fact, students' reactions to the advertisements in the catalogs made it possible to estimate, in a gross manner, which advertisements clearly fell *outside* this "optimum range." It is likely that these advertisements would have been *less* successful than those which fell *within* the optimum range.

Interpretation of the results of the study suggests that processing an optimum amount of information may lead to a more favorable evaluation of the product not simply because customers have greater knowledge on which to base their evaluations, but also because the processing of information about products constitutes a form of commitment to the products. This interpretation implies that, besides providing the proper amount of information, marketers should also influence customers to increase their commitment to a product by, for example, writing for literature about the product.

Customers' commitment, the amount of information they will accept, and the effort they invest in the purchase decision may vary both among products and among individuals. For example, most people gather considerably more information about alternative models before buying a car than before buying a disposable pen. However, considerable individual variation appears to exist both among buyers of cars and buyers of pens. It may be that individual differences in (1) commitment, (2) the amount and complexity of information accepted, and (3) the amount and kind of effort invested in the purchase decision will provide useful bases for market segmentation.

PROPOSITION TWO

Since increased effort leads to a more favorable evaluation of a product, increased convenience (lack of effort) may not always bring about increased satisfaction with a product.

"Effort" also includes the time and energy necessary to prepare the product for use and to use it. The results of this study suggest that a product requiring some effort in preparation and/or use may be evaluated more favorably than a similar product requiring less preparation (and/or use) effort, provided that the effort required does not exceed the maximum customers will readily expend. Put another way: increased convenience may not, beyond a point, lead to increased customer satisfaction with a product. In fact, there may be an amount of effort in preparation and/or use which maximizes customer satisfaction. This amount may vary among individuals, products, and uses of a product. Specifying optimum preparation effort on these bases may add precision to product development and market segmentation.

For example, requiring a customer to perform a simple chore, such as adding an egg to a packaged mix, may result in the customer's evaluating the product much more favorably than another mix which requires less effort (and is, therefore, more convenient), yet yields an identical food.

A similar arugment could be made for photographic equipment. While the new "automatic" cameras reduce the risk of failure for all neophyte photographers, the new one-step operation ignores the notion that some amateurs might be more satisfied with their results (and presumably would take more pictures) if they had expended somewhat greater effort in taking the pictures. There may be a segment of the neophyte market which would prefer to have a camera slightly more complex than the simplest possible model.

PROPOSITION THREE

If failure of a product to meet customers' expectations results in a less favorable evaluation of that product, marketers should endeavor to keep their products and customers' expectations in line with each other. ("Expectations" [or "attitudes," "images," etc.] about a product depend upon information consumers accept from advertisements and other sources.)

The results of this study indicate that a product receives a more favorable evaluation when it comes up to customers' expectations than when it does not. Failure of a product to meet all of a customer's expectations may occur (1) because the expectations are not consistent with one another, and/or (2) because the product does not come up to some or all of a customer's expectations. For instance, a number of advertisements for a novel food product may lead consumers to expect a certain taste, convenience, etc. If these expectations cannot be made consistent with one another and with information from other sources, and/or if the product does not come up to these expectations, customer dissatisfaction is likely to result. The effects of such dissatisfaction are likely to include (1) failure to repurchase and (2) unfavorable comments to others. In any case, the product involved is likely to fare poorly.

A product may do poorly both because it does not come up to the expectations the manufacturer has tried to create for it, and because those expectations are not consistent with expectations customers have formed from experience with similar products. During the depression, The Marlin Company attempted to introduce a line of "high quality" razor blades at less than 2¢ per blade, while Gillette, known as the standard of quality in the industry, sold blades at 5¢ apiece. Since customers had been so accustomed to buying the industry's quality leader at 5¢, they expected that any blade of comparable quality would have to sell for 5¢. They couldn't expect a cheaper blade to be as good. In fact, Marlin's blades apparently did not come up to the quality claimed for them; even if they had, it is unlikely that they could have enjoyed success without a costly program aimed at changing expectations customers had built up over many years.

Even when a product matches claims made for it, customers may be dissatisfied with the product if the claims are inconsistent with their expectations from other sources. Some years ago a manufacturer introduced a new packaged food, whose texture was thick, as the manufacturer had claimed. Customers soon rejected it because their experience had led them to expect this kind of food to have a "thinner," or "light," texture. Since the product could not readily be altered, the company withdrew it, rather than undertaking a program to change customers' expectations.

Dissatisfaction may result from a product not coming up to customers' expectations, even when expectations based on communications from the manufacturer are consistent with those from other sources. In the 1940's, a manufacturer of pens came out with a poor-quality, overpriced model which he named after a high-priced, highly regarded automobile. Expectations for the product based upon his advertisements were perfectly consistent with those which customers had formed from the name of the automobile itself. Customers were dissatisfied, however, because the product did not come up to their expectations, and the product was soon withdrawn. If one were to generalize from this example, he might say that exaggerated or deceptive communication, even if initially credible, is likely to be profitable for a company for only a very short time.

The implications of these examples are that marketers should (1) be aware of the kinds of expectations customers already have relative to a given product or type of product; (2) create expectations about the product consistent with the expectations customers hold, first attempting to alter existing expectations, if necessary and practicable; and (3) insure that the product comes up to the expectations created for it. Put another way: do not create expectations the product cannot meet. While following these implications may not be sufficient to assure success, it is likely that these implications form necessary conditions for continued success.

CONCLUSION

The purpose of this discussion has been to extend to the market place some findings of a laboratory experiment on consumer behavior. The experiment showed that customers' satisfaction with a product was affected by (1) the effort expended in shopping for the product and (2) customers' expectations about the product.

It was argued that a marketer who wished to understand and influence customers' evaluations of, or satisfaction with, a product could do so by understanding and influencing customers' efforts and expectations. Three propositions for marketing action were advanced: (1) there may be an optimum amount of information which marketers should communicate to customers; (2) there may be an optimum amount of preparation (and/or use) effort which some products should require; and (3) marketers should act to keep customers' expectations about a product consistent with each other and with the product itself.

Suggested additional AMA readings

Allison, Ralph, and Uhl, Kenneth. "Influence of Beer Brand Identification on Taste Perception," *Journal of Marketing Research,* August, 1964, pp. 37–43.

Anderson, Lee K.; Taylor, James R.; and Holloway, R. J. "The Consumer and His Alternatives: An Experimental Approach," *Journal of Marketing Research,* Vol. 3 (February, 1967), pp. 62–67.

Arndt, John. "Perceived Risk, Sociometric Integration and Word-of-mouth in the Adoption of a New Food Product," *Science, Technology, and Marketing,* pp. 644–49. Chicago: American Marketing Association, 1966.

Birdwell, A. Evans. "Influence of Image Congruence on Consumer Choice," *Reflections on Progress in Marketing,* pp. 290–303. Chicago: American Marketing Association, 1964.

Bucklin, Louis P. "Testing Propensities to Shop," *Journal of Marketing,* Vol. 30 (January, 1966), pp. 22–27.

Cox, Donald F. "The Measurement of Information Value: A Study in Consumer Decision Making," *Emerging Concepts in Marketing,* pp. 413–21 (ed. by W. S. Decker). Chicago: American Marketing Association, 1962.

Cox, Keith. "The Responsiveness of Food Sales to Supermarket Shelf Space Changes," *Journal of Marketing Research,* Vol. 1 (May, 1964), pp. 63–67.

Cunningham, Scott M. "Perceived Risk as a Factor in Product Oriented Word-of-mouth Behavior: A First Step," in *Reflections on Progress in Marketing* (ed. L. George Smith), pp. 229–38. Chicago: American Marketing Association, 1964.

"Decision Making Process," in *Toward Scientific Marketing* (ed. Stephen Greyser), pp. 44–57. Chicago: American Marketing Association, 1963.

Dommermuth, William P. "The Shopping Matrix and Marketing Strategy," *Journal of Marketing Research,* Vol. 2 (May, 1965), pp. 128–32.

Feldman, Sidney P., and Spencer, Merlin C. "The Effect of Personal Influence in the Selection of Consumer Services," in *Marketing and Economic Development* (ed. Peter D. Bennett), pp. 440–52. Chicago: American Marketing Association, 1965.

Kollat, David T., anud Willett, Ronald P. "Customer Impulse Purchasing Behavior," *Journal of Marketing Research,* Vol. 4 (February, 1967), pp. 21–31.

Munn, Henry L. "Brand Perception as Related to Age, Income and Education," *Journal of Marketing,* January, 1960, pp. 29–34.

Myers, John G. "Determinants of Private Brand Attitude," *Journal of Marketing Research,* Vol. 4 (February, 1967), pp. 73–81.

————. "Patterns of Interpersonal Influence in the Adoption of New Products," *Science, Technology, and Marketing* (ed. R. M. Haas), pp. 750–58. Chicago: American Marketing Association, 1966.

Nicosia, Francisco M. "Opinion Leadership and the Flow of Communications: Some Problems and Prospects," *Reflections on Progress in Marketing* (ed. L. George Smith), pp. 340–58. Chicago, American Marketing Association, 1964.

Silk, Alvin J. "Overlap Among Self Designated Opinion Leaders: A Study of Selected Dental Products and Services," *Journal of Marketing Research*, Vol. 3 (August, 1966), pp. 255–59.

Venkatesan, M. "Experimental Study of Consumer Behavior—Conformity and Independence," *Journal of Marketing Research*, Vol. 3 (November, 1966), pp. 384–87.

Webster, Frederick E. "The Deal Prone Consumer," *Journal of Marketing Research*, Vol. 2 (May, 1965), pp. 186–89.

Part V

RESEARCH INTO CONSUMER DECISION MAKING

Two articles appear in this concluding section. The first by Paul Green takes a searching and analytical look at the requirements for productive experimental research in marketing. Green's insights make his paper required reading for any serious analyst of consumer behavior. Many future directions for research and significant methodological refinements are clarified and elaborated with unusual lucidity.

In the concluding article, a particular type of research—longitudinal analysis—is explored by Granbois and Engel. Consumer behavior is a process that takes place over time, and longitudinal analysis is uniquely adapted to the study of behavior as a process. Its advantages and disadvantages should be understood by all who have a research interest, because it is coming rapidly into widespread use.

19. THE ROLE OF EXPERIMENTAL RESEARCH IN MARKETING: ITS POTENTIALS AND LIMITATIONS

Paul E. Green

INTRODUCTION

One need not belabor the claim that experimental research in marketing is on the increase. A glance at the last few issues of our professional journals would indicate that R. A. Fisher has exerted quite an impact on researchers in marketing. Such terms as "Latin square," "F test," "covariance analysis," "factorial design" and the like are gracing the journals' pages with increasing frequency as even a rudimentary content analysis would show.

*From *Science, Technology, and Marketing,* American Marketing Association, September, 1966, pp. 483–94.

The author is indebted to his colleagues, Irwin Gross, M. H. Halbert, and J. S. Minas, for critical reviews of this paper.

Interest in statistically designed experiments is being reflected in marketing textbooks as well.[1] I would speculate that most future marketing research and quantitative techniques texts will contain at least a chapter or so on experimental design.

The motivation underlying this paper is not exhortation for more experimental research in marketing. The evidence clearly indicates that this is happening already. It seems to me that the issues (and problems) are much more subtle than this. In our zeal to apply these "new" methodological skills—which have been demonstrably successful in the physical sciences—what kinds of errors may be committed? What will happen to those modes of inquiry like observation, case study, and other clinical procedures which have been used in the study of marketing phenomena in the past? What new development in experimental methodology itself should we be made aware of?

Fractionation and clique formation frequently accompany innovation in research technique, whether it be experimental design or other so-called "management science" procedures. Currently, many of the early "hardware" adopters tend to look with disdain upon their "software" colleagues as being methodologically lacking (if not downright inept) and, hence, not satisfying the canons of scientific inquiry. The clinically trained, nonmathematical group often counters with the equally misleading comment: "You can't mathematize the richness of those marketing phenomena that concern me. Moreover, your insistence upon rigorous definition and controlled inquiry will tend to fragment our field and hinder the generation of broad-scale theory."

Part of this paper is concerned with these claims and counterclaims. First, however, I would like to describe what is meant by "experimental research." As we shall see, even defining this term appropriately is not easy. Next, I would like to comment on some of the limitations of traditional design and discuss such terms as "explanation," "prediction," the "elusion experiment," and "extrapolation."

After discussing some of these issues, I shall return to the vexing problems: "What *is* the role of experimental research in marketing?" and "What alternative forms of inquiry exist and can these differing viewpoints be reconciled?"

Finally, in order that the paper not be overly polemical, the concluding section will deal with (some still speculative) thoughts on future methodological innovations in experimental research.

ON DEFINING EXPERIMENTAL RESEARCH

Constructing an appropriate definition of the term "experiment" is extremely difficult. Common usage of the term connotes the notion of

---

[1] See Seymour Banks, *Experimentation in Marketing*, New York, McGraw-Hill Book Co., Inc., 1965.

intervention of the researcher into the system under study, said intervention involving *conscious manipulation* of some (input) variables, beyond that required for recording observations. Under this view—illustrated in the extreme case by the stereotype of the laboratory experimenter—the researcher attempts to hold constant all variables thought to affect the outcome except those variables under test. He consciously manipulates this latter set for the purpose of establishing whether the variations in the controlled variables are necessary and sufficient for yielding the event set. The experimenter's motivation is to establish (or refute) the existence of a prespecified causal relationship between certain "antecedent" variables and certain "consequent" variables.

If the experimenter is dealing with a highly precise and controllable system, he may be able to alter still *other* conditions affecting the system and observe other responses. Finally, he may be able to summarize all of these relationships in terms of "empirical relationships"—and through exercise of that scarce resource called insight—the experimenter may be able to formulate a theory from which *additional* statements can be deduced and tested independently of the relationships found earlier. His use of mathematics at this point involves less description—more deduction.

But the above account of how theories may be developed from experimental data is rather naive and oversimplified, even as applied to the physical sciences. One may be reminded of J. S. Mill's "Canons of Induction" as this idealistic process was described.[2]

In the study of marketing phenomena, however, the preceding description seems highly restrictive. First, one can never control all environmental variables affecting response and, second, the experimenter's intervention can produce undesired "side effects," thus tending to bias the very response which he is trying to measure. Marketing (and agriculture and psychology, etc.) would seem to require a less rigid experimental basis for dealing with phenomena which are marked not only by high variability among test objects but by temporal changes in the state of a single object as well.

Statistically designed experiments—reflecting the pioneering work of R. A. Fisher—have loosened the first restriction.[3] For example, one could argue that statistical control—as reflected in covariance analysis—has reduced the need to hold constant various environmental variables also presumed to affect response. Instead, one measures their effects statistically, and these influences are "removed" during the data analysis.

Accordingly, a new type of mathematics—embodied in analysis of variance procedures—has augmented the descriptive functional relation-

---

[2]See R. L. Ackoff, *Scientific Method: Optimizing Applied Research Decisions* (New York: John Wiley & Sons, Inc., 1962), pp. 312–15.

[3]R. A. Fisher, *The Design of Experiments* (5th Ed., New York: Hafner Publishing Co., 1949).

ships historically associated with experiments on physical systems. Moreover, a new type of deductive mathematics—as reflected in probabilistic models—has been added to the model builder's repertoire, in an effort to deal with the comparatively high variability of the behavioral phenomena being studied.

The second restriction is more tantalizing. One can take the view expressed by many behavioral researchers[4] that the experimenter's manipulation of the system is *not* a necessary condition for experimentation but only a convenient way to establish certain causal patterns of events with due regard for their time sequence; or even that experimentation is also an appropriate descriptor for procedures used to establish *structural* relationships among events. Under this (highly permissive) view, an experiment consists of a "recording of observations . . . made by defined conditions and designed to permit nonsubjective evaluation of the existence or magnitude of relations in the data. It aims to fit these *relations* to parsimonious models, in a process of hypothesis creation or hypothesis checking . . ."[5]

The psychologist, Raymond Cattell,[6] for example, asserts that an experiment can vary along (at least) three bi-polar dimensions:

1. Bivariate to multivariate with regard to the observation of data.
2. Manipulative to non-interfering in the degree of control imposed.
3. Simultaneous to temporally successive in the time sequence of the measurement observations.

Cattell believes that in psychology, at least, the trend is toward multivariate, non-interfering experimental designs, of both a structural (simultaneous)and process (temporally successive) nature.

What we have seen, then, is an evolution of the term "experiment" from the deterministic, one-factor-at-a-time manipulation to the comparatively less restrictive, probabilistic (and, in some cases, non-manipulative) types of design. Judging from the marketing literature, most of the reported experiments have embodied the principles of statistical design in the Fisherian sense. One might add that the procedures used in many marketing models also involve probabilistic rather than deterministic mathematics in the expression of functional relationships as well.

Without debating the respective merits of these views, it would appear that experimentation is *at least* concerned with the establishment of relations among variables for the purpose of explaining and/or predicting specified events. But, from a logical point of view, scientific explanation is identical with prediction, the point of individuation being the *temporal vantage point of the researcher*. In each case there are a set of event

[4]See, for example, R. B. Cattell, "Multivariate Behavioral Research and the Integrative Challenge," *Multivariate Behavioral Research*, Vol. 1, No. 1 (January, 1966), pp. 4–23.

[5]*Ibid.*, p. 9.

[6]*Ibid.*, p. 5.

descriptions, a set of statements describing antecedent conditions, and a set of law-like statements which connect the two. If one grants *this* description, then one can say: "We have an explanation for an event, if and only if (from a different temporal viewpoint) we could have predicted it."[7]

I should emphasize, however, that this symmetry of explanation and prediction is a technical correspondence. As we know, in ordinary discourse, we tend to distinguish between the two terms. However, what we typically call a "prediction," the philosopher of science would call a "predictive statement."

Under this broader view experimentation can be used as *both a means for inquiry and a logic of justification.* That is, experiments can be performed on an exploratory basis for identifying variables thought to be causally related to certain events before articulating a specific model for describing those interrelationships. On the other hand, experiments can be performed for discriminating among alternative models of the system's interrelationship; this, of course, is the usual interpretation of the purpose of experimentation.

In summary, we might say that the term "experiment" has been interpreted in many ways, ranging from: (a) single-variable manipulation the purpose of which is to test the predictive efficacy of a deterministic model in which temporal event sequence is involved; to (b) multivariate, probabilistic, exploratory and non-manipulative designs. While there is a temptation on my part to restrict the term to manipulatory design (in line with historical usage) we should be aware by now that "experimentation" is by no means an agreed-upon concept.

"GOOD" RESEARCH IN MARKETING

If one agrees with the immediately preceding comments, much of the dogma concerning what constitutes "good" research appears open to question. As an illustration of various viewpoints which are held in the behavioral sciences, one could, with over-simplification, identify *three* major methodological camps: (a) the mathematical model builders whose approach to experimentation is largely after-the-fact ("one must have a theory first; data are secondary"); (b) the multivariate behaviorist who views experimentation as much, if not more, as a hypothesis-generating device as it is a hypothesis-testing device; and (c), the clinician who worries about the inability of experimental methods, generally, to capture the subtleties of human behavior. The latter's view of "experimentation" might appear to be less articulated than that of his more quantitative colleagues, but who is to say that his predictive statements are, *prima facie,* inferior.

[7] R. S. Rudner, *Philosophy of Social Science* (Englewood Cliffs, N.J.: Prentice-Hall, Inc., 1966), p. 60.

Thus, it is one thing to talk about different techniques for making predictive statements, for surely different techniques reflect different backgrounds and tastes. It is another thing, I believe, to talk about differences in the logic of validation, since admission of these differences would shake our faith in scientific method, generally. It seems to me that the value of experimentation (if I may be permitted to employ a rather tight interpretation of this term) lies in its major contribution to the logic of validation. That is, models of discovery may be quite varied and, in some cases, inarticulated, while modes of validation represent the essence of scientific method.

This controversy regarding what constitutes "good research" also extends to the content of experimentation. Some researchers feel that fruitful experiments must deal with real-world systems in their natural setting, despite the difficulties and costs associated with control. Other researchers feel that more artificial environments—e.g., the experimental game—permit more rigorous tests, the problems of extrapolation notwithstanding. Clearly, if we knew the appropriate transformation rules by which experimental game results could be extended to less-artificial environments, the latter view would be much more compelling than it currently is.

Thus, despite the enthusiasm with which the principles of statistically designed experiments have been accepted, even cursory reflection reveals rather marked differences of opinion about what an experiment is, what it should be used for, what it should be used on, and why anybody should bother with it all.

THE ELUSIVE EXPERIMENT

Nor do the above difficulties exhaust the set of problems. The traditionalist view of an experiment requires that ". . . one must make sure that the methods of assigning objects to categories remain fixed throughout the experiment. We say, in effect, that if one is going to test whether a treatment cures patients, one must decide at the outset what constitutes a sick patient, what constitutes a healthy one, and what constitutes a treatment."[8]

However, in medicine, for example, it is difficult to decide at the outset just what constitutes the state of a patient and what a "treatment" really is. Thus, the experiment may not only have to reveal the effectiveness of the treatments, but in the process, *define* "effectiveness" and "treatment" as well. I would guess that many marketing experiments reflect the characteristics of the elusive experiment.

Some of our own work on behavioral decision making suggests that

---

[8]C. W. Churchman, "Toward a Mathematics of Social Science," in F. Massarik and P. Ratoosh (eds.), *Mathematical Explorations in Behavioral Science* (Homewood, Ill.: Richard D. Irwin, Inc., 1965), p. 34.

the conclusion of an experiment seldom yields well-defined "terminal" findings. Rather, it provides help for designing *additional* experiments by which alternative explanations of the phenomena can be successively reduced. But, in a way, this viewpoint is closer to that of the clinician than to the "hard-core" statistical design man.

Moreover, one could argue that reliance on the tenets of *strict* experimental design could hamper rather than help the advancement of science in marketing. A little knowledge about F-tests and significance levels can be dangerous. There is something rather "terminal" (and forbidding) about the statement: "At an alpha risk level of 0.05 the hypothesis was rejected." Does this mean that research in this area is to be abandoned? I think not. By manipulation of sample size any hypothesis can be rejected (or accepted). Research is a continuing process. Rarely are the data so unequivocally in favor of a *single* hypothesis that the project can be viewed as completed. More likely is the case that our *credence* in one of the several possible models will be increased with the result that possibilities for future experiments will be suggested. Over-emphasis on statistical tests can be as dangerous as ignorance of the basic requirements for well-designed experiments.

EXTRAPOLATION OF EXPERIMENTAL FINDINGS

Still another problem in experimentation concerns the generalizations we can—or would like to—make from our findings. The results of even large-scale, field-type experiments in which such stimuli as advertising and personal selling are varied by region require many assumptions for policy-making purposes. Have cumulative effects been taken into consideration? Can the environment be presumed to remain reasonably stationary over the next period (when the results are to be put to use)? Is the system flexible enough to permit changes in the input variables, as dictated by the results of the study?

As suggested earlier, in laboratory-like experiments, problems of extrapolation abound. Usually our interest in the study of choice behavior in controlled settings is to make some prediction about behavior in the real world. Some interesting marketing experiments have been performed in controlled settings[9] and, yet, quite appropriately, we are concerned about their validity in larger, real-world systems. Donald Rice and Vernon Smith[10] have recognized the types of assumptions that underlie the extrapolation of experimental gaming results and have proposed a model, incorporating the experimenter's judgment, for making these extrapolations. The point to be made is that such generalization of results is *essentially subjective;* one may never be able to perform economically

---

[9]For example, see W. T. Tucker, "The Development of Brand Loyalty," *Journal of Marketing*, Vol. 1 (August, 1964), pp. 32–35.

[10]D. B. Rice and V. L. Smith, "Nature, the Experimental Laboratory, and the Credibility of Hypotheses," *Behavioral Science*, Vol. 9 (July, 1964), pp. 239–46.

the direct experiment which would be required to test the results of the extrapolation. Such "validation" may have to come from quite indirect sources, where the criteria of relevance are also subjective.

To a large extent, one faces the same problem in choosing among alternative explanations of specific experimental results, even omitting the problem of extrapolation to other environments. In behavioral experiments particularly, it is a rare case in which alternative models are directly contradictory. Rather, either model could explain the data. The question, then, is to determine the credence to be placed in alternative explanations rather than outright acceptance of a particular model.[11]

STATISTICIAN VERSUS CLINICIAN

I hope that my comments thus far have not been too gloomy for the budding methodologist, eager to take up the gauntlet for "rigorous" experimentation; nor too arcane for the non-quantitatively-oriented researcher, puzzled by all of the emphasis on analysis of variance and covariance techniques.

Actually, the current controversy between methodologist and clinician is neither new nor unique to marketing.[12] In 1954 Paul Meehl published a study dealing with the comparative efficacy of statistical versus clinical prediction in the behavioral sciences. His findings led him to state: "There is no convincing reason to assume that explicitly formalized mathematical rules and the clinician's creativity are equally suited for any given task, or that their comparative effectiveness is the same for different tasks. Current clinical practice should be much more critically examined with this in mind than it has been."[13]

Meehl's research indicated that in some 20 studies in which statistical and clinical predictions were compared, in all but one, the statistical predictions were either approximately equal, or superior, to the clinical predictions. But the nature of these predictive statements involved such comparatively well-defined outcomes as "success in schooling" and "recidivism." Meehl makes no claim that statistical methods are superior for all predictive tasks. He does argue, however, for recognition of statistical procedures as a feasible alternative to clinical prediction and presents some persuasive evidence for their adoption in appropriate applications.

It seems to me that the controversy between methodologist and clinician represents "no contest" if we are concerned with the *procedures by*

---

[11]For an approach to this problem, see E. G. Hunt, "The Evaluation of Somewhat Parallel Models," *Mathematical Exploration in Behavioral Science, op. cit.,* pp. 37–55.

[12]See M. H. Halbert, *The Meaning and Sources of Marketing Theory* (New York: McGraw-Hill Book Co., Inc., 1965).

[13]P. E. Meehl, *Clinical Versus Statistical Prediction* (Minneapolis: University of Minnesota Press, 1954).

which theories are to be validated. Using Rapoport's terminology,[14] manipulative causality (established through experimentation) is "stronger" evidence than either observational or postulational causality. By "observational" causality is meant, essentially, that the results are obtained by correlation analyses. "Postulational" causality refers, roughly, to the agreement we express when given an explanation of some event sequence. Under this latter view, we seek neither current manipulations nor observations; an explanation is "adequate" to the extent that it is subjectively congruent with certain assumptions about how the world works. This is a type of arm-chair theorizing which need only obey the rules of logic.

Much of current marketing theory seems to be postulational—rather than manipulative—in character. But such was the case in the early days of physical science. Moreover, it is difficult to perform experiments in large (or even small) social systems, and I am prepared to accept the fact that much of marketing theory—and social science generally—will remain postulational for years to come.

On the question of hypothesis *generation,* however, it seems to me that the adduced evidence is still equivocal concerning the efficiency of alternative procedures. Usually the clinician's model is richer than that of the methodologist (who has to worry about solution techniques), and one can obviously say trivial things in mathematical symbols just as easily as in words. I would guess that this form of the controversy will be with us for some time, in one disguise or another, although there are signs that mature methodologists are starting to learn some marketing and that their counterparts in marketing are starting to learn some methodology.

EXPERIMENTAL RESEARCH IN THE FUTURE

If one grants the contribution which experimental research (however interpreted) can make to the advancement of marketing theory, it seems reasonable (or at least, entertaining) to speculate about future innovations in experimental design.

Current emphasis in research methodology is on statistically designed experiments. With regard to industry application of experimental design, I would guess that covariance techniques will assume increasing importance in the design of field experiments in marketing.[15] Covariance designs provide an efficient way to cope with the effects of major environmental influences on response variables and can often increase the precision of the results at little added costs.

---

[14]A. Rapoport, *Operational Philosophy,* New York, John Wiley & Sons, Inc., pp. 51–64.

[15]P. E. Green and D. S. Tull, "Covariance Analysis in Marketing Experimentation," *Journal of Advertising Research,* Vol. 6, No. 2 (June, 1966), pp. 45–53.

I would also speculate that *adaptive* experimentation will receive increasing attention by marketers. John Little, for example, has proposed an interesting model for determining promotional budgets which embodies a sequential procedure for updating portions of the model through field experimentation.[16] In principle, this approach is similar to optimal-seeking methods which are used for updating production process specifications when one is dealing with nonstationarity.

Multivariate research methodology is also undergoing extension in the breadth and power of its techniques. I would speculate that a wide variety of nonlinear multivariate designs will become operational in the not-too-distant future. In addition, it seems reasonable to suppose that multivariate techniques will find increasing use in the study of behavioral processes (as opposed to structure). This will require sequential designs of some complexity but should still be tractable under today's computer technology.

One class of multivariate techniques—so-called clustering methods—appear particularly appropriate for classification problems in marketing.[17] Furthermore, these techniques can free the analyst from making *a priori* assumptions about customer populations when analyzing data appropriate for segmentation or media measurement studies.

It is in the area of experimental gaming, however, that the most dramatic methodological advances may be made. From the standpoint of data manipulation, work is already underway at a number of universities and research centers on extremely flexible "data analyzers"; that is, computers with visual display devices that enable the researcher to test, quickly and inexpensively, a large variety of hypotheses on the assembled data bank.

For example, the experimenter may be interested in the sequential behavior of subjects' choices over some set of experimental trials. After keying in certain instructions on the console the computer would process the data in the desired fashion and the results would be displayed visually. Various significance tests could be conducted automatically, if desired. The researchers may then wish to summarize the data in another form, and so on. This rapid feedback of results can be extremely valuable in allowing the experimenter to follow various "hunches" about alternative models for explaining the data.

I would also speculate that experimental research in general will become more "sequential" in character. That is, the experimenter of the future will tend to design *sequences* of experiments in which choices between presuppositions and hypotheses are varied over experiments in a systematic attempt to narrow down alternative explanations of the

---

[16]J. D. C. Little, "A Model of Adaptive Control of Promotional Spending," Sloan School of Management, Massachusetts Institute of Technology, Cambridge, Mass., 1965; also see P. E. Green, P. T. FitzRoy, and P. J. Robinson, "Advertising Expenditure Models: State of the Art and Future Prospects," *Business Horizons* (in press).

[17]For one such application, see P. E. Green, R. E. Frank, and P. J. Robinson, "Cluster Analysis in Test Market Selection," *Journal of Marketing* (in press).

response data. Illustrations of this general approach are already appearing in experimental research on conflict and cooperation. In effect, the researcher attempts to predict behavior on successively richer environments from results in simpler environments. This approach may be one way to respond to the charge that experimental gaming results are not close enough to the "real world" to be of much value.

One additional consideration comes to mind in speculating about future experimental work in marketing. It is rather surprising that so little formal experimentation is being conducted by marketers (or other social scientists) in conjunction with governmental activities. One could view many governmental programs (the War on Poverty, the Peace Corps, etc.) as large-scale "social experimentation." It is almost ironic that formal design techniques have been utilized so little. I would guess that increasing attention will be paid by methodologists in the future to these large-scale and important social activities.

CONCLUSIONS

In conclusion, the future outlook for experimental research in marketing appears provocative, both from the basic and applied viewpoints. The *philosophical* questions of experimental research will probably remain controversial for years to come. But, fortunately, these unsettled issues do not halt the *practice* of research.

After all, one could just as easily ask: "What is probability?" Despite the tantalizing semantical complexities of this concept, probabilistic models in marketing (and other disciplines) have become almost commonplace. Certainly, one should be self-conscious about his methods of inquiry even though the foundations of a discipline are usually the constructs which are most in dispute. We need not worry that such reflection will stultify research activity in marketing or any other discipline. Our methodological consciences, the philosophers of science, will keep us honest—and appropriately unsure of ourselves.

20. THE LONGITUDINAL APPROACH TO STUDYING MARKETING BEHAVIOR*

Donald H. Granbois and James F. Engel

INTRODUCTION

One result of the growing influence of behavioral concepts in the study of marketing has been a heightened interest in the processes that underlie the actions of participants in the marketing system. A recent attempt to

*From *Marketing and Economic Development*, American Marketing Association, September, 1965, pp. 205–21.

synthesize the contributions to marketing of several behavioral disciplines emphasized the usefulness of behavioral theory in the study of both consumers and business firms in the performance of their marketing roles, particularly when these roles are conceptualized as problems of human choice or decision making.[1] The study of consumer behavior, for example, has increasingly viewed the consumer as a decision maker, emphasizing the performance of various stages of the decision-making process, such as learning about alternatives and changes in attitudes and information states preceding the final decision, the relative roles of household members in the decision, and the comparative influence of "stored" and various "outside" sources of influence at each stage.[2] The notion of treating decision making by executives as a behavioral phenomenon has been stimulated by the work of Cyert and March, who have persuasively argued the merits of a "positive" or behavioral theory of the firm as a useful complement to the more usual normative approach.[3]

Further progress in conceptualizing marketing in terms of decision-making processes seems to be directly related to our ability to conduct empirical studies of actual on-going marketing behavior, both as a means of suggesting generalizations and of testing hypotheses. Research of this kind usually involves an investigation of the behavior of some relevant population through time, with particular attention to changes in overt acts (such as shopping or actual purchases) and changes in information and attitude states (such as knowledge of certain alternative products or images of specific retailers) for the whole population or for subgroups. The present paper will be concerned with longitudinal analysis as a means of studying changes in marketing behavior, with some attention given to alternative research techniques to highlight the particular contribution offered by this method.

APPROACHES TO STUDYING MARKETING BEHAVIORS OVER TIME

Sampling procedures and analytical strategies for four methods of studying marketing behavior over time are summarized in Exhibit 1. By far the most common method—and the one that is often least satisfactory—uses cross sectional analysis of single samples as a means of discovering important dimensions of the process being studied. Respondents' current purchasing behavior, attitudes or plans or their "retro-

[1]John A. Howard, *Marketing: Executive and Buyer Behavior* (New York: Columbia University Press, 1963).

[2]For a review of some of the literature of this type, see Donald H. Granbois, "The Role of Communication in the Family Decision-Making Process," in Stephen A. Greyser (ed.), *Toward Scientific Marketing* (Proceedings of the Winter Conference of the American Marketing Association, 1963) (Chicago: American Marketing Association, 1964), pp. 44–57.

[3]Richard M. Cyert and James G. March, *A Behavioral Theory of the Firm* (Englewood Cliffs, N.J.: Prentice-Hall, Inc., 1963).

spective histories" of past actions must be employed. Analysis of the resulting data by respondents' "stage" in some relevant process is assumed to reveal changes associated with movement through such stages.

When this method is replicated through the use of successive samples, certain trends in the data may become apparent (for example, change in the proportion of consumers purchasing a certain brand), but the interpretation of these trends is clouded by the researchers' inability to trace patterns of change from individual respondents from one wave to the next. The degree of change that actually occurs may be far greater than such studies indicate, because the method cannot account for compensating changes that "cancel out."

Cohort studies offer distinct advantages in sample design and sometimes in cost, since the same respondents are studied repeatedly. These studies do not offer the unique advantage of the remaining method— longitudinal analysis—in that individual patterns of change in response are not traced from one wave to the next. True longitudinal studies capitalize on panel design with analytical procedures for following individual patterns of change and therefore can be used to discover "predictive relationships" between sets of variables, complex patterns of change or "turnover" within the sample, or relationships between experimental or quasi-experimental variables and the pattern of behavior being studied. Furthermore, longitudinal studies can overcome some of the problems of bias and error inherent in the other methods. Before proceeding with further discussion of the flexibility of application of longitudinal methods in marketing, the subject of bias and response errors deserves further attention.

RESPONSE ERRORS AND RESEARCH DESIGN

It is now recognized that all survey research is fraught with the perils of response bias and chances for error in survey data. The basic question thus becomes, how can we get accurate empirical information using survey techniques?

Some kinds of information are difficult to record accurately using the cross sectional approach because of certain fundamental characteristics of human behavior. When a problem is being researched in which these fundamental behavioral characteristics are a *known* factor, error often can be minimized through use of the longitudinal approach.

Let us look briefly at several important types of response error and examine the potential of longitudinal analysis to sharpen the accuracy of empirical information.

Errors in Reporting Past Behavior

Human memory has been studied extensively, and it is now known that inaccuracies can enter for two reasons: (1) memory decay and (2) motivated forgetting.

EXHIBIT 1
ALTERNATIVE METHODS FOR STUDYING MARKETING PROCESSES OVER TIME

Method	Sampling Procedure	Analytical Strategy	Sample Marketing Application
Cross section	**Single sample** A sample of respondents representing various stages of a single process is studied once with respect to one or more variables of interest that are measured by asking respondents about current or past behavior.	**Stage Comparison** The variables of interest are compared among respondents at different stages; differences are assumed to represent changes in individuals' experience as they move through these stages.	**Traditional market analysis studies** Differing patterns of consumption and purchasing behavior among families in varying stages of the life cycle are assumed to reflect patterns that shift through time.
Trend study	**Successive samples** The variables of interest are studied in samples periodically taken from the same population using the same sampling technique each time; essentially, this method is a series of carefully replicated cross sections.	**Trend analysis** The samples are assumed to be equivalent; changes in the variables through time are therefore assumed to reflect actual changes in the population.	**Annual budget studies** The proportion of respondents purchasing certain categories of goods is computed in annual studies (such as those conducted by metropolitan newspapers).
Cohort study	**Periodic censuses or panel** The variables of interest are measured continuously or periodically in population censuses or in a single sample (panel) maintained over time (often with periodic additions to replace drop-outs or to maintain representativeness).	**Cohort analysis** Individual responses are not compared through time; analysis is similar to trend analysis.	**U. S. Census of Population data analysis** Household ownership of certain appliances is compared among censuses.

Longitudinal
analysis

Panel
  The variables of interest
  are measured continuously
  or periodically in a single
  sample (panel) maintained
  over time (often with
  periodic additions to re-
  place drop-outs or to maintain
  representativeness).

Prediction studies
  Individual scores on different variables are compared over time to determine, for example, the
  extent to which responses
  for variable a at time t
  predict responses for
  variable b at time $t + 1$.

Gross and net change analysis
  The same variables are
  studied repeatedly. Individual scores are compared each
  time with previous responses;
  both aggregate patterns of
  change (net change) and
  patterns of "switching"
  (gross change) are studied.

Experiments
  Assessment is made of the
  effects of either "natural"
  or artificially introduced
  experimental variables on
  the variables of interest,
  by comparing before and
  after scores of exposed
  respondents with measures
  of those not exposed.

Purchase intention studies
  Panel members are re-
  peatedly asked about
  purchase plans and recent
  purchases; degree of
  fulfillment of plans is
  studied over time.

Brand switching studies
  Purchase panel data are
  analyzed to study changes
  in market share and to
  detect and measure the
  incidence and magnitude of
  changes in brands pur-
  chased.

Advertising effectiveness studies
  Purchase rates of respondents reporting exposure
  to ad-carrying vehicles are
  compared with those reporting
  no exposure.

Memory decay.[4]   The early work of Ebbinghaus showed that the pattern of memory decay usually takes the form of a sharp initial drop and a subsequent leveling off. In retention, however, it is common to smooth out irregularities or items that do not seem to fit in the context of the original event (leveling), and certain outstanding details tend to become sharpened or clearly embedded in memory. In addition, details often are recalled more accurately if they are consistent with a culturally meaningful pattern or context. Bartlett, in particular, has shown how the customs and mores of a society are instrumental in determining what is recalled and what is forgotten.[5]

Every marketing researcher knows that recall is greatly enhanced when the event to be recalled is important to the individual and when recall is pleasant to him. Zeisel has documented the strong likelihood of memory fade regarding recent purchases of convenience goods.[6] It is unlikely, for example, that ice cream purchases over the past month will be recalled with much clarity, whereas the respondent no doubt could more readily recreate the set of circumstances surrounding the purchase of an automobile and report the decision-making process with some clarity even though the event happened as long as two years ago. Even when the event is important, however, memory decay is usually of such a magnitude that survey data tend to be highly inaccurate.

Finally, isolated events are remembered more readily than those of a repetitive nature. The automobile purchase, for example, stands in isolation whereas the greater frequency of ice cream purchases no doubt serves to diminish memory of early purchases. It is interesting that the intervention of recent events may also distort the recall of earlier events. Withey reports that the past income is recalled accurately if present income is substantially unchanged relative to the past.[7] If present income has increased, however, the size of the past income is likely to be inflated.

Motivated forgetting.   Much forgetting is motivated, and motivated distortion of memory is known to take several forms: (1) diminished recall of events of ideas that are inconsistent with important values or attitudes; (2) selective recall of dissonant information; and (3) defensive memory distortion.

1. *The influence of attitudes and beliefs.*   A large body of evidence

[4]Relevant evidence on memory decay is reviewed concisely in Bernard Berelson and Gary A. Steiner, *Human Behavior, An Inventory of Scientific Findings,* (New York: Harcourt, Brace & World, Inc., 1964), pp. 162–88 and in Ernest R. Hilgard, *Introduction to Psychology* (2d ed.; New York: Harcourt, Brace & Co., 1957), chap. 12.

[5]Frederic Charles Bartlett, "Social Factors in Recall," in Theodore M. Newcomb and Eugene L. Hartley (eds.), *Readings in Social Psychology,* (1st ed.; New York: Henry Holt & Co., 1947).

[6]Hans Zeisel, *Say It with Figures,* Fourth Edition (New York: Harper & Bros., 1957).

[7]S. B. Withey, "Reliability of Recall of Income," *Public Opinion Quarterly,* Vol. 18 (1954), pp. 197–204.

documents that experiences and events in harmony with existing attitudes and beliefs are learned and recalled better than those in conflict. Among the many studies that document this proposition, Edwards found that students recall political propaganda that is consistent with their party preference while forgetting contradictory propaganda.[8] Taft reports the Negroes repressed recall of items unfavorable to Negroes while readily recalling favorable items,[9] and Levine and Murphy found that pro-communist respondents recalled propaganda favorable to the Soviet Union much more readily than anti-communists.[10]

2. *Selective recall of dissonant information.* The theory of cognitive dissonance states that when two or more ideas or knowledges (cognitions) are inconsistent (dissonant) with each other, a state of tension called cognitive dissonance is created.[11] Dissonance can arise for many reasons, and it frequently is seen following a commitment to a course of action or to a belief. The individual then is often motivated to discard any thoughts or knowledges that are inconsistent with this commitment.

Several studies have demonstrated that dissonant information will either be forgotten or distorted. Brock and Blackwood showed that recall of information under highly dissonant conditions is distorted to make it consistent with the individual's own commitment.[12] Similarly, Brehm and Cohen report an experiment in which information that contradicted a commitment to a point of view was forgotten to a significantly greater extent than non-discrepant information.[13]

One might expect that dissonance of high magnitude would be created when an individual commits himself to the purchase of a product that is important to him, for the costs of a wrong decision can be high. He still may have doubts that his decision was correct, especially when other products offered important satisfactions. Under these circumstances, it is probable that he will defend his purchase psychologically by over-looking all dissonant thoughts, for failure to do so would be to encourage the continuation of a state of tension. He thus will tend to forget many of the troubling circumstances surrounding the purchase and will most readily recall favorable ones. A major appliance manufacturer discovered, for example, that consumers who undertake buying action other

[8]A. L. Edwards, "Political Frames of Reference as a Factor Influencing Recognition," *Journal of Abnormal and Social Psychology*, Vol. 36 (1941), pp. 34–50.

[9]R. Taft, "Selective Recall and Memory Distortion of Favorable and Unfavorable Material," *Journal of Abnormal and Social Psychology*, Vol. 49 (1954), pp. 23–28.

[10]J. M. Levine and G. Murphy, "The Learning and Forgetting of Controversial Material," in Theodore M. Newcomb and Eugene L. Hartley (eds.), *Readings in Social Psychology* (1st ed.; New York: Henry Holt & Co., 1947), pp. 108–15.

[11]Leon Festinger, *A Theory of Cognitive Dissonance* (Evanston, Ill.: Row, Peterson & Co., 1957).

[12]T. C. Brock and J. E. Blackwood, "Dissonance Reduction, Social Comparison, and Modification of Others' Opinions," *Journal of Abnormal and Social Psychology*, Vol. 65 (1962), pp. 319–24.

[13]J. W. Brehm and A. R. Cohen, *Explorations in Cognitive Dissonance* (New York: John Wiley & Sons, Inc., 1962), pp. 92–97.

than that stated in a buying plan, often deny that they ever had stated a conflicting buying plan.

3. *Defensive forgetting.* Few people are without defense mechanisms that serve to protect the individual's self esteem from attack. Perhaps some of the examples of motivated forgetting discussed above are illustrations of repression of information that is unpleasant or unacceptable, and the memory then becomes buried in the unconscious. Other defense mechanisms also can result in distorted memory.

While space does not permit an extensive discussion, it seems apparent that rationalization can distort recall. Socially acceptable reasons are frequently substituted for true reasons, and these rationalizations come to be accepted as true. It is not unusual for the purchaser of a new automobile to defend his decision for mechanical reasons where, in reality, he might be "keeping up with the Joneses." The evidence on defensive forgetting is scanty, but it is reasonable to expect that it can and does serve to distort survey responses.

Longitudinal analysis and the problem of memory.   In the cross sectional approach, consumers are interviewed *once* to obtain the desired information. All of the possible forms of memory distortion discussed above become an ever-present danger, and there is no effective way, through cross sectional analysis, to overcome the problem of memory inaccuracy.

The longitudinal approach, on the other hand, requires the recording of actual behavior as it occurs over short periods of time so that little reliance is placed on the respondent's memory. When actual behavior is measured, such as purchases of products or media exposure, behavior diaries are commonly used. Thus memory errors either are substantially minimized or avoided completely. This avoidance of the memory problem is a powerful advantage of longitudinal analysis.

INTERACTION BIAS

An interview is a social situation requiring interaction between two distinct personalities—respondent and interviewer. The interviewer becomes an important part of the respondent's psychological field, and this social influence can bias responses considerably. The respondent frequently will tell the interviewer what he thinks the interviewer wants to hear or what he *wants* the interviewer to hear or thinks the interviewer *should* hear.

The bias resulting from interaction between respondent and interviewer has been widely documented and only a few examples need be cited. Lucas and Britt note that many respondents will give false reports on magazine readership to impress the interviewer with their sophistication.[14] The number of claimed readers of socially acceptable and prestigious magazines sometimes exceeds reported circulation by fifteen or

[14]Darrell B. Lucas and Steuart H. Britt, *Measuring Advertising Effectiveness* (New York: McGraw-Hill Book Co., Inc., 1963), p. 223.

more times. Similarly, Parry and Crossley report that 34 percent of those interviewed in one study claimed to have given to charities whereas a check of actual giving disclosed that they had not.[15]

One of the most thorough studies on response error was undertaken by Lansing *et al.* from 1958 through 1961.[16] An opportunity existed to check respondents' claims of reported savings accounts and small loans against actual records. In one survey, 24 percent of respondents did not mention the existence of a savings account, and the average error in reported account balance was nearly $1,700. While certain classes of respondents were less accurate than others, a general tendency seemed to exist to distort both the existence of the account or loan and its magnitude. It should be pointed out, however, that conscious distortion may have been only *one* reason for these response errors.

Many other studies could be cited to demonstrate the general agreement that the danger of distortion of replies during the interview is a fact of life in survey research. There is some evidence that the type and wording of questions can partially overcome interaction bias, although the evidence is inconclusive on this point.[17]

It should be obvious to the reader that the longitudinal approach also requires an interaction between respondent and interviewer, and it would appear that the danger of interaction bias is not affected by this method. Ferber, however, reports that the longitudinal design can reduce interaction bias to a considerable extent. As he points out:

1. Rapport between interviews and respondents improves dramatically over time and refusals to give information drop sharply (for those who stay in the panel).
2. The accuracy of reported information (on savings accounts and the amount saved) increased, because the presence of many assets and debts were not reported during early interviews.[18]

Thus, Ferber's studies indicate that the respondent comes to trust the interviewer to a greater extent, better rapport is established, and the accuracy of reporting is significantly improved. It should be noted, however, that some surveyors are not as optimistic as Ferber on this point.

Errors from response style

Finally, errors can arise from tendencies which cause a person consistently to respond differently to questionnaire items than he would

---

[15]Hugh Parry and Helen Crossley, "Validity of Responses to Survey Questions," *Public Opinion Quarterly,* Vol. 14 (1950), pp. 61–80.

[16]John B. Lansing, Gerald P. Ginsburg, and Kaisa Braaten, *An Investigation of Response Error* (Studies in Consumer Savings, No. 2) (Bureau of Economic and Business Research, University of Illinois, 1961).

[17]For one example see James F. Engel and Hugh G. Wales, "Spoken Versus Pictured Questions on Taboo Topics," *Journal of Advertising Research,* Vol. 2 (1962), pp. 11–17.

[18]Robert Ferber, *Collecting Financial Data by Consumer Panel Techniques* (Bureau of Economic and Business Research, University of Illinois, 1959), pp. 62–66.

if the content were presented in a different form. This type of error is referred to as "response style" (or response set).

Cronbach has isolated several important response styles:[19]

1. Gambling—a tendency to use or lack caution in selecting answers to multiple choice questions.
2. Inclusiveness—a tendency to give many responses where no limit is placed on the number of replies that might be given.
3. Acquiescence—a general tendency to agree or disagree regardless of actual feelings.

To this list Jackson and Messick add a tendency to reply in a socially desirable way and a contrary tendency to reply negativistically in a socially undesirable or rebellious fashion.[20]

Other response styles no doubt could be added to these lists, and it is apparent that they present real problems to survey researchers. Of these response styles, acquiescence or "yea-sayer"–"nay-sayer" bias is perhaps of greatest concern. Couch and Keniston report that some people consistently reply yes or no as a manifestation of deep-seated personality traits,[21] and Wells reports rather conclusive evidence that "yea-saying" can bias marketing research survey answers to a disturbing extent.[22]

Unfortunately the biases resulting from response style are present in *all* forms of survey research. There is little basis to claim that this type of bias will be reduced significantly by reinterviews through the longitudinal approach.

THE POTENTIAL OF LONGITUDINAL ANALYSIS IN
MARKETING RESEARCH

In this section we have examined certain behavioral characteristics (inaccurate memory, interaction bias, and response style) which can interfere with the collection of accurate information in survey research. These behavioral characteristics are part-and-parcel of human nature, and they must be accepted and adapted to in research design. The problem clearly is to determine a research approach which minimizes response bias or avoids it completely if possible.

No research design is free from *all* forms of response bias, but the

---

[19]See L. J. Cronbach, "Response Sets and Test Validity," *Educational and Psychological Measurement*, Vol. 6 (1946), pp. 475–94; and "Further Evidence on Response Sets and Test Design," *Educational and Psychological Measurement*, Vol. 10 (1950), pp. 3–31.

[20]D. N. Jackson and S. Messick, "Content and Style in Personality Assessment," *Psychological Bulletin*, Vol. 55 (1958), pp. 243–52.

[21]Arthur Couch and Kenneth Keniston, "Yeasayers and Naysayers: Agreeing Response Set as a Personality Variable," *Journal of Abnormal and Social Psychology*, Vol. 6 (1960), pp. 151–74.

[22]William D. Wells, "How Chronic Overclaimers Distort Survey Findings," *Journal of Advertising Research*, Vol. 3 (1963), pp. 8–18.

reinterview approach of longitudinal analysis effectively overcomes memory errors, and this is its most basic advantage. Moreover, the gain in rapport and accuracy of response over time through reinterviews can be an effective weapon against interaction bias. While the errors from response style still remain, the reinterview approach appears to be the *only* effective empirical device which combats memory error and, to a lesser extent, interaction bias. This is not to say, of course, that the single interview approach is of no value, for it will always be used in situations where memory accuracy is not needed and when research funds are limited. Longitudinal design is no panacea, but its virtues are sufficient to warrant its more extensive use in marketing research.

ILLUSTRATIVE APPLICATIONS OF LONGITUDINAL ANALYSIS

Despite its potentially important contributions, longitudinal analysis has not been widely used in marketing. Still, a review of the literature has revealed several illustrative adaptations that will be briefly summarized.

PREDICTION STUDIES

Several researchers have explored the relationships between consumers' stated purchase intentions and their fulfillment of these plans by scheduling waves of reinterviews at regular intervals following an initial study of purchase intentions. These reinterviews have typically measured actual purchasing behavior for the period following the original interview and have sought the underlying reasons for non-fulfillment of plans. Such studies offer marketing students insight into consumer planning processes. Moreover, they are potentially useful for aggregate economic forecasting, since they help to evaluate the degree to which intentions studies may be used to predict changes in consumer durables spending.

Namias compared durable goods intentions data from the 1952 Survey of Consumer Finances with purchase data gathered in a reinterview study conducted in 1953.[23] Only 54 percent of those intending to buy in 1952 had carried out their plans before the reinterview, and 70 percent of those *not* planning to buy "held fast to their intentions." Fulfillment of plans varied directly with family income, liquid asset holdings, the proportion of income owed in personal debt, favorable attitudes toward the household's financial position and toward market conditions, residence in smaller cities, and the presence of children (in families in which the head was under 45).[24]

Lininger, Mueller and Wyss compared car purchase plans and their fulfillment in a series of five interviews based on an initial sample of

---

[23]Jean Namias, "Intentions to Purchase Compared with Actual Purchases of Household Durables," *Journal of Marketing*, Vol. 24, No. 1 (July, 1959), pp. 26–30.

[24]*Ibid.*, pp. 27–29.

450 urban families in 1954.[25] They studied, among other things, the effects of characteristics of plans (degree of certainty, cash vs. credit, new vs. used, etc.) on the degree of plan fulfillment and the effects of attitude on ultimate purchasing behavior.

A somewhat different use of panel data comparing car purchase intentions and purchases was reported by Brown, who analyzed monthly data from 6,000 families in the J. Walter Thompson panel for a year.[26] The initial interview in the sequence obtained intentions data and personal preference as to make of car from each adult family member. Subsequent analysis of actual purchasing behavior revealed the comparatively small influence of children in choice of make, and the fact that in 42 percent of the families who purchased, the make selected corresponded with the expressed preference of both husband and wife.[27]

Somewhat similar studies have been conducted by Ferber, Juster, and Hill.[28] Ferber's data covered a ten-month period in which monthly waves of interviews with a panel of 150 families in Decatur, Ill., obtained intentions and purchase data for a large number of durable items, clothing and shoes. Detailed analyses uncovered patterns relating to the incidence and characteristics of these purchases, the existence of unplanned purchases, the length of the planning horizon, characteristics of plans and of planners, and some suggested correlates of plan fulfillment.

Juster experimented with alternative phrasings of the purchase intentions question in a series of reinterview studies using questionnaires mailed to member-subscribers of Consumers Union. He found that buying intentions reflect estimates of purchase probabilities and suggested that future studies "attempt to estimate mean purchase probability in a population, not the proportion with sufficiently high probabilities to report that they 'intend to buy'."[29]

Detailed results of Hill's study have not yet been presented, but he has reported plans to include a series of intentions and purchase questions on household durable goods in a series of five interviews with a sample of 360 inter-generationally linked families in Minnesota.

[25]Charles Lininger, Eva Mueller and Hans Wyss, "The Contribution of Panel Studies to Forecasting the Automobile Market," *Proceedings of the American Statistical Association*, 1957.

[26]George H. Brown, "The Automobile Buying Decision within the Family," in Nelson N. Foote (ed.), *Household Decision-Making, Consumer Behavior, Vol. 4* (New York: New York University Press, 1961), pp. 193-99.

[27]*Ibid.*, p. 194.

[28]Robert Ferber, "Factors Influencing Durable Goods Purchases," in Lincoln N. Clark (ed.), *The Life Cycle and Consumer Behavior* (New York: New York University Press, 1955), Vol. IV, pp. 75–112; F. Thomas Juster, *Anticipations and Purchases—An Analysis of Consumer Behavior* (National Bureau of Economic Research, No. 79 General Series) (Princeton, N.J.: Princeton University Press, 1964); Reuben Hill, "Patterns of Decision-Making and the Accumulation of Family Assets," in Foote, Nelson N. (ed.), *Household Decision-Making, Consumer Behavior* (New York: New York University Press, 1961), Vol. 4, pp. 57–80.

[29]Juster, *op. cit.*, p. 15.

Finally, although we normally don't think of impulse buying studies as longitudinal, studies that combine an entrance interview with a brief reinterview as the shopper leaves the store are conceptually identical with the purchase intentions studies for durable goods. Most published studies unfortunately have not reported detailed analyses of correlates of high and low proportions of unplanned purchases nor of unfilled purchase plans, but future studies may well explore the in-store decision-making process using this technique.[30]

GROSS AND NET CHANGE ANALYSIS

Perhaps the largest number of studies with implications for marketing falls into this category. Only a few will be cited here to illustrate the range of applications that have been explored.

Consumption economists have used panel data in several ways. Katona and Fisher used two reinterview waves in a household income study to evaluate responses from a single cross section study designed to estimate past income patterns.[31] Crockett obtained data on food expenditures for 1,000 families in the Market Research Corporation of America's panel for 1951 and 1953 so that resulting calculations of income elasticity could be compared with data from time series and cross sectional analyses.[32]

Houthakker and Haldi attempted to obtain precise measures of the effects of income changes and current "investment" in automobiles on automobile purchases by comparing data from two years on current ownership and purchases of member families in the J. Walter Thompson panel.[33]

An interesting attempt to test hypotheses derived from Stigler's formulation of the value of information was recently published by Farley, who utilized data from the purchases reported to MRCA in 1957 by 199

[30]A study of super market shoppers currently being conducted at Indiana University by David T. Kollat and R. P. Willett promises to contribute much in this area. The study entails a large number of entrance interviews to determine purchase intentions, a complete recording of actual purchases, and follow-up interviews in the home of a sample of respondents from the store interview to collect further data on household characteristics, shopping behavior, and personality variables. See Ronald P. Willett and David T. Kollat, "Impulse Puchasing as a Special Case of Customer Decision Making," in Smith, L. George (ed.), *Reflections on Progress in Marketing* (Proceedings of the Education Conference of the American Marketing Association, 1964) (Chicago: American Marketing Association), pp. 212–28.

[31]George Katona and J. A. Fisher, "Postwar Changes in the Income of Identical Consumer Units," in National Bureau of Economic Research, *Studies in Income and Wealth* (New York: National Bureau of Economic Research, 1951), Vol. 13, pp. 61–122.

[32]Jean Crockett, "Demand Relationships for Food," in Irwin Friend and Robert Jones, *Proceedings at the Conference on Consumption and Service*, (Philadelphia: University of Pennsylvania, 1960), Vol. I, pp. 293–310.

[33]H. S. Houthakker and John Haldi, "Household Investment in Automobiles; An Intemporal Cross-Section Analysis," in I. Friend and R. Jones, *Proceedings of the Conference on Consumption and Saving* (Philadelphia: University of Pennsylvania, 1960), Vol. I, pp. 175–225.

Chicago Metropolitan Area families.[34] Out of the notion that search (which requires expenditures of time and resources) will proceed as long as the expected savings resulting from search exceed its marginal cost, Farley hypothesized that heavy users of a product would search more extensively for lower-priced brands (and thus be less brand loyal) than light users, for whom additional search would return smaller savings. His analysis tended to confirm this hypothesis but did not support two further hypotheses: (1) higher income families were expected to value time relatively higher and therefore search less than lower income families, and (2) larger families were thought to value money more highly and thus search more extensively than smaller families. Earlier literature exploring a variety of mathematical models for the prediction of brand shares based on panel data are too well-known (and much too extensive) for review here.[35]

Finally, Frank, Massy, and Morrison have reported an interesting use of panel data to study the diffusion of a new product by tracing the time sequence of adoption among panel members. Their study was based on data from 538 Chicago Tribune panel families and explored correlates of primary adoption, secondary adoption, other adoption and non-adoption of Folger's Coffee following its introduction into the Chicago market.[36] Very briefly, they found no socio-economic predictors but did find adoption more likely among non-working wives, families for whom beverages were a relatively important part of total consumption, families who clustered many purchases on shopping trips, Friday shoppers, and families with low brand loyalty for coffee.[37]

EXPERIMENTS

Perhaps the most promising use of longitudinal analysis is to assess the effects of an independent variable (either one occurring naturally in the environment of the panel members or one artificially introduced by the researcher) on one or more dependent variables, such as attitudes or rates of purchase of a product. The use of panel members as experimental subjects is actually a special application of the more general research approach of using experimental design in natural settings and is therefore affected by the same problems of research design and meth-

[34]John U. Farley, " 'Brand Loyalty' and the Economics of Information," *Journal of Business*, Vol. 37, No. 4 (October, 1964), pp. 370–81.

[35]A good review of this literature is found in John U. Farley and Alfred A. Kuehn, "Stochastic Models of Brand Switching," in George Schwartz (ed.), *Science in Marketing* (New York: John Wiley & Sons, Inc., 1965), pp. 446–64.

[36]Ronald E. Frank, William F. Massy and Donald G. Morrison, "The Determinants of Innovative Behavior with Respect to a Branded, Frequently Purchased Food Product," in L. George Smith (ed.) *Reflections on Progress in Marketing* (Proceedings of the 1964 Education Conference of the American Marketing Association) (Chicago: American Marketing Association, 1965), pp. 312–23.

[37]*Ibid.*, pp. 318–20.

odology as any field experiment.[38] The panel feature of these studies, however, permits the investigation of somewhat longer and more complex processes than can be handled by single before-after studies. The search for a new house is an example.

Panel experiments seem ideally suited for research in one of marketing's most perplexing areas—the effects of promotional variables on audience members. Much has been said about the communication objectives approach to advertising since the publication of Colley's DAGMAR,[39] and there seems to be substantial agreement with the notion that advertising objectives and subsequent evaluations of performance should be based upon specific, measured changes in the information and attitude states of target audiences, provided that communications achievements can be shown to bear a predictable relationship to changes in audience purchase behavior

As early as 1942, panel analysis was suggested as a means of relating advertising exposure to purchase behavior,[40] but no means of relating intermediate changes in attitudes and product knowledge were suggested. Recently, Gail Smith of General Motors has reported on methodology that seems to add these dimensions, using a reinterview schedule in conjunction with a series of six audience surveys each year.[41] Each survey gathers data on media exposure as well as makes currently considered as possible candidates for the next purchase and the preferred make. A battery of 35 semantic differential items is presented for each make considered a potential choice. The panel feature of these surveys facilitates the assessment of the effect of advertising on product awareness, image and preference over time. Because actual purchases of reinterviewed respondents can be related back to earlier responses, purchase probabilities can be estimated for various levels of awareness and preference.

CONCLUDING COMMENTS

Although the bulk of this discussion has centered on the various longitudinal approaches to the study of change in marketing, the more conventional methods clearly still have much to offer in specific situations. What should be emphasized, therefore, is the notion that each approach has characteristics that suit it to certain problem settings and not to

---

[38]Many of these problems are discussed in Seymour Banks, *Experimentation in Marketing* (New York: McGraw-Hill Book Co., Inc., 1964).

[39]Russell Colley, *Defining Advertising Goals for Measured Advertising Results* (New York: Association of National Advertisers, 1961).

[40]Alfred R. Root and Alfred C. Welch, "The Continuing Consumer Study: A Basic Method for the Engineering of Advertising," *Journal of Marketing*, Vol. 7 (July, 1942), pp. 3–21.

[41]Gail Smith, "How GM Measures Ad Effectiveness," *Printers' Ink*, May 14, 1965, pp. 19–29.

others. Despite the several excellent examples of longitudinal applications in marketing cited here, great potential remains for further use of these methods. Marketing researchers would do well to consider this potential in framing future projects.

Suggested additional AMA readings

Andreason, Alan. "Potential Marketing Applications of Longitudinal Methods," in *Marketing and Economic Development* (ed. Peter D. Bennett), pp. 261–73. Chicago: American Marketing Association, 1965.

Hempel, Donald J. "An Experimental Study of the Effects of Information on Consumer Product Evaluations," in *Science, Technology, and Marketing* (ed. Raymond M. Haas), pp. 589–97. Chicago: American Marketing Association, 1966.

Holloway, Robert J. "Laboratory Research in Marketing at the University of Minnesota," in *Science, Technology, and Marketing* (ed. Raymond M. Haas), pp. 507–10. Chicago: American Marketing Association, 1966.

Hughes, G. David. "The Measurement of Changes in Attitude Induced by Personal Selling," in *Toward Scientific Marketing* (ed. Stephen A. Greyser), pp. 175–85. Chicago: American Marketing Association, 1964.

Kassarjian, Harold H., and Nakanishi, Masao. "A Study of Selected Opinion Measurement Techniques," *Journal of Marketing Research*, Vol. 4 (May, 1967), pp. 148–54.

Massey, William F. "Applying Factor Analysis to a Specific Marketing Problem," in *Toward Scientific Marketing* (ed. Stephen A. Greyser), pp. 291–307. Chicago: American Marketing Association, 1966.

Mittelstaedt, C. "An Experimental Study of the Effects of Experience on Consumer Decision Making," in *Science, Technology, and Marketing* (ed. Raymond M. Haas), pp. 617–25. Chicago: American Marketing Association, 1966.

Nicosia, Francesco. "Panel Designs and Analysis in Marketing," in *Marketing and Economic Development* (ed. Peter D. Bennett), pp. 222–43. Chicago: American Marketing Association, 1965.

Pessemier, Edgar A. "A New Way to Determine Buying Decisions," *Journal of Marketing*, Vol. 23 (October, 1959), pp. 41–46.

Pessemier, Edgar A., and Teach, Richard D. "Pricing Experiments, Scaling Consumer Preferences, and Predicting Purchase Behavior," in *Science, Technology, and Marketing* (ed. Raymond M. Haas), pp. 541–60. Chicago: American Marketing Association, 1966.

Pratt, Robert W., Jr. "Understanding the Decision Process for Consumer Durable Goods: An Example of the Application of Longitudinal Analysis," in *Marketing and Economic Development* (ed. Peter D. Bennett), pp. 244–60. Chicago: American Marketing Association, 1965.

Schendel, Dan E. "Operation of the Behavioral Laboratory at Purdue University," in *Science, Technology, and Marketing* (ed. Raymond M. Haas), pp. 497–506. Chicago: American Marketing Association, 1966.

Uhl, Kenneth P. "Field Experimentation: Some Problems, Pitfalls, and Perspective," in *Science, Technology, and Marketing* (ed. Raymond M. Haas), pp. 561–72. Chicago: American Marketing Association, 1966.

Venketesan, M. "Laboratory Experiments in Marketing: The Experimentor Effect," *Journal of Marketing Research,* Vol. 4 (May, 1967), pp. 142–47.